THE OPERAS OF ALBAN BERG/ *WOZZECK*

THE OPERAS OF alban berg

VOLUME ONE / *WOZZECK*

GEORGE PERLE

UNIVERSITY OF CALIFORNIA PRESS

BERKELEY / LOS ANGELES / LONDON

Illustration credits: Numbers 1, 2, 13, 14, and 21 courtesy of Dr.
Volker Scherliess. Number 4 courtesy of Rowohlt Taschenbuch
Verlag GmbH. Number 5 courtesy of Stadtgeschichtliches
Museum, Leipzig. Numbers 6, 16, and 18 courtesy of Metropolitan
Opera Guild/Opera News. Number 7 courtesy of
Theatersammlung der Österreichische Nationalbibliothek.
Number 11 courtesy of Universal Edition, Vienna, and the John
Herrick Jackson Music Library, Yale University. Number 12
courtesy of Universal Edition, Vienna, and The Library of
Congress, Washington, D.C. Number 15 courtesy of Ullstein
Bilderdienst. Number 17 courtesy of Universal Edition, Vienna.
Number 19 is reproduced from an article by Luigi Colacicchi in
Musica 43 by courtesy of G. C. Sansoni Editore Nuova S.p.a.
Number 20 courtesy of The Mary Flagler Cary Music Collection in
The Pierpont Morgan Library, New York.

TO BARBARA

CONTENTS

ILLUSTRATIONS

1. Berg in 1909.

2. Berg in his army uniform, 1915.

3. Georg Büchner.

4. Johann Christian Woyzeck, 1780–1824.

5. A contemporary engraving: "J. C. Woyzeck meets his death as a repentant Christian, at the Marketplace in Leipzig, August 27, 1824."

6. "Fünfkreutzertanz" by Michael Nader, painted in 1829.

7. Program of the first performance of Büchner's play in Vienna, at which Berg was present (May 5, 1914).

8, 9, 10. Berg's own handwritten notations in a copy of the play now in the possession of an American collector.

11. Sketch for *Wozzeck*, Act I, Scene 5, mm. 682–690.

12. Autograph score of *Wozzeck*, Act I, Scene 5, mm. 681–683.

13. Berg's announcement of the private publication of the vocal score.

14. Alban Berg ca. 1923.

15. Erich Kleiber, *Generalmusikdirektor*, Staatsoper, Berlin, 1925.

16. Advance announcement of the world première of *Wozzeck* at the Berlin Staatsoper, December 14, 1925.

17. The Doctor's study (Act I, Scene 4). Sketch by Panos Aravantinos for the first Berlin production.

ACKNOWLEDGMENTS

I, and others of my generation, lived with and studied the vocal score for many, many years before Dimitri Mitropoulos's revival of *Wozzeck* in a concert performance with the New York Philharmonic on April 12, 13, and 15, 1951, gave us our first opportunity to hear the opera. It is only fitting that a list of acknowledgments should first of all recall this debt to a great and dedicated musician.

This book was already under way while I was living in England in 1966–1967. It was my great good fortune to be able to spend many hours during this period in the company of that indefatigable and generous Berg scholar, H. F. Redlich, who not only encouraged me in my work by the warm interest he showed in it, but also kept me abreast of his own continuing studies and discoveries. It was Dr. Redlich who first proposed (in a letter to me on March 9, 1964) the foundation of the International Alban Berg Society, and from that moment until his sudden death in the autumn of 1968 he worked for the successful realization of this project with his characteristic enthusiasm, energy, and wisdom.

The ban on Act III of *Lulu* has finally been lifted, more than 43 years after the composer's death, and there is every indication that by the time this book appears an authentic edition of the complete opera may at last be available. In August, 1963, when that ban was still in effect, I was permitted to examine the *Particell* and vocal score of Act III, through the extraordinary kindness and generosity of the late Dr. Alfred A. Kalmus, one of the directors of Universal Edition. In Volume Two I have incorporated material from several of the articles in which I reported the results of my studies: "*Lulu:* The Formal Design,"

Acknowledgments

Journal of the American Musicological Society, XVII/2 (Summer 1964); "*Lulu:* Thematic Material and Pitch Organization," *Music Review,* XXVI/4 (November 1965); "Die Personen in Bergs *Lulu,*" *Archiv für Musikwissenschaft,* XXIV/4 (November 1967); "The Complete *Lulu,*" *Musical Times,* CXX/2 (February 1979).

Some of the material which appears in Volume One is adapted from three previously published articles: "Woyzeck and Wozzeck," *Musical Quarterly,* LIII/2 (April 1967); "The Musical Language of *Wozzeck,*" *Music Forum,* I (1967); "Representation and Symbol in the Music of *Wozzeck,*" *Music Review,* XXXIII/4 (November 1971).

A special debt is owed to Donald Harris, who is presently collaborating with Laurence Lyon on an annotated edition of the Berg-Schoenberg correspondence, and who very generously put his survey of this correspondence at my disposal. Mark DeVoto, to whom we owe the definitive study of Berg's *Altenberg Lieder,* has been in correspondence with me on matters relating to this book since its inception. Many of the chapters were sent to him as soon as they were written and he was unfailingly helpful with his criticism and suggestions. I am grateful also to Claudio Spies and Hugo Weisgall for many fruitful discussions and much helpful advice. A portion of the manuscript was read by Max Massey, who made many useful editorial suggestions.

For permission to reprint copyrighted material I am especially grateful to Universal Edition, A-G, Vienna, the exclusive publisher of Berg's music.

My earlier books, as well as this one, have benefited from the invariably apposite advice of Alain Hénon, associate editor of the University of California Press. Jane-Ellen Long edited the whole manuscript in its final stages, and I doubt that there is a page that is not more lucid and readable as a result of her skill, discernment, and patience. I am glad of this opportunity to thank them both.

To the American Council of Learned Societies my thanks are due for a grant which defrayed some of the costs I incurred in the initial stages of my work.

PREFACE

As I write these lines the full three-act version of Alban Berg's posthumous masterpiece *Lulu* is receiving its world première in Paris. Advance attention and international press-coverage are on a scale comparable only to that which greeted the première of *Wozzeck* fifty-four years earlier. That the excitement and worldwide interest surrounding the first performances of both of Berg's operas can hardly be due to their intrinsic merits probably goes without saying. The weeks that preceded the première of *Wozzeck* on December 14, 1925, were a time of crisis for the Berlin State Opera, a crisis which originated in personal, political, and factional disputes that had nothing whatever to do with Berg's opera. The public knew nothing at all of Berg's music, and even critics and connoisseurs especially concerned with avant-garde composition knew very little of it. Nevertheless, the forthcoming production of an "unperformable" opera by an "atonal" composer who was characterized in contemporary newspaper accounts as "the most intransigent of all the Schoenbergians" was made the focal point of controversy. By the time the first curtain rose on opening night Alban Berg's name was already widely known, but as a prescient critic asserted after that opening night, "The work that we have before us is one whose great intrinsic qualities will still be valid when there is no one left who remembers the current crisis of the Berlin Opera."[1]

Today the composer of *Wozzeck* is universally recognized as one of the outstanding masters of twentieth-century music, and it is hardly surprising that the unveiling of the final and culminating act of his second opera forty-three years after his death should be the occasion for "perhaps the most important and glamorous operatic première since the end of World War II," as we are told in a front-page story in the *New York Times*. *Lulu*, like *Wozzeck*, will be with us for a long time, and it will continue to hold our interest and attention for its intrinsic merit, not because of the intrigue and controversy surrounding the long suppression of its third act.

Both operas add new dimensions to the dramatic range of the operatic theater and extend its relevance to life and to the world of ideas as radically and significantly as any work—even such a one as *Tristan und Isolde*—of the past. They hold a most important place in the history of music as the first atonal and the first twelve-tone works to become a part of the repertory and to prove that the revolution in the language of music embodied in the works of Schoenberg, Berg, and Webern in the early years of this century was not merely a cultist self-centered tendency that could have no significance for musical culture in general. They solve the perennial problem of operatic form in a new and unique way, integrating characteristic self-contained pieces that recall the classical "number" opera within an overall cyclic and recapitulative design whose unity and scale are comparable only to the most impressive achievements in the literature.

The present study began as an investigation of pitch organization in *Wozzeck* and *Lulu*. Such a study could not be kept within purely musical limits, even in dealing with the most abstract devices of the twelve-tone system, as when we find an otherwise inexplicably contrived procedure, a single set-statement that cyclically permutes, on two different pitch-levels, both the inversion and the retrograde inversion of Alwa's tone row, explained by the words to which these notes are set: "Nobody knows what to write!" A study of dramatic content and characterization soon led to an exhaustive investigation of the literary background of the two operas. Thus it was that this book became one which should in large part be accessible to the general reader as well as to the specialist. I found myself becoming more and more involved in the evolution of the musical language of *Wozzeck* and in the remarkable transformation that had taken place in Berg's style and technique by the time he came to write his second opera, and eventually my project came to include discussions in depth of all of Berg's work. Finally, new discoveries about Berg's life and associations revealed that both operas are involved with the biography and character of the man in most intimate, explicit, and astonishing ways, so that an understanding of their genesis and implications inevitably called for a presentation not only of the man's work as a whole, but also of the life and character of the man himself.

My first article on Berg was published twenty years ago.[2] It was the earliest analysis of the music of *Lulu* to go beyond a recapitulation of Reich's

2 "The Music of *Lulu*: A New Analysis," *Journal of the American Musicological Society* XII/2–3 (1959): 185ff.

summary description of the procedures Berg had used in deriving the numerous twelve-tone sets in the opera from a single basic tone row. The speciousness of Reich's so-called analysis can be easily demonstrated. It was, nevertheless, based on oral and written communications from the composer himself to his official biographer, and this authorization carried more weight than the illogicality of Reich's arguments and their irrelevance to the actual music of the opera. My early studies of Berg's twelve-tone methods in *Lulu* soon led me to question another accepted view, that Berg is a less "systematic," a less "mathematical," composer than either Schoenberg or Webern, and that this explains the greater accessibility and wider acceptance of his music. On the contrary, he is at least as "systematic" and "mathematical" (whatever that may mean), if not more so, but not at all in the same ways. By the time I had come to prepare the second edition of my book, *Serial Composition and Atonality*,[3] I had come to the view expressed in its concluding paragraph: "Berg's twelve-tone music, though its coherence depends on the same properties of set structure as the twelve-tone music of Schoenberg and Webern, suggests an independent line of development, one that still awaits its continuation beyond his special and personal *Klangideal*. The implications of his unprecedented technical discoveries have still to be investigated, not only by theorists, but, above all, in the work of other composers." This, too, was a departure from a conventional view, that Berg's music was retrogressive compared to Schoenberg's and especially Webern's, that it looked more to the past than to the future. Since then I have investigated "the implications of his unprecedented technical discoveries" and come to the conclusion that Berg was the most forward-looking composer of our century and that he had progressed further than anyone else in the direction of that comprehensive reformulation of postdiatonic compositional procedures that had motivated Schoenberg's discovery of the twelve-tone system in the first place.[4]

That one can place no confidence in the "authorized" analyses of Berg's music and the accepted interpretations of its character and significance has been clear to me for a long time. It took me somewhat longer to realize that simple statements of fact about his life and work that have come to us from Berg's first biographer and from other authorized sources are equally untrustworthy, though by this time they have been reconfirmed through mere repetition in numberless magazine articles, program notes, critical reviews, encyclopedias, and books. Thus, for example, the liner notes of all three commercially recorded versions of *Wozzeck* repeat the account of the genesis of the opera that was published by Willi Reich shortly after the composer's death on

3 Berkeley: University of California Press, 1968.

4 The first volume of this book was already in the hands of the publisher and most of the second volume had already been written by the time Douglas Jarman's book, *The Music of Alban Berg*, was published. Professor Jarman supports the views set forth in the paragraph above, not only in his detailed commentary on my earlier publications but also in his own cogent and extensive analytical studies.

Christmas Eve, 1935.[5] According to this account: (1) Berg began to prepare the libretto soon after seeing the first performance of the play in Vienna in May, 1914, but this work was interrupted by his call to military service at the outbreak of World War I, so that it was not until the summer of 1917 that he finally got the libretto into shape and could begin the actual composition of the opera. (In fact, the only changes that Berg made in the text of the individual scenes are such as would occur to a composer in the actual course of composition. No preliminary draft of the libretto was necessary and Berg did not prepare one.) (2) The composer radically revised the sequence of the scenes, working only from the chaotically arranged version which Franzos, the first editor of the play, had prepared from Büchner's rough drafts. (In fact, Berg derived his ordering from the edition of Landau, published in 1909, which retained Franzos's reading of the individual scenes, but not his ordering of them.) (3) The full score was completed in April of 1921. (In fact, the full score was completed in the spring of 1922.)

Though I had long found it impossible to accept the oft-repeated characterization of Berg's widow as "the most faithful guardian of his works"[6] in view of her suppression of a major portion of his last and greatest composition, I did not reject the familiar account of their idyllic domestic life until I discovered, a few months after the death of Mrs. Berg on August 30, 1976, a miniature score of the *Lyric Suite* containing, in Berg's own hand, detailed annotations of a secret program inspired by his love for another woman.[7] In a moving letter to that woman the composer rejected the myth of an untroubled and blissful domestic existence, which he himself helped to fabricate and perpetuate during his own lifetime and which his widow successfully perpetuated until her own death forty-one years later: "Everything that you may hear of me, and perhaps even read about me, pertains, insofar as it is not completely false—as, for example, this, which I read today by chance in a Zurich programme: 'A completely happy domesticity, with which his wife has surrounded him, allows him to create without disturbance'—pertains to what is only peripheral."[8] And now we have this same judgment confirmed in Mrs. Berg's own words in her recently revealed letters to her closest friend, Alma Mahler Werfel.[9]

In short, in making use of authorized sources for information about the life and work of Alban Berg we must keep in mind the earnest warning that Joseph Kerman urges upon the Beethoven scholar in respect to the best-known of authorized biographers, Anton Felix Schindler: "Every statement of fact and every shade of implication requires verification or, if verification is not possible, the stern exercise of judgment."[10] To the considerable extent that the present book may be taken as a biography of Berg as well as a specialized study of the two operas, I am pleased to claim that it is neither authorized nor uncritically

5 Reich 37, pp. 12, 64f.   6 Reich 65, p. 35.
7 Perle 77d, *IABSN*.   8 Berg 78, *IABSN*.   9 Perle 78, *IABSN*.
10 Kerman, "Schindler's Beethoven," *The Musical Times* 108/1 (January 1967): 3.

dependent upon authorized sources. This explains not only what one will find   xvii
in this book but not in others, but also what one will find in other books but
not in this. For example, Reich refers, without any further elaboration, to "a
love affair which culminated in a suicide attempt in the autumn of 1903."[11]
With whom was Berg in love? How did he attempt suicide? Who told Reich
about it? If his source was reliable, why has he so little to tell us about it?
Perhaps this "suicide attempt," if any, was only an adolescent gesture that
should not be treated as a significant biographical detail? I have preferred to
omit all reference to the supposed "suicide attempt," but other biographical
studies of the composer merely repeat, without any additional comment and
more or less verbatim, Reich's simple assertion that there was such a "suicide
attempt."

The production that Berg's three-act *Lulu* was given in its première at the
Opéra in Paris on February 24th is consistent with a long tradition. Paris saw
its first *Magic Flute* in 1801 and its first *Freischütz* in 1824 in productions that not
only drastically revised the original characterizations, settings, and action, but
the text and music as well. Patrice Chéreau is only the most odious example in
the current generation of a type whom Arnold Schoenberg characterized almost fifty years ago: "Producers who look at a work only in order to see how to
make it into *something quite different*."[12] If Chéreau revises the action, settings,
and characterizations of Berg's opera without troubling at all about the text and
music, this only shows greater indifference to, not greater understanding of,
the implications of text and music. In his memoirs Berlioz invoked a curse on
the adapters of Mozart and Weber. His words are more eloquent than current
taste finds acceptable, but I will nevertheless take the liberty of borrowing
them: "Your crime is ridiculous. *Despair!* Your stupidity is culpable. *Die!* Be
thou rejected, derided, accursed of men. *Despair and die!*"

G. P., FEBRUARY 1979

11 Reich 65, p. 16.   12 Schoenberg 65, p. 139.

FROM THE EARLY SONGS TO *WOZZECK*

In a brief essay written two years before his death Arnold Schoenberg recalled his first meeting, forty-five years earlier, with Alban Berg: "When [he] came to me in 1904, he was a very tall youngster and extremely timid. But when I saw the compositions he showed me—songs in a style between Hugo Wolf and Brahms—I recognized at once that he had real talent."[1] The title page of the last of twelve unpublished early songs at the Library of Congress in Washington, D.C., bears the inscription, "unter Schönberg's Aufsicht," and may well be the first piece that Berg wrote under Schoenberg's, or, for that matter, anyone's supervision. Berg, born February 9, 1885, was already in his twentieth year, and it is difficult to discover what promise Schoenberg could have seen in these puerile efforts.[2] It seems more likely that Schoenberg's recognition of Berg's "real talent," which induced him to accept the timid young man as a student in spite of his inability to pay for lessons at the time, was based on an estimate of his personal and intellectual qualities.

Two of Berg's student compositions, both presumably belonging to the year 1908, have been published: the song *An Leukon*[3] and a set of piano variations.[4] The variations, a routine exercise in the style of Brahms, were performed on November 8, 1908, at a concert of works by Schoenberg's pupils; at the same concert Anton Webern conducted his Passacaglia, Op. 1. The vast

1 Redlich 57b, pp. 245f.
2 For a survey of the early songs, including those composed after Berg began his studies with Schoenberg, see Chadwick 71, *ML*.
3 Reich 37, 63, 65.   4 Redlich 57b.

disparity between these two works—all the more remarkable when one considers that Webern was hardly more than a year older than Berg and that his studies with Schoenberg had commenced at the same time as Berg's—is a reflection of the great difference in their respective musical backgrounds. "He took piano lessons from his sister's governess," wrote the friend of Berg's youth, Hermann Watznauer (quoted by Reich, who makes no reference to any other musical instruction before the meeting with Schoenberg).[5] Webern, on the other hand, had studied piano, cello, and theory as a child, and when his lessons with Schoenberg began he had already attended the University of Vienna for two years, taking courses in harmony and counterpoint and studying musicology with the noted Guido Adler. *An Leukon* is more successful than the piano variations, but only because it is less ambitious.

Yet by January 5, 1910, Schoenberg, in a letter to his publisher in which he bitterly complains of the Vienna Music Academy's refusal to offer him a teaching post, was able to describe Berg's progress as

> really extraordinary testimony to my teaching ability. . . . [He] is an extraordinarily gifted composer. But the state he was in when he came to me was such that his imagination apparently could not work on anything but *Lieder*. Even the piano accompaniments to them were songlike in style. He was absolutely incapable of writing an instrumental movement or inventing an instrumental theme. You can hardly imagine the lengths I went to in order to remove this defect in his talent. . . . I removed this defect and am convinced that in time Berg will actually become very good at instrumentation.[6]

In the same year Berg published at his own expense two works that may be compared with Webern's Passacaglia both for their intrinsic quality and as signposts of the composer's personal style: the Piano Sonata, Op. 1, and the Four Songs, Op. 2.

It is difficult to reconcile the dates of composition assigned by both Reich and Redlich to the former and by Reich to the latter with those assigned to the piano variations and *An Leukon*. Can the Piano Sonata have been completed in the summer of the same year as the variations, an utterly derivative academic exercise by a diligent but inexperienced student who has not yet learned how either to correct or to avoid some elementary crudities in harmony, rhythm, and instrumental writing? Why should this puerile exercise have been selected for public performance in preference to the Sonata? Is it conceivable that the song composer who in the spring of 1908 was still capable of the conventional prosody and primitive chromaticism, the literal formal relationships and mechanical rhythmic patterns, the unimaginative instrumental writing of *An Leukon* could by that summer[7] compose a cycle of four immensely subtle and complex songs, pieces that show a profound assimilation of the revolutionary

---

5 Reich 65, p. 13.   6 Schoenberg 65, p. 23.

7 This is the date given in Reich 63 and 65 for Opus 2, but Reich 37 gives the beginning of 1909 for the same work.

stylistic conceptions which were only just emerging in Schoenberg's work at that time? Redlich's assignment of the Four Songs to 1909–1910 seems more acceptable. Perhaps the manuscripts of these two works could tell us something about Berg's remarkable metamorphosis from a diligent but backward student handicapped by his late start into the "extraordinarily gifted composer." Unfortunately, however, they are lost, according to Hans Redlich's descriptive catalogue of Berg's works.[8]

It is doubtful that the tonal setting of "Schliesse mir die Augen beide," published by Reich in a magazine article on Berg in 1930, can serve as an authentic example of a student composition, even though it is dated 1907, for Berg would probably have revised it in 1925 when he composed its companion piece, a twelve-tone setting of the same text.[9] In this instance as well, scholarly research is frustrated by the loss (according to Redlich) of the manuscript. Nor should one be misled by the date of 1907 that appears on the title page of what some writers have taken to be the original version for voice and piano of the *Sieben frühe Lieder,* published in 1928, which is probably in fact essentially a reduction of the orchestral setting that received its first performance in that year. In this later version, a remarkable evocation of the musical language of late German romanticism reminiscent of Schoenberg's *Gurrelieder,* the original songs must have been revised to some extent, as well as orchestrated.

Gurrelieder and other early tonal works of Schoenberg were an important influence on Berg throughout his career;[10] the final interlude of *Wozzeck,* for example, in its very sound and texture reveals its antecedents in the orchestral interludes of *Gurrelieder.* More important than these external similarities, however, is the general formal conception that both of Berg's operas share with Schoenberg's romantic masterpiece—the integration within a large-scale design of self-contained individual numbers that remain clearly differentiated in spite of thematic and harmonic interrelations. A formal procedure exploited in *Lulu* with the most far-reaching consequences upon both the musical and the dramatic structure of the opera finds its only precedents in two other works of Schoenberg's tonal period, the First Quartet and the First Chamber Symphony. Both of these employ the traditional cycle of movements of the classical sonata, but the four movements are combined into one, and their formal elements interspersed throughout the work. In *Lulu* the formal components of a single

---

8 Redlich 57b.

9 The two songs were dedicated to Emil Hertzka in honor of the twenty-fifth anniversary of Universal Edition, the publishing house he founded. They were originally published as a supplement to Reich 30, M. Reich 63 assigns the first version of the song to 1907. Redlich, in his edition of the two songs (U. E. 1955), disputes Reich and gives the year of composition as 1900, on the basis of a literal interpretation of the concluding sentence of Berg's dedicatory preface: "They were composed—one at the beginning, the other at the end of the quarter-century (1900 to 1925)—by" (there follows a photograph of Berg). The style and quality of the setting, its place in Watznauer's listing (Reich 65, p. 109), and the first letter in Berg 65 support the date given by Reich.

10 Berg's pupil, Gottfried Kassowitz, reports that in the course of his lessons Berg made frequent use, for illustrative purposes, of the works of Schoenberg, "above all, the tonal compositions of the latter" (Kassowitz 68, ÖM).

4

well-defined design are distributed throughout each act (sonata-allegro in Act I, rondo in Act II, theme and variations in Act III) and separated by sections that are not components of that design. Berg's special interest in Schoenberg's early compositions is further reflected in his arrangements of the piano-vocal score of *Gurrelieder* and the piano-vocal score of the third and fourth movements of the Second Quartet; his published thematic analyses of *Gurrelieder, Pelleas und Melisande,* and the First Chamber Symphony; and his essay on the First Quartet, "Why Is Schoenberg's Music So Hard to Understand?"[11]

Only thirty years old when Berg became his pupil, Schoenberg was still close in temperament and outlook to the generation that represents the final florescence of Austro-German romanticism, the generation of Mahler, Wolf, and Strauss. From the beginning of their association with Schoenberg, Berg and Webern shared in the creative experiences that led Schoenberg through a series of radical stylistic changes, beginning with the First Quartet in 1905. With this work Schoenberg turned away from the programmatic content, extravagant timbral resources, and grandiose dimensions of *Gurrelieder* and *Pelleas* toward a more classical conception of formal design and tonal structure that he carried progressively further in the Chamber Symphony, Op. 9, in 1906, and the Second String Quartet in 1907–1908. It was this very attempt to preserve the articulative and integrative possibilities of the traditional tonal system that led Schoenberg to introduce structural elements external to and eventually destructive of that system. The whole-tone scale and series of perfect fourths are thus exploited as additional means of defining and characterizing the harmonic material of the Chamber Symphony. The musical language of Berg's Piano Sonata is unmistakably derived from this work.

With the Second Quartet Schoenberg reverted to the traditional cycle of four self-contained contrasting movements. In spite of the extravagant use of modal mixture, elliptical harmonic progressions, and chromaticism, each of the first three movements is strongly unified around a key center. But in the final movement, though at the very conclusion the tonality of the first movement is restored, the concept of a tonal center as represented in the major-minor system is discarded, its rejection explicitly indicated by the absence of a key signature. A similarly radical questioning of the traditional concept of a tonal center is apparent in each of the three Mombert songs of Berg's Opus 2. The first, with its signature of six flats, is presumably in E♭ minor, but it concludes with a chord of the "augmented sixth" (Ex. 1). The second, in A♭ minor, ends on the dominant harmony of that key. The last song has no key signature, and concludes with a progression and a cadential chord that cannot be defined in terms of the harmonic categories of diatonic tonality (Ex. 2).

Permanent hallmarks of Berg's personal style are already found in this early work, particularly in the concluding song: the rhythmic variation of a re-

11 The arrangements and analyses are published by Universal Edition, the essay in Reich 37, 63, 65.

Example 1

Berg, Op. 2, No. 2

Example 2

Berg, Op. 2, No. 2

Example 3

iterated melodic interval in mm. ♩ 6–9♩;[12] the symmetrical progression in the left hand of the piano part, mm. 12–14 (Ex. 3); progressive transformations through the imposition of a strictly ordered pattern of changes in the right hand, mm. ⌐12–15⌐ (Ex. 3); a statement of the total content of the semitonal scale, through simultaneous white-key and black-key *glissandi*, in m. 15; successive downward octave-transpositions at the climax of the movement, against chromatically ascending minor ninths, mm. ⌐15–16; a series of perfect

12 Where it has seemed desirable to indicate exactly at which point in a given bar a cited passage begins or ends, this will be shown by durational symbols giving the portion of the initial and concluding bars comprised in the citation.

fourths in one-to-one alignment with a semitonal progression moving in the opposite direction, mm. 20–23; and the subtle fluctuations of tempo, expressed both in the notated durational values and in verbal directions to the performer. (It should be pointed out, however, that the characteristic alternation of *accel.* and *rit.* is only found in the later, revised edition.)

The special quality that marked Berg's musical language to the end of his life, the conjunction of an emotional intensity that is typical of full-blown romanticism with the most rigorous and abstract formalism, is already fully asserted in this final number of Opus 2. Though in a technical sense their innovative features are undoubtedly derived in part from Schoenberg's earliest atonal compositions, the Four Songs are fully representative of a personal *Klangideal*.

"I already feel the opposition that I shall have to overcome," wrote Schoenberg in a program note for the première of the first works in which he dispenses completely with triadic functional harmony—the cycle of fifteen songs from Stefan George's *Das Buch der hängenden Gärten*, Op. 15, and the Three Piano Pieces, Op. 11, both completed in 1909.[13] In the same year Schoenberg also composed, within the space of a few months, both the Five Pieces for Orchestra, Op. 16, and *Erwartung*, Op. 17. These four works mark not only the beginning of a new period in Schoenberg's creative life but also the beginning of a new era in the history of music. New concepts in the treatment of dissonance had been primary factors in earlier stylistic transformations, but the implications of Schoenberg's "liberation of the dissonance" were far more radical. With the dissolution of the functional relations of the major-minor system, the range of harmonic and melodic possibilities was expanded to the point where all *a priori* restrictions governing the twelve notes of the chromatic scale disappeared.

Webern took his place as a colleague of Schoenberg's in the evolution of the new music with his Five Movements for String Quartet, Op. 5, also composed in 1909, and Berg did the same in the next year with his String Quartet, Op. 3, the last work he was to write under Schoenberg's direction. In the String Quartet Berg brilliantly fulfilled, only a few months after Schoenberg's letter of January 5, Schoenberg's prediction that "in time Berg will actually become very good at instrumentation." In its exploration of the sonic resources of the medium the String Quartet already points to the *Lyric Suite* of fifteen years later. Erwin Stein's description of the latter as "essentially unsymphonic . . . in contrast to the pronounced symphonic character of the majority of compositions for string quartet" applies to the earlier work as well. As in the *Lyric Suite*, "the development is not symphonic-epic, but lyric-dramatic; a climax of atmosphere and expression."[14]

The headmotif and principal figure (Ex. 4) of the Quartet consists of a five-note segment of the whole-tone scale plus one odd note, a type of pitch-

13 Reich 68, p. 71.   14 Prefatory note to the *Lyric Suite*, 1927.

Example 4

class collection destined to play a significant structural role in *Wozzeck*. The opening bars are filled with characteristic Bergian details: the chromatic expansion of the final semitone of the initial motive; rigorous linear patterns—semitones against perfect fourths—generating the harmonic progression in the viola and cello parts; the abstract rhythmic pattern imposed upon this progression, with the first dyad stated once, the second twice, the third three times; and the symmetrical prolongation of this progression. The significance of the formal conception of the String Quartet and of the relation between detail and large-scale design have been pointed out by Theodor W. Adorno:

> At a time when Schoenberg and Webern had been deferring this question of the larger instrumental forms and had contracted the time dimension or had allowed its articulation to depend upon the poetic word, Berg followed the impulse of his own creative drive, which he himself felt to be architectural. . . . He did not obediently receive the larger forms from tradition: he did not pour new wine into old bottles; he did not merely cover the unaltered schemata of the sonata, the variation, and the rondo with chromatics and enharmonics in a modernistic manner. On the contrary, right from the start he shows himself determined to develop them with severity and originality from the motivic and thematic structural principles worked out by Schoenberg and adapted by Berg in the Piano Sonata.[15]

"The String Quartet," wrote Schoenberg shortly after Berg's death, "surprised me in the most unbelievable way by the fulness and unconstraint of its musical language, the strength and sureness of its presentation, its careful working and significant originality. That was the time when I moved to Berlin (1911) and he was left to his own devices. He has shown that he was equal to the task."[16]

In spite of the "strength and sureness" of the String Quartet, Berg undertook the composition of his first orchestral work and his first work not written under Schoenberg's supervision—the Five Orchestral Songs on Picture-Postcard Texts by Peter Altenberg, Op. 4, completed in the autumn of 1912—with some trepidation. In a letter dated January 17, 1913, he told Schoenberg "how happy your judgment that the songs are not altogether bad has made me. Especially in respect to the orchestration, where I feared, in view of my unfortunate beginnings, that in every bar—though it urged itself upon me with the intensity of something *heard*—I might have committed some imbecility.

15 In Reich 37, p. 36.   16 Reich 65, p. 29.

8   Even Webern's contrary view (he only saw two songs) could not reassure me. Only the kind words in your letter!" Ten weeks later Schoenberg conducted a concert in Vienna which included two of the *Altenberg Lieder*. A segment of the audience, determined to provoke a disturbance, succeeded in creating enough of a tumult during the Berg songs that the concert could not be continued. For Berg this was no *succès de scandale* like the riotous première of Stravinsky's revolutionary work that took place in Paris two months later, but a humiliation. Yet fifty years later the composer of *Sacre du Printemps*, commenting upon this moment in the history of music, writes: "I did not know then what I know now, which is that Schoenberg had written a body of works we now recognize as the epicenter of the development of our musical language."[17] And of the *Altenberg Lieder* he offers the well-considered judgment that they "are one of the perfect works composed in this century and worthy of comparison with any music by Webern or Schoenberg up to the same date."[18]

Two months after the abortive première of the two songs of Opus 4, Berg visited Schoenberg in Berlin. His subsequent letters to Schoenberg show that Schoenberg not only did nothing to reassure Berg as to the excellence of the work, but even added his own censure to that of the critics and the public. Reich suggests that "it must have been the aphoristic form of the latest pieces—the Altenberg songs and the Four Pieces for Clarinet and Piano, Opus 5, completed in the spring of 1913—that occasioned Schoenberg's vehement censure; they were so brief as to exclude any possibility of extended thematic development."[19] But Webern had written nothing since 1909 that was not "so brief as to exclude the possibility of extended thematic development," and Schoenberg himself had turned to "aphoristic form" in 1911, in his Six Little Piano Pieces, Op. 19, and again in the following year in *Pierrot lunaire*, which Berg heard for the first time during his visit with Schoenberg in Berlin. Why should the brevity of the *Altenberg Lieder* and the clarinet and piano pieces have "occasioned Schoenberg's vehement censure?" It is even more difficult to understand, in view of Schoenberg's invariably uncompromising insistence on the authentic presentation of his own works in performance, why he should ever have been willing to offer the *Altenberg Lieder* in a partial performance that under the best circumstances would have been a fatal misrepresentation of the work. In any event, Berg never again attempted to bring this work, perhaps his finest composition after the two operas and the *Lyric Suite*, to performance. The earliest survey of Berg's work, an article by his fellow student, Erwin Stein, published in January of 1923, introduces Berg as the composer of *Wozzeck* and lists the preceding compositions by opus numbers, but consigns the *Altenberg Lieder* to oblivion, leaving an unexplained gap between Opus 3 and Opus 5.[20] In spite of Ernst Krenek's enthusiastic essay on the songs in the memorial volume that appeared shortly after Berg's death, "this astonishing work, which

17 Stravinsky 63, p. 54.   18 Stravinsky 60, p. 122.   19 Reich 65, p. 41.
20 Stein 23, *Anbruch*.

fell, after its first alarming appearance, like a stone into the abyss of the forgotten from which no one has as yet fetched it"[21] had still to wait another sixteen years for what was in effect its first performance.[22]

Apart from their brevity, these pieces have little in common with the aphoristic statements of Anton Webern. They are miniatures rather than aphorisms; far from excluding "the possibility of extended thematic development," they are perhaps above all remarkable for unfolding, within such circumscribed durational limits, an extraordinarily complex and extensive system of motivic interrelationships. In similar contrast to these limits are the variety and scope of the timbral resources (solo voice, tripled and quadrupled winds and brasses, a large percussion section, glockenspiel, xylophone, harp, celesta, piano, harmonium, and strings, with individual sections of the last sometimes divided into as many as five parts). The aural imagination, skill, and boldness that Berg had displayed in his first work for string quartet are equally evident in this, his first work for orchestra.

The opening bars are a striking musical example of what Sokel calls the "paradox in Expressionism, where the greatest sense of formal abstraction exists side by side with the most chaotic formlessness."[23] Six simultaneous *ostinato* figures, no two identical in duration, create a dense and shifting chaos of sound (at a dynamic level of *ppp!*). In the fifth bar the *ostinato* figures begin to be subjected to different types of sequential ascent: one sequential pattern generates a five-note motive (Ex. 5) that plays a dominant melodic and harmonic role and, both as simultaneity and as melodic motive, brings the cycle to

Example 5

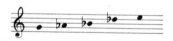

a close; another figure ascends by whole steps; another generates the interval series 1, 2, 3, 4, 5, 6, 7 in its ascent;[24] the other figures ascend along the degrees of the semitonal scale. These abstract, but in their aggregate effect chaotic, transformations are brought to a climax by a *fortissimo* statement of a basic harmonic figure (Ex. 6), a signal for the musical "curtain" that opens upon the

Example 6

21 In Reich 37, p. 47.

22 For the history of the work in publication and performance, as well as a careful analysis, see DeVoto 66a, the definitive study of the *Altenberg Lieder*. DeVoto 66b, *PNM*, is a revised version of portions of this study.

23 Sokel 59, p. 13.

24 The integers are "interval numbers," showing differences in semitones.

soloist as the complex mass of sound is reduced to a quiet "accompaniment."[25] Symmetrically opposed to this in the finale is the reversed statement of the same figure, marking the closing of the "curtain" upon the soloist. The first word of the vocal part, "Seele" ("soul"), is anticipated by two notes that are to be attacked and released "like a breath"; the first, *ppp*, is hummed with lips closed, the second, *pp*, with lips open. Articulate song thus gradually emerges from silence, just as coherent instrumental motives emerged from a mist of chaotic sound in the orchestral introduction.

The first theme of the work (as distinct from its motives) is a twelve-tone series (Ex. 7), apparently the earliest example of an ordered twelve-tone set in the history of music. The final movement of the cycle is a passacaglia based on two subjects, this twelve-tone series and the five-tone series of Example 5.

Example 7

Thus the finale of the *Altenberg Lieder* anticipates, as early as 1912, the twelve-tone passacaglia theme of the scene in the Doctor's study in *Wozzeck*. The opening and closing bars of the third song present a vertical twelve-tone set, anticipating the twelve-tone chords of *Wozzeck* and *Lulu*. It serves here as a musical counterpart for the word "All" in the line that opens and, with its verb tense changed, closes the text: "Über die Grenzen des All blicktest [blickst] du [noch] sinnend hinaus!" ("Beyond the bounds of the universe musingly you looked [still look]!") Even the unexpected change of tense from past to present—a delightful example of the singular contrariety of Altenberg's literary style—is reflected in the musical imagery. The vertical set is dissipated in the opening section of the song, each note, from the lowest to the highest, dropping out in turn. The opposite procedure occurs in the concluding section: the complete chord is built up through the accumulation, in ascending progression, of one note at a time. In the finale there is a leitmotivic association between text and music at the words "keine Ansiedlungen" ("no settlements"); the orchestra at this point recapitulates the setting of "Hattest nie Sorge um Hof und Haus!" ("without a care for house and hold!") in the third song.

The composer of *Wozzeck* can already be perceived in these musical metaphors and symbols, as he can in the connecting of verbal and musical design in the contrasting ideas of the third and fourth songs. The third song concludes with a twelve-tone simultaneity as a musical symbol for the key word "All"; the next commences with a new, diametrically opposed, key word, "Nichts," musically represented in the extreme high range of the flute by a single *pianissimo* note that ascends through a semitone into the nothingness of

25 In m. 15 the first note in the second trumpet part should be *f♯* (sounding *b*), not *f♮* (cf. DeVoto 66a, p. 134).

space. Even the curtains of *Wozzeck* are suggested at the conclusion of the orchestral introduction to the cycle in the mechanical patterns of the descending figures that accompany the second chord of Example 6 in m. 15: simultaneous series of semitones, whole-tone scales, and diminished-seventh chords.

The sources of the *Altenberg Lieder* may be traced in Berg's own Four Songs and String Quartet, and in the *Gurrelieder,* Second Quartet, and Five Pieces for Orchestra of Schoenberg. The passacaglia seems to have been significantly influenced by the variation movement of the Second Quartet, a conjecture that finds support in the fact that Berg completed the *Altenberg Lieder* a few months after completing his arrangements of that movement and of the finale of the Second Quartet. But whatever its derivations from prior compositions and whatever its adumbrations of subsequent ones, as an artistic entity Opus 4 stands alone among Berg's works, deprived of successors by the traumatic impression that its humiliating "failure" made upon him.

Though Opus 5 is paired with Opus 4 as Berg's only other essay in the "aphoristic form" that was characteristic of all of Webern's atonal music and that Schoenberg had temporarily adopted, it is a work which departs radically in style and means from its predecessor. Where the *Altenberg Lieder* has motives and themes, the Four Pieces for Clarinet and Piano has only cells. The clarinet and piano pieces employ the procedures of repetition, symmetrical structures, chromatic inflection, and progressive transformation patterns that in the last song of Opus 2 generate what might be described as "normal" harmonic continuity in an atonal idiom (procedures that play a far larger role in the "free," i.e., non-dodecaphonic, atonal works of Berg than they do in those of Schoenberg and Webern). Where the earlier work was diffuse and lacked direction, Berg now knew how to use these procedures to give each of the Four Pieces extraordinary structural coherence, unity, and direction.

Webern's Six Bagatelles for String Quartet, written in the same year, exists in another world of musical time and rhetoric from Berg's Four Pieces. Berg's is in effect a large-scale work based on traditional conceptions of overall balance and contrast. Adorno calls attention to the analogy with the four-movement classical sonata: the relatively more complex and extensive outer movements of Berg's miniature cycle correspond to the sonata-allegro and finale of the classical model, the second movement to the adagio, and the third to the scherzo.[26] Such correspondences, in spite of the disparity in dimension and in means, point to the composer of *Wozzeck*. The basic harmonic language of the two works is also the same, though Opus 5 has neither room for nor need of "themes" or such special structural devices, described in Chapter Five, as vertical sets, chord series, or tone-rows. Even the "expressive" character and dramatic power of the opera is foreshadowed, as far as this is possible in a miniature piece of "absolute" music for two instruments.

Redlich's suggestion that "the psychological roots of the Three Orchestral Pieces [Op. 6] can be traced back to a personal crisis in Berg's life"[27] is

26 In Reich 37, pp. 49ff.   27 Redlich 57b, pp. 66ff.

confirmed by the attitudes and concerns expressed in Berg's letters as well as by the character of the work itself. A few weeks after his return from Berlin, Berg wrote to Schoenberg (July 9, 1913) of his plans for an extended symphonic work: "If in the last few months I have given so much and such intense thought to the working out of a symphony, this has surely happened chiefly because I wanted to make up for that which I would have had the benefit of doing *under your direction,* dear Mr. Schoenberg, *had you remained in Vienna.*" The "symphony" did not materialize, however, though portions of the projected work found their way into the *Präludium* of the Three Pieces for Orchestra.[28] Berg's continuing self-doubt is still painfully evident in a letter to Schoenberg dated July 20, 1914, in which he referred to his work on the Three Pieces for Orchestra: "But I must always be asking myself whether that which I'm expressing there . . . is any better than the last things I've done. And how can I judge this? Those I hate, so much so that I've been close to destroying them, and of these I have no opinion yet, since I'm right in the middle of them."[29] On September 8, 1914, he sent Schoenberg the first and third movements of Opus 6, with the hope that the work was "something I could confidently dedicate to you without incurring your displeasure." Self-criticism and the outbreak of the war ("the urge 'to be in it,' . . . to serve my country") slowed work on the second movement.[30]

If the composition of the Three Pieces was to some extent conceived as a project in self-improvement and as a means of winning Schoenberg's approval by the successful completion of a large orchestral work, it seems also to have been strongly motivated by Berg's intense preoccupation with and affection for the music of Mahler. The overwhelming impression that the Ninth Symphony, above all, had made upon him—the first performance had taken place in Vienna in June of 1912—is affirmed as clearly in the Three Pieces for Orchestra as it is in his letters.[31] The Ninth Symphony, in its fragmentation of thematic material, its prismatic distortion of simple diatonic motives, its pointillistic orchestration, its sudden expressionistic outbursts, its grotesque juxtaposition of the grandiose and the banal, its disruption of the tonal balance that is the very basis of the symphonic form (the four movements are in the keys of D major, C major, A minor, and Db major, respectively), may be said to have as its "program" the demise of the classical-romantic tradition of which it is one of the last significant products. Berg's Three Pieces persists in this tradition beyond Mahler, and with explicit reference to Mahler, while affirming the collapse of the musical language on which the tradition is based. More specifically, those

---

28 Berg 65, p. 258; Berg 71, pp. 162f. According to Redlich 57a, p. 65, the final symphonic interlude of *Wozzeck* incorporates a fragment of the unrealized symphony. Presumably, this refers to the principal theme, in D minor, and the sections based upon it, since everything else in the interlude is derived from material found elsewhere in the opera. But Willnauer 66, *NZfM,* p. 133, cites as the source of the D minor theme an unfinished piano-piece that Berg had planned for his wife and to which he refers in Berg 65, p. 253 (Berg 71, pp. 158f.).

29 Redlich 57a, p. 358.   30 Redlich 57b, p. 68.   31 Berg 71, pp. 147f.

characteristic aspects of Mahler's style which play such an important role in the Three Pieces persistently reappear in Berg's work to the end of his life: in both *Lulu* and the Violin Concerto, his last compositions, there are episodes that still show the strong influence of Mahler, and that still stand close to the Three Pieces.

If the Three Pieces is, in a sense, retrogressive, coming as it does after Schoenberg's Five Pieces for Orchestra, *Erwartung,* and *Pierrot lunaire,* and after Berg's own *Altenberg Lieder* and the clarinet and piano pieces, it was nevertheless essential preparation for the composition of *Wozzeck.* The musical idiom of *Erwartung* and *Die Glückliche Hand,* the two works for the musical theater which Schoenberg had completed in 1909 and 1913, respectively, but which were performed for the first time only in 1924, two years after Berg had completed the opera, could not serve the musico-dramatic conception of *Wozzeck* beyond providing suggestions for incidental details. Essential elements of the musical idiom to serve that conception were evolved by Berg in the Three Pieces for Orchestra.

A straight line of development can be traced from the Piano Sonata through the String Quartet to the Three Pieces. The problem explored in these three works is that of generating, in an ambiguous harmonic idiom, a large-scale musical structure by means of complex thematic operations. The articulative procedures of tonality that still serve in Mahler's Ninth to establish stable referential patterns, to differentiate these from subordinate and transitional material, and to limit the range of variational possibilities, are no longer available to Berg. The distorted form in which the principal theme of the first movement of the Ninth Symphony is recapitulated (Ex. 8) is recognizable as a chromatic transformation of a simple diatonic melody (Ex. 9) whose priority is never in doubt. In the Three Pieces for Orchestra, on the contrary, it is often impossible to say which explicit version of a given theme is to be regarded as its normal form, since the referential elements are frequently definable only in terms of their general shape and rhythmic character. Thus the first more or less

Example 8

Mahler, Symphony No. 9

Example 9

ibid.

14 extended melodic idea in the *Präludium* (Ex. 10) is almost immediately restated in an inverted form (Ex. 11) whose contour only approximately complements that of the model. An upbeat figure (Ex. 12) that occurs six times in its original form and four times in its inverted form between mm. 27 and 44 of the *Marsch*

Example 10

Example 11

Example 12

employs different intervals at almost every restatement, a procedure that clearly foreshadows the concluding scene of Act I of *Wozzeck*. In the major-minor system such deviations would reflect a change in mode or in the position of the given pattern relative to the scale degrees. Thematic transformation is still dependent on such harmonic factors in the Ninth Symphony, though there the scope of thematic variation is drastically and even dangerously extended, embracing banal and primitive assertions of traditional tonal functions at one extreme and extravagant uses of harmonic mixture and chromaticism at the other. The diffuse and ambiguous harmonic language of the Three Pieces for Orchestra, however, provides no comparable rationale for thematic transformation.[32]

An insufficiency of harmonic criteria leaves a composer so many possible ways of handling his themes that chaos, in conjunction with abstraction and literalness, is likely to ensue. These are opposite sides of the same coin. We have again the "paradox in Expressionism, where the greatest sense of formal abstraction exists side by side with the most chaotic formlessness." In tonal music exact imitation (except at the octave and to a restricted degree at the

32 The harmonic language of the second movement of the Three Pieces is discussed in Archibald 68, *PNM*.

fifth), exact inversion, and exact sequential displacements (such as occur in the *Marsch* at mm. 84–86) are rarely to be found, since the preservation of the semitonal content of each interval of the original pattern would contravene the tonality of that pattern. In the absence of the restrictive criteria of simultaneity and progression that are characteristic of tonal music, a rigorous contrapuntal scheme such as the three-part fugue, exact double canon in diminution, and exact triple canon in retrograde, simultaneously unfolded in the seven polyphonic voices of the eighteenth number of *Pierrot lunaire*, is not the formidable achievement that it is often taken to be. Employment of such strict polyphonic devices was a new departure in Schoenberg's atonal music and may have suggested the canonic episode at mm. 115–120 of the third of the Three Pieces, where three three-part canons occur simultaneously. Exact as well as approximate inversions appear in profusion throughout this movement. The simultaneous *ostinato* figures of unequal duration in mm. 83–93 of the second movement recall the opening bars of the *Altenberg Lieder*.

The primary themes of all three movements have their genesis in the *Präludium*. As in the opening bars of the *Altenberg Lieder*, coherent musical ideas emerge only gradually. The *Präludium* commences with vague figures in unpitched percussion instruments, against which the timpani enters *pianissimo*. The obscure pitch values of the timpani are gradually clarified by doublings in other instruments. Against a continuing harmonic background from which the percussion instruments gradually withdraw, an isolated *a♭* appears in the top line, then *g-a♭*, then *e-g-a♭*, the primary melodic cell of the work. The further evolution of linear and harmonic material is interrupted at mm. 9–11 by a special rhythmic motive, enunciated in a single reiterated note against sustained chords. This rhythmic motive, which recurs in mm. 13–15, 36–37, 42 –44, and at the conclusion of *Reigen*, is an early example in Berg's work of a device that plays, in a much more sophisticated treatment, an important role in both operas. The evolution of thematic material is resumed with a melodic motive entirely generated by the basic cell (Ex. 13); it will return, at its original pitch level and with its original harmonic background, near the conclusion of the finale (mm. 160–161).

Example 13

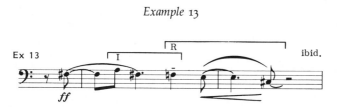

There follows, after an emphatic restatement of the rhythmic motive, an episode that anticipates the music of Act I, Scene 5 of *Wozzeck*, a complex polyphonic development of melodic themes whose linear contours are subtly varied at each repetition. The basic cell marks the beginning of this episode (mm. 15–17); the inverted basic cell marks its climax and initiates (mm. 24–27) a

16 second section, culminating in a *fortissimo* presentation of one of the two chief themes of the second movement (Ex. 14). A recapitulation of the initial statement of the rhythmic motive introduces the second of these themes (Ex. 15) and is followed by a quasi-retrograde version of the opening section, with the

Example 14

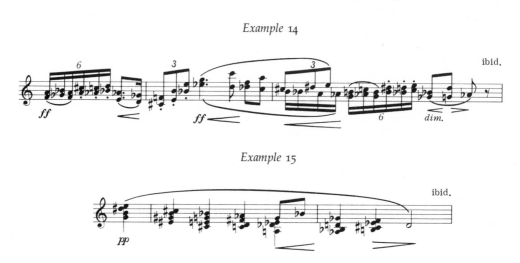

Example 15

return to the single note, *a♭*, of the basic cell, the gradual disappearance of the pitched instruments except for the timpani as the unpitched instruments return, and finally the disappearance of the timpani as well, so that the movement ends as it began, with a single stroke on the tamtam. The obvious symmetry of the overall formal design is in striking contrast to the elusive quality of the thematic content. There are unmistakable correspondences with the first movement of Mahler's Ninth Symphony—in the character and function of the opening and closing sections, in the melodic material, and in the monotone rhythmic motive.[33]

Stravinsky describes Berg as "the only one to have achieved large-scale development-type forms without a suggestion of 'neo-classic' dissimulation. . . . The essence of his work is thematic structure, and the thematic structure is responsible for the immediacy of the form. However complex, however 'mathematical' the latter are, they are always 'free' thematic forms born of 'pure feeling' and 'expression.' " He cites the Three Pieces for Orchestra as "the perfect work in which to study this."[34] The second movement of this work, *Reigen* (round-dances), is based on the idiomatic stylistic features of the waltz and *Ländler*, and the third movement on those of the march. Thus, they share with the music of the later neo-classical tendency a dependence on preestablished and widely known conventional "forms." Stravinsky's point is nevertheless well taken, and Berg himself dismisses any attempt to "connect

33 Redlich 57b, pp. 69ff.   34 Stravinsky 59, pp. 71f.

this employment of old forms in *Wozzeck* with the atavistic movement 'Back to——,' which incidentally started much later."[35]

In the scherzo of Schoenberg's Second Quartet, simple diatonic functionality, as opposed to the chromatic and elliptical harmony of the remainder of the work, is consigned to the domain of the popular and the vulgar in the literal quotation of a Viennese street ballad, *Ach du lieber Augustin.* A similarly grotesque exploitation of quotations and pseudo-quotations of banal *Ländler* and march tunes dominates many of the movements of Mahler's symphonies. The idiomatic elements of waltz, *Ländler,* and march in the Three Pieces for Orchestra are more abstract, since they are removed from their conventional harmonic context, unlike the necessarily (in view of their dramatic function) more realistic dance and march episodes in *Wozzeck.* They are nevertheless an adumbration of the latter, and also of the popular elements in the later works. Above all, the significance for Berg's subsequent development of *Reigen,* the *Marsch,* and the *Altenberg Lieder* passacaglia is that in these three movements he discovered the essential role that traditional forms and traditional stylistic details could play in restoring the possibility of coherent large-scale structure which the dissolution of the classical tonal system had destroyed. For Berg this restoration was a pressing need, whose conditions he worked out independently almost a decade before Schoenberg resolved the same problem for himself in the principles of the twelve-tone system.

The thematic organization of the Three Pieces for Orchestra integrates the separate movements into a single large-scale design. In this respect Berg's work is totally unlike Schoenberg's Five Pieces for Orchestra (1909) and Webern's Six Pieces for Orchestra (Op. 6, 1913) and Five Pieces for Orchestra (Op. 10, 1913). For the thematic techniques on which this integration chiefly depends Berg is indebted to the pre-atonal works of Schoenberg—above all, perhaps, to the First Quartet, the First Chamber Symphony, and *Pelleas und Melisande.* In these works complex transformation processes, germ motives, and the assignment of multiple functions to individual thematic elements (so that variants of the same theme or motive are employed at one point melodically and at another as subordinate accompanying figures) are elaborated to a degree that goes significantly beyond comparable thematic procedures in the works of Schoenberg's immediate forerunners and contemporaries. In this respect Berg remains as much a devoted disciple of Schoenberg in the Three Pieces for Orchestra as he was in the Piano Sonata and the String Quartet. The transformation of the sextuplet figure of Example 14 into the "slow waltz" theme of the second movement of Opus 6 (Ex. 16) and the transformation of the upper line of Example 15 by inversion and rhythmic revisions into one of the principal subjects of the *Marsch* (Ex. 17) are entirely representative of thematic procedures found in Schoenberg's First Quartet.

35 In Redlich 57b, p. 267.

Example 16

Example 17

Though its harmonic language is obviously dependent to a certain extent on conceptions underlying those atonal works of Schoenberg that had preceded it, these conceptions do not play a comparably extensive and obvious role in Opus 6. The Five Pieces for Orchestra had been performed by the time Berg composed the Three Pieces, but *Erwartung* and *Die Glückliche Hand* had not. Berg commenced the work, beginning with the third movement, in March of 1914, shortly after a trip to Amsterdam where he heard the Five Pieces for Orchestra for the first time. He referred to the influence of this work on his own composition in a letter to his wife (July 11, 1914): "I shall be dedicating the new pieces for orchestra to Schoenberg. As my teacher he has long been due for a large-scale work dedicated to him by me. He asked for it outright in Amsterdam as a present for his fortieth birthday. He 'ordered' it, in fact, and was my inspiration for it, not only through my listening to his own pieces for orchestra (but remember, mine don't derive from them, they will be utterly different), but because he urged and advised me to write character pieces."[36]

The *Marsch* was completed in the weeks immediately following the assassination at Sarajevo and is, in its feeling of doom and catastrophe, an ideal, if unintentional, musical expression of the ominous implications of that event. Fragmentary rhythmic and melodic figures typical of an orthodox military march repeatedly coalesce into polyphonic episodes of incredible density that surge to frenzied climaxes, then fall apart. It is not a march, but music *about* a march, or rather about *the* march, just as Ravel's *La Valse* is music in which *the* waltz is similarly reduced to its minimum characteristic elements. In spite of the fundamental differences in their respective musical idioms, the emotional climate of Berg's pre-war "marche macabre" is very similar to that of Ravel's post-war "valse macabre." The composer's own conception of the expressive character of the *Marsch* is suggested in his next work, *Wozzeck*, by Wozzeck's

36 Berg 71, p. 159.

portentous words, "Es wandert was mit uns da unten!" ("Something's follow-ing us down there below!") in Act I, Scene 2, the musical setting of which is drawn from the *Marsch* (mm. 79–84).

It is even possible that the passage is derived from material that Berg had originally sketched for *Wozzeck*. Berg had seen the Vienna première of Büch-ner's play early in May and, according to a letter he wrote to Webern three years later, "at once decided to set it to music."[37] Gottfried Kassowitz, who was studying with Berg at the time, reports that Berg began sketches for two scenes almost immediately after seeing the play for the first time.[38] In addition to the explicit quotation mentioned above, a number of passages in the opera are strikingly anticipated in the Three Pieces: the curtain music at the conclu-sion of Act I (mm. 113–119 of *Reigen*); the canonic episode that represents Marie's struggle with the Drum Major in I/5 and Wozzeck's struggle with him in II/5 (mm. 72–77 of the *Marsch*); the famous *tutti* unison at the conclusion of the murder scene (m. 135 of the *Marsch*); and the rising semitonal transposi-tions of a single chord as Wozzeck drowns (mm. 161–163 of the *Marsch*).

The date, "August 23, 1914," that stands at the conclusion of the pub-lished score of the Three Pieces evidently refers to the completion of the scor-ing of the last movement rather than to the completion of the work as a whole. The second movement was finally sent off to Schoenberg twelve months later, just about the time of Berg's induction into the Austrian army. In the *Altenberg Lieder* and the Three Pieces for Orchestra Berg had brilliantly fulfilled the pre-requisites for the next project he boldly set for himself, composition of the first full-scale atonal opera, but he could not have known this. The partial perfor-mance of the *Altenberg Lieder* did not contribute to his self-assurance, as we have seen, and the Three Pieces were performed for the first time only after he had completed the opera. Thus the work was composed and scored without Berg ever having had the experience, so important to the maturing composer, of comparing the imagined sound of an orchestral score of his own creation with the actual effect in performance of its abstract symbols.

Work on the composition of *Wozzeck* was brought to an abrupt halt by Berg's induction into military service, and he was only able to return to it, or rather to begin once again, two years later, while still in the service. In spite of his precarious health—seven years earlier he had suffered his first attack of the bronchial asthma which was to plague him recurrently for the rest of his life—he underwent the usual basic training. After a serious physical break-down he was judged unfit for active service and assigned to guard duty in Vienna, but the conditions and rigors of his military life remained harsh. Trans-ferred at last to an office job at the War Ministry, where he remained until the end of the war, he was eventually able to resume work on the opera, at least intermittently. On August 13, 1917, during a leave of absence, he wrote to Schoenberg: "The musical setting of Büchner's play, *Wozzeck*, planned more

37 Reich 53, *SM*, p. 50.　　38 Kassowitz 68, *ÖM*.

20 than three years ago, occupies me again. But it cannot come to the coherent writing down of any considerable section, for in another week my freedom will be gone again, and once more my slavery in Vienna will begin, and continue, perhaps, for years." A year later, on leave again, he informed Webern that he had been able "to finish something." The same letter, dated August 19, 1918, indicates that he had already made some progress toward the unique formal conception that governs the work:

> It is not only the fate of this poor man, exploited and tormented by *all the world*, that touches me so closely, but also the unheard-of intensity of mood of the individual scenes. The combining of 4–5 scenes into *one* act through orchestral interludes tempts me also, of course. (Do you find anything similar in the *Pelleas* of Maeterlinck-Debussy!) I have also given thought to a great variety of musical forms to correspond to the diversity in the character of the individual scenes. For example, normal operatic scenes with thematic development, then others *without* any thematic material, in the manner of *Erwartung* (understand me rightly: this is a question of *form*, not of the imitation of a style!), song forms, variations, etc. Up to now I've completed one scene and I hope to complete another, a large one, here.[39]

A few weeks earlier he had written Schoenberg that he had "once again seized upon [his] old plan of composing *Wozzeck*, after several unsuccessful attempts to write some piano pieces, or chamber music." The composition of smaller works for one or a few instruments would certainly have seemed a more reasonable endeavor, considering the circumstances under which Berg had to work and the long periods during which work was impossible, but his self-identification with the poor soldier of Büchner's tragic drama had made the composition of the opera a spiritual necessity that could not be fulfilled by the composition of "piano pieces, or chamber music." "There is a bit of me in his character," he wrote to his wife on August 7, 1918, "since I have been spending these war years just as dependent on people I hate, have been in chains, sick, captive, resigned, in fact humiliated."[40] The project he had first conceived under the overwhelming impression that the staged drama had made upon him a few months before the outbreak of the war could only be resumed after the composer's own experiences in the intervening years had led to this self-identification. That first impression had been temporarily obliterated when Berg, like so many other persons of refinement, sensibility, intellect, and culture, succumbed to the war fever and joined the general chorus of philistine banalities. Can it be the composer of *Wozzeck*, under the spell of Büchner's spirit, who writes to his wife of his indignation at the sight of an Englishman because the latter "is merely required to report every other day" while "in England the Austrians are imprisoned and starving in unheated stalls,"[41] and who sends her this New Year's message (December 31, 1914): "Yes, the war has to continue. . . . The war's great surprise will be in the guns, which are going to show a frivolous generation their utter emptiness. Perhaps the truth will

39 Reich 53, *SM*, p. 50.   40 Berg 71, p. 229.   41 Berg 65, p. 266.

dawn then—that there exist different values from those which up to now have been taken as the only salvation. . . . The war must go on until its true task is completed."[42]

Berg's experiences during the war years and the change in his outlook it effected are summed up in a letter (November 27, 1919) to Erwin Schulhoff, an early admirer and promoter of his work and a radical antimilitarist. By that time Berg had forgotten that he had ever supported the war. He described himself as a "fierce antimilitarist" whose "strongest support" in August of 1914 was Karl Kraus:

> Believe me, though I was not in the field and not wounded, I suffered no less than you in the military service (somewhere Kraus says, "It is still worse to be forced to salute!"). I was in the ranks for three and a half years, in "training" for months, until, at Bruck, my weak constitution (I am asthmatic) broke down completely; then hospital, frightful details as sentry, relief duties; finally the war ministry, where *daily* for *two and a half years* from 8 o'clock in the morning until 6 or 7 o'clock in the evening I was occupied with the most difficult paperwork under a frightful superior officer (an idiotic drunkard); these long years of suffering endured in the rank of *corporal*, not composing a note—oh, it was dreadful, so that today, though I am actually freezing and have nothing to live on, I am *happy* in comparison to that period, when *physically* it was still bearable. I don't think you will soon again find such an enraged antimilitarist as I am.[43]

Berg goes on to cite as opponents of chauvinism and militarism, in whom Germans can take pride, the murdered communist leaders Rosa Luxemburg and Karl Liebknecht: "What names does the Entente have (outside of Russia) that ring of idealism as these do?" he asks.

Knight's argument against the interpretation of Büchner's drama as a *pièce à thèse* in support of the social revolution is convincing and applies equally to Berg's opera: "A political or social or economic moral can be drawn from it all, but . . . one will draw that moral at one's own risk; the dramatist has not told one to do so."[44] Nevertheless, the revolutionary impeachment of that social order for whose overthrow Büchner had called in his seditious tract, *The Hessian Courier*, is implicit in every line of his drama, and the musical setting of that drama was written against a background of war and revolution that bridged the gap between an author who was only beginning to emerge from the obscurity in which he had died eighty years earlier and the still-unknown composer.

42 Berg 71, pp. 177f.
43 Vojtěch 65, pp. 52f. Schulhoff, a pianist and composer, died in a German concentration camp in 1942.
44 Knight 51, p. 132.

2

WOYZECK AND WOZZECK

When the play that was to serve as the libretto of Alban Berg's *Wozzeck* was published for the first time, its author, Georg Büchner, had been dead for thirty-eight years.[1] Another thirty-eight years elapsed before the Staatstheater in Munich presented the first theatrical production on November 8, 1913. Berg saw the first production in Vienna in May of the following year, only three months before the outbreak of World War I—the beginning of an epoch during which the degradation Büchner's poor soldier suffers at the hands of the representatives of "organized society" was to become the common experience of millions of human beings. *Woyzeck* (as the title is given in most editions since that of Witkowski),[2] a work that has come down to us only in the preliminary drafts and sketches recovered after the author's death in 1837, retains the immediacy and contemporaneity today that it had for Karl Emil Franzos, the Galician–Jewish novelist who first deciphered the faded and almost illegible manuscripts, and for those later and greater writers whose revolutionary revision of dramatic conventions, decisively influenced by this work, led in turn to its acceptance as a living classic of the German theater.

The respects in which Gerhart Hauptmann, Frank Wedekind, and Bertolt Brecht found Büchner relevant to their own aesthetic and ideological principles

---

1 Prior to its publication in the first complete edition of Büchner's works (Büchner [Franzos] 1879), *Wozzeck* appeared in the *Neue freie Presse* (Vienna) in September and October, 1875, and in the Berlin weekly *Mehr Licht* in January of 1877, according to Franzos 01, *DD*, pp. 293, 298.

2 Büchner (Witkowski) 20. Franzos's spelling (Wozzeck) will be retained where the reference is to his edition, to other editions in which his spelling is followed, or to the opera itself.

are as diverse as their literary personalities. "[Hauptmann] saw him primarily as the portrayer of simple and suffering beings. Frank Wedekind absorbed the grotesque and rebellious elements of his plays, and through Wedekind Büchner came to be one of the spirits presiding over German Expressionism. For the young Bertolt Brecht, Büchner helped provide a language which was earthy and poetic at once. The French *avant garde* dramatists of the 1950's have seen Büchner as a poet of existential anguish and absurdity."[3] For central European socialists at the turn of the century, among whom Büchner's revolutionary pamphlet, *The Hessian Courier*, "became something of a household book of socialism side by side with Karl Marx and Ferdinand Lasalle" after its publication in Franzos's *Gesamtausgabe* in 1879,[4] *Wozzeck* can only have been a drama of social protest, a restatement in another medium of the revolutionary message of Büchner's proto-socialist pamphlet of 1834. But for Rainer Maria Rilke it was

> a monstrous affair . . . powerfully setting forth how around the most trivial existence, for which even the uniform of a common infantryman seems too wide and too much emphasized, how even around the recruit Wozzeck all the greatness of existence stands, how he cannot prevent now here, now there, before, behind, beside his dull soul, horizons from being torn open onto violence, immensity, the infinite; an incomparable play, the way this misused person in his stable-jacket stands in universal space, *malgré lui*, in the infinite relationship of the stars.[5]

One may suppose that the author of *Danton's Death* and *Woyzeck* was committed to a literary career, but it is doubtful that he arrived at this point during his short life. He was the son, grandson, and nephew of medical men, and his studies at the University of Strasbourg and the University of Giessen were intended to prepare him for the same profession. At Giessen Büchner assumed a leading role in the underground political activity that the example of the July Revolution in Paris had revived in the German universities. The same realism that sets him apart from his contemporaries as a writer separates him from his colleagues in politics. The masses, argued Büchner, will be moved, not by the liberal professors' demand for Freedom of the Press and similar abstractions, but only by an appeal based on their economic plight. *The Hessian Courier*, intended for surreptitious distribution among the peasants, was such an appeal. Büchner's original draft, which has not survived, was revised, to his great distress, by Pastor Weidig, Büchner's senior in the revolutionary band, to bring it into line with his own religious orientation and less radical political convictions. The difference in their aims is suggested by Weidig's substitution of "the aristocrats" for Büchner's "the rich" in every reference to the class enemy. The pamphlet was printed, but the conspiracy was soon betrayed and several of the participants were arrested. The authors, who were not yet known as such to the authorities, were put under surveillance but were temporarily allowed to remain at liberty.

3 Lindenberger 64, pp. 17f.   4 Hauch 29, *PMLA*, p. 897.   5 Rilke 48, p. 133.

Büchner returned to the family home in Darmstadt, prepared to flee at a moment's notice should he be threatened with arrest. Here, within five or six weeks in January and February of 1835, he composed *Danton's Death*, surely one of the most remarkable first plays ever written. Like *Woyzeck*, it has been subjected to radically diverse interpretations, according to the ideological tendencies of the interpreter. No comment on the drama itself is more succinctly relevant to it than the following words from a letter Büchner wrote to his fiancée:

> I have been studying the history of the Revolution. I felt annihilated by the terrible fatality of history. I find in human nature a frightful sameness, in human relations an inexorable power, given to all and to none. The individual only froth on the wave, greatness sheer chance, the splendor of genius a puppet show, a ridiculous struggle against an iron law, the recognition of which is the greatest achievement, the mastery of which is impossible.[6]

In a desperate attempt to raise some money he sent the manuscript of the play to Karl Gutzkow—already, though not much older than Büchner himself, a well-known writer—in the hope that Gutzkow's political and literary sympathies would lead him to respond favorably to this extraordinary plea from a total stranger for aid in securing a publisher and an advance. Without delay, Gutzkow sent a reply assuring him of both, but before it arrived Büchner, learning that his arrest was imminent, fled to Strasbourg. There he resumed his scientific studies and wrote the satirical romantic comedy, *Leonce and Lena*, and the remarkable prose narrative, *Lenz*, which was based on the diary of a witness to the mental derangement of J. M. R. Lenz, a poet and dramatist of the *Sturm-und-Drang* period. A scientific paper, written in French, "The Nervous System of the Barbel," was published by the Strasbourg Natural History Society and earned for Büchner a doctorate from the University of Zurich, where he was appointed lecturer in natural history in the autumn of 1836. Three months later, on February 19, 1837, at the age of twenty-three, he died of typhus.[7]

It is known that Büchner completed a play entitled *Pietro Aretino* shortly before his death, but no trace of this work survives. *Woyzeck* remained unpublished and possibly even unread until 1875, when it was discovered by Franzos among the manuscripts submitted to him by the author's brother, Ludwig.[8] Of his literary works only *Danton's Death* was published during Georg Büchner's lifetime, and that with numerous falsifications intended to make the text more attractive to the public and less offensive to the censor. *Lenz* and an incomplete version of *Leonce and Lena* were published shortly after Büchner's death in a

6 Büchner (Bergemann) 58, p. 374.
7 Weidig died in prison a few days afterward, driven to suicide, or possibly murdered, after a year in confinement. An absorbing account of Büchner's political activities and associates, as well as other interesting background material, is found in Mayer 60. See also Viëtor 49.
8 The circumstances are described in Franzos 01, *DD*, pp. 195–203, 289–300.

periodical edited by Gutzkow, whose project for a complete edition of Büchner's works fell through because he could not come to an agreement with the author's family. An edition was finally published under Ludwig Büchner's direction in 1850,[9] but *Woyzeck* was not included and little concern for textual accuracy was shown in the editing of the remaining works. By 1874 Georg Büchner had become, as Franzos's old bookdealer put it after searching out a copy of the 1850 edition for the young novelist, "surely—though it isn't safe to use a superlative in this connection—the most obscure of German writers."

The *Woyzeck* manuscripts, by the time they came into Franzos's hands, were so faded that it was necessary to treat the pages chemically in order to restore the script, and this was only the first of many difficulties that Franzos faced in deciphering the text. The handwriting was not only "microscopically small," but "the most illegible imaginable," and numerous abbreviations peculiar to the author had to be decoded. None of the manuscripts contained a continuous draft of the complete play. It could be reconstructed only through the collation of segments representing different stages in the creation of the work. The same characters appear under a variety of names in these different portions of the manuscripts. More serious than the problem of arriving at a literal transcription was the difficulty of determining the proper sequence of the different scenes, which are neither numbered nor grouped into acts, and which, according to Franzos, "offered not the slightest indication" of the intended ordering other than what might be inferred from their content.[10] It is in the nature of the play itself that such evidence remains open to widely divergent interpretations.

When the Büchner manuscripts were sent to Franzos in 1875 nothing could have seemed less probable than that the works of their long-deceased brother should add any luster to a name already made famous by his younger siblings: Wilhelm, factory-owner and member of the German Reichstag; Luise, noted novelist and fighter for women's rights; and above all, Dr. Ludwig Büchner himself, a popular and distinguished materialist philosopher and "freethinker" whose celebrated book, *Force and Matter,* had already appeared in numerous editions, reprints, and translations. Like the Doctor in *Woyzeck,* Ludwig Büchner was much concerned with the question of free will, and though his position on this question was diametrically opposed to that of his fictional counterpart, the conclusions of the two doctors are remarkably similar. "Mankind is free!" exclaims the Doctor in *Woyzeck.* "Have I not proved that the bladder muscle is subordinate to the will!" Dr. Ludwig Büchner, on the other hand, in a little pamphlet translated and published by Annie Besant in one of her pre-theosophist phases, maintained that the will is *not* free, but is determined by heredity and education as well as by instincts and innate propensities, from which he concluded that "since the will is not rigid or unchangeable, it is therefore in the power of man himself by progressive training, molding,

9 Büchner (Büchner) 1850.   10 Büchner (Franzos) 1879, pp. 202ff.

26   and improvement to free himself from these animal instincts more and more, and thereby to make himself better, happier, and more contented than he has hitherto been." Woyzeck's words, reiterating a recurring motif in Georg Büchner's letters, "Man is an abyss—it makes one dizzy to look into it!" would have been as incomprehensible to the real doctor as to the fictional one. "I recall," wrote Dr. Büchner to Franzos, "that it was not only the difficulty of deciphering [*Woyzeck*] but also its content, so far as I could decipher it, that led me to omit [it] from the *Nachgelassene Schriften.*" Dr. Büchner was distressed not only by the "cynicism" of the work, but also by what he euphemistically termed its "trivialities." Much of his correspondence with Franzos concerns such questions as whether the offensive word in the drunken Drum Major's "Ich will ihm die Nas ins Arschloch prügeln" was to be replaced by "A-loch" (Franzos) or "A—" (Dr. Büchner).

Franzos successfully resisted the efforts of the eminent "freethinker" to censor the projected edition, but failed in his attempts to rescue that portion of Georg Büchner's legacy that had passed into the hands of Minna Jaegle, the author's fiancée. Fräulein Jaegle, surviving her lover by forty-three years, remained devoted to his memory to the end, loyally protecting the papers that had come into her possession upon his death from what to her was the impertinent curiosity of one whose interests were merely professional. Franzos' importunities were definitively rejected:

> In your esteemed letter of February 17 [1877] you say I have a moral duty to assist in the publication of Georg Büchner's works by making available such papers of his as are in my possession. To this I have the honor to reply to you that I feel no moral duty whatever to make the said papers public. Some of them concern only me personally. Others are incomplete abstracts and notes. The memory of Georg Büchner is so dear to me that I cannot wish to expose anything of his that is unfinished to review by literary critics. Having been prevented by serious illness from replying to you sooner, I have had to postpone it until today. I would be obliged to you, esteemed sir, if you would permit this explanation to suffice for the future.[11]

Whatever writings of Büchner's Minna Jaegle may still have possessed had vanished without a trace by the time of her death three years later, and it is assumed that she destroyed them when she felt her end approaching. Franzos was convinced that the manuscript of *Pietro Aretino* was in her possession. Other scholars dispute this assumption and suggest that the manuscript may have been destroyed in a fire in the Büchner home, in which the letters that Ludwig Büchner had neglected to publish in his edition of 1850 are known to have perished. It has been conjectured that a final fair copy of *Woyzeck* was in fact completed, but its fate, if such a manuscript ever existed, is equally unknown.

Though Franzos describes his *Gesamtausgabe* as the "first critical edition," it is clear that he was not governed by scholarly considerations in preparing the

---

11 Büchner (Bergemann) 58, pp. 597f.

text of *Wozzeck* for its first publication. Franzos was not a "literary historian," but a novelist who found himself, as he points out, "obliged to undertake literary-historical tasks because of a special interest" in a writer of supreme genius whom the professional scholars had ignored. Later researchers have established that the claim in his editorial postscript to *Wozzeck*, "The foregoing is a literally faithful reproduction of the wording of the manuscripts," is unjustified. Of the two distinct tasks laid upon an editor in this instance, the preparation of a coherent version of the drama and the faithful reproduction of the text, he really concerned himself only with the first and, at the time, more urgent one. Even here he succeeded only insofar as the actual wording of the individual scenes was concerned, not in their overall ordering. A new and more coherent arrangement of the Franzos reading appeared in 1909 in Paul Landau's edition of *Georg Büchner's Collected Works*.[12] New readings of the original manuscripts appeared only in 1920 (Witkowski) and 1922 (Bergemann). Both of these offered "scholarly" transcriptions of Büchner's text for the first time, but Witkowski made no attempt to provide a dramatically feasible version, and Bergemann's attempt to base such a version exclusively on extrinsic aspects of the manuscripts proved to be abortive. In subsequent editions of what was to remain for forty-five years the standard *Gesamtausgabe* of Büchner's writings, Bergemann radically revised his stage version of the drama, with the explanation that the manuscripts give "only suggestions for the ordering of the scenes, but no definitive solution."[13]

On the authority of Berg himself, his authorized biographer Willi Reich let it be known that the composer had worked exclusively with Franzos's edition in preparing the libretto. Berg's ordering of the scenes, however, corresponds to that of Landau. A particularly striking example of the extent of this correspondence is found in their respective treatment of the twelfth and seventeenth scenes of Franzos's edition. Landau took these to be variants of a single scene and therefore included only Franzos's seventeenth scene in the body of his text, appending the twelfth scene as an alternative version directly below it, in the form of a footnote. In the opera the two scenes are integrated into a single episode. With the deletion from Landau's version of those scenes which Berg excluded from the opera, the succession of scenes in Landau and in Berg is identical. According to Reich, "Rudolf Schäfke points out (in an article in *Melos*, Berlin, May 1926) various refinements of Berg's textual arrangement, and errs only insofar as he assumes that Berg used Paul Landau's critically sifted edition of 1909, whereas in fact the composer worked from Karl Emil Franzos's first edition of 1879 and only compared his version with other editions after the opera was completed."[14] In Berg's own copy of Schäfke's article an interlinear note in his own hand seems to indicate that he did in fact base his libretto on the Franzos edition.

12 Büchner (Landau) 09.
13 Bergemann's 1922 transcription, on which all of his subsequent editions were based, has finally been supplanted by a transcription, in Büchner (Lehmann) 67, from which the literal content of the *Woyzeck* manuscripts can be reconstructed for the first time.
14 Reich 65, p. 118.

28   It can nevertheless now be affirmed that the remarkable correspondence between Berg's libretto and the Landau edition of the drama is not coincidental. In 1967 a copy of the play containing Berg's own handwritten notations adapting it to the libretto came to my attention. It is a cheap, popular edition, No. 29 of a series called "Orplidbücher," published by Axel Juncker Verlag. Neither the editor nor the year is indicated, but on a slip of paper pasted below the title on the title page Berg wrote the following:

(in der Fassung von Karl Emil Franzos)
Oper
in
drei Akten
(15 Scenen)
von
Alban Berg
Op. 7
(Textbuch)

This version of the drama, however, is "in der Fassung von Karl Emil Franzos" only in the *reading* of the individual scenes, which was the only one available when the Landau edition was published in 1909. The order of the scenes is that of Landau. On a blank page preceding the text the composer has provided a handwritten "Scenarium." In the text itself Berg has deleted the scenes omitted from the opera by pasting together or striking out the pages containing these scenes. The sequence of the remaining scenes is identical with that of Berg's "Scenarium" (see Plates 8–10.)

        The *Kayser Deutsches Bücherverzeichnis* gives the year of publication as 1919. On June 17, 1921, Berg was still, as he writes to his wife, working on the "Wozzeck-Szenen-Disposition."[15] Thus Berg's annotations must have been made on or after this date. The disposition of scenes in Act I had already been fixed by this time, since Berg describes this act as completed in a letter to Schoenberg dated July 29, 1919. Berg's fusion of Franzos's twelfth and seventeenth scenes (II/5 in the opera), which Landau, taking them to be variants of a single scene, grouped together, cannot have been suggested by "Orplidbücher" No. 29. This modest, pasteboard-bound, unscholarly publication omits the twelfth scene of Franzos's edition altogether, as it does all editorial comment and even the name of the editor. The particular correspondence in question suggests that Berg was acquainted with the original Landau *Gesamtausgabe*.[16]

15 Berg 65, p. 463.
16 I first pointed out the correspondence between Berg's libretto and the Landau edition in an earlier version of this chapter (Perle 67c, *MQ*), completed just before Berg's own copy of the Landau edition came to my attention. A second article on the same subject (Perle 68, *NZfM*) is derived from the present version of this chapter. My review of the recordings of the opera in Perle 67d, *SR*, also disputes Reich's account of the genesis of the libretto. Gerd Ploebsch did not have an opportunity to consult these articles when he was preparing his doctoral dissertation; he arrived independently at the same conclusion, that Berg must have based his libretto on Landau (Ploebsch

In any event, Berg's "new dramaturgical treatment" did not involve the composer in a preliminary "project of organizing the poet's sketchy design," as everyone has assumed on the basis of the above-quoted statement by Willi Reich.[17] There is, in fact, no good reason to assume that he prepared a libretto in advance of the composition at all. With a few exceptions, the only changes that Berg made in the text of the individual scenes are such as would occur to a composer in the actual course of composition. Quite unlike the case with *Lulu*, no preliminary draft of the libretto was necessary. The "new dramaturgical treatment," insofar as this is reflected in the libretto apart from its musical setting, is found above all in the grouping of its fifteen scenes into three acts of five scenes each, as opposed to the uninterrupted sequence of the original. As

---

68). It comes, then, as something of a surprise to discover the following statement in a monograph (Hilmar 75) published for the fiftieth anniversary of the première of the opera: "Bisher war man der Meinung, dass Berg die Ausgabe von Franzos zur Komposition der Oper vorgelegen hat" ("Until now it has been assumed that Berg worked from the Franzos edition in composing the opera"). Since the credentials of the new book make it likely that it will supplant Reich as the authorized history of the composition (the publisher, Universal Edition, is also the publisher of Berg's works; the author, Bibliotheksoberkommissär Dr. Ernst Hilmar of the Municipal Library in Vienna, was supported in this project by the "special interest" and the "indefatigable assistance" of the composer's widow), we cannot ignore it, even though the author overlooks Perle entirely in a specialized bibliography that comprises almost 200 entries on Berg's opera. Unfortunately, Dr. Hilmar's unjustified claim is only the first in a succession of more serious and even more inexplicable errors, all comprised within the space of two short paragraphs.

Although Redlich, like everyone else, accepted Reich's assertion that the libretto is based exclusively on the Franzos edition, in his "Table of Concordances" he compared Berg's libretto with Arnold Zweig's edition (1923) of the play. The latter is a practical performing edition partially based on the first revised text (Witkowski's), published in 1920. Redlich notes that "here and there the composer improved Büchner's text, as in the fourth scene of the first act, where his replacement of 'Wozzeck, let me feel your pulse' by 'Wozzeck, show me your tongue' leads to a 'curtain' of grotesque, daemonic effectiveness." But Berg did not have before him the Büchner text as restored by Witkowski. Redlich is correct in attributing "Wozzeck, let me feel your pulse" to Büchner, but he is incorrect in attributing "Wozzeck, let me see your tongue" to Berg. It is Franzos who is responsible for the improvement.

In 1913 a separate printing of *Wozzeck* and *Lenz*, No. 92 of the "Insel-Bücherei" series, was published from Hausenstein's new edition of Büchner's collected works. Like "Orplidbücher" No. 29, this earlier edition gives *Wozzeck* in the Landau reordering of Franzos's text. A hitherto unreported copy of this 1913 printing containing Berg's own marginal notes on the opera was put at Dr. Hilmar's disposal by Helene Berg. Dr. Hilmar somehow overlooks Redlich's explicit statement that his comparison is based on "Büchner's *Woyzeck* (Ausgabe A. Zweig)," and makes the really extraordinary assumption that the 1913 edition of *Wozzeck* (not yet *Woyzeck!*) is a restoration of Büchner's original text. He "corrects" Redlich by attributing Büchner's "Wozzeck, let me feel your pulse" to Franzos, and Franzos's "Wozzeck, let me see your tongue" to Büchner.

Like "Orplidbücher" No. 29, "Insel-Bücherei" No. 92 lacks the footnote in which Landau gave what he took to be a variant scene. Since this scene is incorporated in Act II, Scene 5 of the opera, Dr. Hilmar concludes that Berg must have known the Franzos edition, as well as the Landau. The grounds he gives for this assumption, however, are incorrect: "Insel-Bücherei" No. 92 *does*, in fact, contain the "missing" scene, in an "Afterword" which Dr. Hilmar overlooked.

(This new authorized version of the genesis of Berg's libretto bids fair to provide future Ph.D. candidates with a continuing subject, where I had thought I had succeeded in eliminating one. A word of warning to them: A later edition of the play, edited by Ernst Hardt and based on the revised texts in the Witkowski and Bergemann editions, was also incorporated into the "Insel-Bücherei" series. For some reason the publisher assigned the same number to it as to the Landau–Hausenstein. Thus we have two entirely different editions of the play, both of them known as "Insel-Bücherei" No. 92.)

17 See Perle 67d, *SR*.

30   late as August 19, 1918, the composer was only tentatively feeling his way toward this conception.[18]

Berg's identification of the anonymous editor as "Franzos" was justified by the *reading* of the individual scenes, and the inclusion of this attribution in the then-intended full title of the work (the same attribution is given in the full title of the short score)[19] may have seemed necessary in order to differentiate his basic text from the new critical edition of Witkowski, especially since in this title he corrects Franzos's misspelling of the protagonist's name, altering it to "Woyzeck," as given for the first time in Witkowski's 1920 edition. In the fair copy of the full score, completed in the spring of 1922,[20] the same year in which Bergemann brought out the first edition of his *Gesamtausgabe*, Berg likewise initially used the authentic spelling, "Woyzeck," but then restored the name to "Wozzeck." The omission of the diphthong is, from a musical point of view, sufficient reason for restoring the version that Berg had already employed in composing the musical setting of the drama. But the title *Wozzeck*, rather than *Woyzeck*, is also appropriate as a sign that his conception of the drama was, fortunately, derived from Franzos and Landau, rather than from the "critically sifted" editions of subsequent literary historians.

The conscientious efforts of Bergemann himself and of other "scientifically" minded scholars to deduce from their valuable historical and textual investigations implications as to the form and content of the drama were, on the whole, until recent studies had made some further corrections in their work, more damaging than Franzos's mistakes—more damaging even than what some critics have described as his falsifications. The principal difficulties concerned the denouement of the drama. The series of scenes on which the final act of the opera is based is identical in Franzos and in Landau. In the Franzos-Landau-Berg version Wozzeck's tragic fate culminates in his drowning in the pond beside which his victim lies, after he wades into the water to retrieve the discarded murder weapon. Knight points out that Franzos's "wilful insertion of the stage-direction 'ertrinkt' . . . begs the question of Büchner's final intentions. . . . It is not known just how *Woyzeck* was intended to end. . . . Franzos supported his assumption . . . with an emendation which almost

18 See the letter to Webern of that date: Reich 53, *SM*. The assertion in Reich 37, "In the summer of 1917 the arrangement of the text of *Wozzeck* was completed," is a surmise based on the assumption that Berg would have prepared an independent libretto before commencing serious work upon the composition. But according to Reich 65: "In the summer of 1917 he had already begun on the composition (Act II, Scene 2), although the text was not yet finished." The two statements are equally misleading.

19 According to Albrecht 53. The date given at the end of the short score, as cited in Albrecht, is July 16, 1922. Since the piano reduction of the full score was in preparation several months before this, this date cannot refer to the completion of the short score. According to Reich 37, the short score was completed by the autumn of 1920. But Reich 65 states that "the short score of the work was finished in October 1921." The latter date is probably correct. A letter to his wife dated September 6, 1918, makes it clear that Berg orchestrated at least a portion of the work long before completing the short score.

20 Reich 37 has "1921," but this is an error. It is corrected in Reich 63, 65, but in the meantime the erroneous date was given general currency in the literature on *Wozzeck*.

amounts to a forgery."[21] One of the scenes omitted by Franzos and published for the first time in the editions of Witkowski and Bergemann was taken to prove that Büchner could not have intended to let Woyzeck drown. The manuscripts fall into two sets of sketches, an incomplete revision that includes some scenes not found among the sketches, and two "separate" scenes, one of which is the scene in question. It is given here in its entirety, as it appears in Bergemann:

DER IDIOT. DAS KIND. WOYZECK

KARL *hält das Kind vor sich auf dem Schoss.* Der is ins Wasser gefallen, der is ins Wasser gefallen, mir, der is ins Wasser gefallen.
WOYZECK. Bub, Christian!
KARL *sieht ihn starr an.* Der is ins Wasser gefallen.
WOYZECK *will das Kind liebkosen, es wendet sich weg und schreit.* Herrgott!
KARL. Der is ins Wasser gefallen.
WOYZECK. Christianchen, du bekommst en Reuter, sa sa *das Kind wehrt sich; zu Karl:* da, kauf dem bub en Reuter!
KARL *sieht ihn starr an.*
WOYZECK. Hop! hop! Ross.
KARL *jauchzend.* Hop! Hop! Ross! Ross! *läuft mit dem Kind weg.*[22]

Regardless of a transcriber's intentions, the condition of the manuscripts excludes an objectively literal reading of the text in many places. Scientific impartiality will necessarily give way to subjective evaluations based on plausibility, prejudice, or even unconscious word-associations. The resulting unintentional emendations of the original text may be even more problematic than the deliberate emendations of a less scholarly editor. Variants between the readings of Witkowski and Bergemann illustrate these difficulties repeatedly. Thus, where Bergemann has "Ross" (horse), Witkowski saw "Nass" (wet), associating the word in question with "Wasser" (water) rather than with "Reuter" (hobby-horse). This water motive unfortunately led Bergemann and almost all subsequent editors and scholars to make another mistaken association that affected their conception of the play as a whole. The idiot's refrain was, plausibly enough, understood to refer to Woyzeck, dripping wet after his return from the pond. The child's reaction to his father's appearance seems to confirm this interpretation. If this scene was not to be ignored as a completely

21 Knight 51, pp. 116f.
22   THE IDIOT. THE CHILD. WOYZECK
KARL *(holding the child on his lap).* That one fell in the water, that one fell in the water, that one fell in the water.
WOYZECK. Son! Christian!
KARL *(staring at him).* That one fell in the water.
WOYZECK *(tries to embrace the child, who shrinks away and cries out).* My God!
KARL. That one fell in the water.
WOYZECK. Christy, you'll get a hobby-horse. Trot! trot! *(The child resists him.) (To Karl):* Here, buy the boy a hobby-horse!
KARL *stares at him.*
WOYZECK. Giddyap, giddyap, horsey!
KARL *(shouting gleefully).* Giddyap, giddyap! Horsey, horsey! *(Runs off with the child.)*

32 discarded sketch that implied nothing whatever about the author's intentions for the conclusion of the play, what could be surmised regarding these intentions? The scholars found grounds for their speculations in information that had not been available to Franzos. It was now known that there had been an historical model for the protagonist of Büchner's tragedy.

The real Woyzeck (Büchner changed only his Christian name in the play) was the protagonist of a scene enacted before a large audience in the marketplace at Leipzig on August 27, 1824—his public execution. Three years earlier the despised and poverty-stricken ex-soldier, by trade a wigmaker and barber, forty-one years of age, had stabbed to death his faithless mistress, a forty-six-year-old widow. At his trial the defense pleaded insanity, and a prominent expert, Hofrat Dr. Clarus, was appointed to investigate Woyzeck's mental condition. After lengthy interrogations and observations Clarus reported that in spite of certain aberrations and delusions Woyzeck could not be regarded as mentally unbalanced. The date for his execution was set, but then a postponement was granted pending a second investigation by Clarus, who reaffirmed his earlier conclusions. Doubts about the accuracy of Clarus's diagnosis continued to be expressed after the execution, in reply to which Clarus published a report "on the sanity of Johann Christian Woyzeck." The latter appeared in a medical journal that would have been available in the Büchner household, since the elder Büchner was himself a contributor.[23]

The story of the real Woyzeck not only suggested the content of the drama but was also the source of explicit verbal motives, employing Woyzeck's own words as reported by Clarus. A scene of twenty-five words, found only at the conclusion of the first draft,[24] led Bergemann and other scholars to project parallels beyond those indicated in the manuscripts themselves. This scene was thought to indicate that Büchner proposed to show Woyzeck in the custody of the law, and perhaps even to confront him eventually, in the courtroom, with the representatives and agents of a criminal social order that should itself be on trial. In Franzos's edition this scene is given in an "emendated" version at the conclusion of the play, after Wozzeck's death by drowning:

Seziersaal

CHIRURG. ARZT. RICHTER

RICHTER. Ein guter Mord, ein ächter Mord, ein schöner Mord, so schön, als man ihn nur verlangen kann. Wir haben schon lange keinen so schönen gehabt.
ARZT.————[25]

23 The historical antecedent of the drama was first brought to attention by Hugo Bieber in *Literarisches Echo,* June 1, 1914.
24 Since the revision on which Büchner was working at the time of his death breaks off before this point in the drama, we do not know whether or not he planned to retain this scene.
25   *DISSECTING ROOM*
SURGEON. PHYSICIAN. JUDGE
JUDGE. A good murder, a real murder, a lovely murder. You couldn't ask for a nicer one. We haven't had one so nice in a long time.
PHYSICIAN. ——

Bergemann gives the following version:

GERICHTSDIENER. BARBIER. ARZT. RICHTER

POL. Ein guter Mord, ein ächter Mord, ein schöner Mord, so schön als man ihn
nur verlangen tun kann; wir haben schon lange keinen so schönen gehabt.
BARBIER. *Dogmatischer Atheist. Lang, hager, feig, gutmutig, Wissenschaftl.* [26]

Franzos, as he explained in his notes, suppressed the "Barbier," whose
role he saw, on the basis of another scene that had been indubitably discarded
by the author, as a preliminary sketch for the Drum Major. Bergemann et al.,
noting the presence of a figure identified by the profession of the historical
Woyzeck (and, presumably, of the fictional one as well, since it is one of the
latter's duties to shave the Captain), took this as confirmation of Woyzeck's
return after he had waded into the pond, implied earlier in the Idiot's refrain,
"Der is ins Wasser gefallen." They concluded that the "Barbier" represented
Woyzeck, apprehended by the police after the discovery of Marie's corpse. Yet
a more inappropriate collection of attributes for either the historical or the fictional Woyzeck can hardly be imagined than that which describes the "Barbier"
in Bergemann's version of the scene. Moreover, in the only other scene in
which the "Barbier" appears he is assigned a text that the author eventually
distributed among characters that offer the strongest possible contrast to
Woyzeck—the Captain, the Doctor, the Drum Major, the Apprentices.
Nevertheless, this interpretation was unaccountably accepted by most scholars
and editors of the work, including many who followed Franzos's version of
Woyzeck's fate as a matter of practical necessity in the absence of any other
resolution of the drama, as Bergemann himself did.

The arguments for hypothesizing another denouement have finally been
disposed of once and for all. Hermann van Dam has shown that the Idiot's
refrain, "Der is ins Wasser gefallen," may possibly be taken as foreshadowing
the scene in which Woyzeck wades into the pond, but that there is less than no
reason for it to be taken as a reference to Woyzeck's appearance after his supposed emergence from the pond. "These words of the Idiot can (and almost
must) be otherwise understood. They are nothing else than a fragment of a
counting-rhyme, which the Idiot Karl continually babbles, and which does not
first occur in this scene."[27] In the earlier scene that shows the remorseful Marie
reading from the Bible, the Idiot is acting out fairy tales on his fingers. One of
his lines, "Der hat die goldne Kron," is found in the same children's game.[28]

34   Strangely enough, van Dam continues to accept the view that the "Barbier" is
"undoubtedly the barber Woyzeck, after his arrest." This egregious misconcep-
tion will not long survive, it is to be hoped, the objections since raised against
it in an article by Wolfgang Martens.[29]

In addition to the negative proof of the gross textual inconsistencies that
must follow from an identification of the "Barbier" with Woyzeck, Martens
offers conclusive positive evidence for his opinion that the "Barbier" is an independent role. In the first place, the "Barbier" is the traditional barber-
surgeon, one of whose functions it was to assist the legal authorities in investigations of homicide by examining the corpse. Büchner had obviously intended,
before dropping the role altogether, to represent him as another anonymous
agent of the Establishment, identified, like the Captain and the Doctor, only by
the title of his profession. Second, the only scene in which the "Barbier" is
given any dialogue is the discarded sketch mentioned above,[30] which shows
him to be garrulous, sentimental, grotesque, and conceited about his professional attainments—all attributes of the typical barber of literature and opera.[31]

Thus, after forty years of critical research, we are brought back to Franzos's conception of the denouement of the drama. His emendation of the text
by the stage direction *ertrinkt* "almost amounts to a forgery" only because he
failed to provide any critical apparatus whatever to show that this was indeed
an emendation. But it is not an emendation of the content of the drama.
Woyzeck does *not* re-emerge after he wades into the pond. Franzos, who, to be
sure, did not have to cope with the historical facts about the real Woyzeck,
recognized the function of the "Barbier" in the final scene and substituted
"Chirurg" for the title of the role. This scene could well have been omitted
altogether by Franzos, as it was by Berg.[32]

---

29 In 60, *ZfdP.*
30 Büchner (Bergemann) 58, pp. 488f.; Büchner (Lehmann) 67, pp. 148f.
31 The recent translation in Büchner (Mueller) 65 includes *both* of the scenes in which the
"Barbier" appears, and identifies him both times, without any editorial comment, by the name of
the title role. The earlier scene was crossed out in the MS by Büchner himself, after he had incorporated an improved version of segments of its text in later drafts. Even the description of the
"Barbier," as deciphered by Bergemann but deleted heretofore from the practical editions that
incorporate the scene in which it is found, is given by Mueller. The character of Woyzeck is thus
made into an absurdity, though this, presumably, is not what the translator means when he describes the drama as having served "as the impetus for literary movements down to the present
day's Theatre of the Absurd."
32 Cf. Lindenberger 64, p. 99: "I, for one, have always felt uncomfortable with this scene,
for the crudeness of its irony seems to me out of keeping with the tone of the other later scenes of
the play; moreover, drawn as it is from an early draft, it need carry no more authority than other
scenes from these drafts which editors have chosen to eliminate." Before dropping the "Barbier" it
should be pointed out that there are many places in the MSS where the identity of a character must
be conjectured, rather than deciphered, and that such a conjecture may not be used as evidence for
the validity of the assumption on which it depends in the first place. For example, where Witkowski attributes the statement, "Ich bin ein dogmatischer Atheist," to a "Student," Bergemann
offers a conjectural identification of the speaker as "Franz," i.e., Woyzeck, thus speciously sup-
porting his thesis that the "Barbier" ("Dogmatischer Atheist") and Woyzeck are the same person.
Similarly tendentious attributions are found in Witkowski's edition.
Lehmann accepts Martens's arguments against the identification of the "Barbier" as
Woyzeck, but, seemingly unaware of van Dam's earlier arguments against a literal interpretation of

At least two of Franzos's "wilful insertions" are so extraordinarily apposite and effective that it is difficult to believe that they do not originate with Büchner. In the Doctor's study Wozzeck, becoming increasingly disturbed and fearful as he describes his delusions to the Doctor, suddenly interjects the exclamation, "Ach, Marie!" This seemingly unmotivated interpolation marvelously epitomizes that one aspect of Wozzeck's existence which enables him to survive his superstitious terrors and the humiliations to which he is subjected—his relationship with Marie and the child. Robert Craft reports Albert Camus's remark after a performance of the opera: "The way the name of Marie comes to Wozzeck's lips is a stroke of genius."[33] If so, it is a stroke of genius that must be credited to Franzos rather than to Büchner. (In the opera there is simultaneously an implied allusion to the child as well, through the setting of "Ach, Marie!" to Marie's "Komm, mein Bub!" *Leitmotiv* [Ex. 40].) The other of these "wilful insertions" occurs in the scene of the children playing before Marie's door the morning after the murder. (The stage directions are Franzos's.) A child turns from his playmates, who have just learned of the discovery of Marie's body, and calls out to Marie's son, "Du! Dein Mutter ist todt!" ("You! Your mother is dead!"). What could be more characteristic of Büchner than the realistic childlike callousness of this line?

On the other hand, Franzos is accountable for the disturbing fact that the single appearance of the Idiot, and his words, "Ich riech Blut!", lack motivation in the opera, as they do in Franzos's edition of the play. By deleting the other appearances of the Idiot, Franzos reduces his appearance in the Tavern Garden to an arbitrary device and deprives his crucial words of a context without which they are inexplicable. The Idiot, here and in the later scenes in which he appears, is innocently babbling words belonging to the child's world of fairy tale and counting-rhyme, words—"Blut!", "Wasser!"—which are fearfully transformed in Wozzeck's mind, which are portents of his fate.

Berg's libretto is now seen to be a remarkably authentic practical version of the drama, one that finds more support in recent critical studies than the versions of those editors who conscientiously attempted to conform closely to the speculations of Bergemann and other scholars regarding Büchner's ultimate intentions. His setting of the libretto, however, is based on formal principles totally dissimilar in technique and effect from those that seem to govern the drama. Though the play remains unfinished, in the sense that no final fair-copy revision is known, the fact that it consists of "loosely constructed, partly fragmentary scenes"—the reason offered by Berg to explain his imposition of a tightly constructed, systematically planned musical framework[34]—cannot be entirely attributed to its unfinished state. Many of the scenes in *Danton's Death*,

---

the Idiot's "Der is ins Wasser gefallen," fails to follow Martens's conclusion that it was indeed Büchner's intention that Woyzeck should drown in the pond. Regarding Lehmann's placement of the two "verstreute Bruchstücke" in his synoptic arrangement of the MSS, see Chapter Three, fn. 7, below.

33 Stravinsky 66, p. 181.   34 Berg 27, *MM*.

36 a play that Büchner *did* finish, are also mere sketches, "loosely constructed, partly fragmentary scenes." Of these Knight has written:

> It seems certain that Büchner, with immense boldness and originality, was deliberately aiming at an almost entirely new technical effect, . . . whereby the action is presented in a series of apparently, but not really, disconnected flashes, which ultimately, but only ultimately, form a picture that makes sense. . . . He evolved, partly from his Sturm-und-Drang predecessors, this disconnected, kaleidoscopic technique, which results in something rather like the scenario of a film, and foreshadows the Expressionist methods of eighty or ninety years later, though not so obviously as does *Woyzeck*.[35]

Woyzeck is even "more episodic, less logically connected and fitted together" than *Danton's Death*.

> The events *seem* to follow one another with less precision, indeed they sometimes seem actually inconsequent or disconnected, as is shown by the fact that one can quite reasonably fit the scenes together in various sequences. But this inconsequence is only apparent: actually the events are linked together with an almost perfect inner logic, the theme develops with an economy and inevitability seldom found in the work of any dramatist.[36]

Within a few months after the world première of Berg's opera, presented in Berlin under the direction of Erich Kleiber on December 14, 1925, Manfred Gurlitt conducted the first performance of his own setting of the drama. Gurlitt's *Wozzeck* is based, like Berg's, on the Landau edition. Unlike Berg, he does not group the scenes into acts and provides no musical interludes to bind the scenes to one another. The "expressionistic" elements of the play are preserved, but the dramaturgic metamorphosis that would justify transference of the drama from the spoken to the musical stage is not achieved.[37]

In Berg's opera the "economy and inevitability" and the "inner logic" of the drama are not merely inferred from a series of seemingly disconnected events; they are objectively and powerfully expressed through an autonomous musical structure of unprecedented rigor and symmetry. As in Mozart, the sound and the sense of the text are projected through a non-verbal material that imposes its own logic and its own proportions. In Berg as in Mozart, a constant and inevitable order subsumes the dramatic details, but Berg's order, unlike Mozart's, is irrational, meaningless, non-human, indifferent, for it embraces the casual and the essential, the momentous and the trivial, with equal impartiality. If "the episodic, scene-by-scene, 'expressionist' style" of the drama disappears, all the more powerfully projected is a characteristic theme discussed by Knight in connection with the *Lenz* narrative: "The perpetual, poignant, horrifying contrast between men, so hopelessly involved in a universe not made by them and hostile to their interests and efforts, and that

---

35 Knight 51, p. 81.   36 Ibid., p. 133.
37 There are some interesting incidental parallels between the two versions. In both operas an orchestral epilogue follows the drowning scene, and in both "Wir arme Leut!" is a primary *Leitmotiv*.

universe itself, as it mechanically functions in the manifestations of external nature."[38] What could be more expressive of Wozzeck's isolation and estrangement, which have led to Marie's death and to his own, than the quiet, rhythmical croaking of the toads as he drowns in the pond beside which lies the corpse of his murdered mistress? The dramatic relevance of this "nature music" is inseparable from its objective role within an autonomous musical structure.

Was Berg correct in assuming that the conversion of Büchner's "loosely constructed, partly fragmentary scenes" into a opera could only be realized through the imposition of such a structure? Schoenberg had already composed his revolutionary "expressionist" monodrama *Erwartung* in the "disconnected, kaleidoscopic technique" of the so-called athematic style. It was the nature of the composer rather than the nature of his subject that led Berg to impose order and discipline through the rigorous formal framework that governs the work as a whole and upon which the significance of the smallest structural detail depends. Berg's special kind of form-consciousness manifests itself not only in his two operas but in each of his major works, from the *Altenberg Lieder* to the Violin Concerto.[39]

"*Woyzeck*," writes George Steiner, "is the first real tragedy of low life. It repudiates an assumption implicit in Greek, Elizabethan, and neo-classic drama: the assumption that tragic suffering is the sombre privilege of those who are in high places."[40] In Berg's *Wozzeck* this assumption was repudiated on the operatic stage as well.[41]

38 Knight 51, p. 147.

39 Lindenberger 64, p. 129, suggests that the "form-consciousness which is manifest [in the opera] is indicative . . . of a kind of classicism peculiar to much of the art of the 1920's. It seems to me analogous, for instance, to the mythological framework and charts of correspondences around which James Joyce constructed *Ulysses*; T. S. Eliot's well-known description of the function of Joyce's mythological framework—'It is simply a way of controlling, of ordering, of giving a shape and a significance to the immense panorama of futility and anarchy which is contemporary history'—is perhaps applicable to the function of the tight musical forms which Berg employs to contain the chaotic and characteristically modern materials that he found in Büchner's play."

40 Steiner 61, p. 274.

41 The foregoing chapter had already been prepared for publication by the time Maurice R. Benn's recent study of Büchner (*The Drama of Revolt* [Cambridge: Cambridge University Press, 1976]) came to my attention. It includes a comprehensive and valuable essay on the *Woyzeck* manuscripts and the sources of the drama.

3

THE TEXT AND FORMAL DESIGN

Aside from the omission of a number of scenes and some minor roles, the libretto of *Wozzeck* almost literally reproduces the Franzos–Landau text. Fragments of the omitted scenes and of the dialogue assigned to the deleted roles have been transferred to other scenes and characters in the libretto. A very few passages are rearranged for the sake of the musical design; such changes, considering the exigencies of this design, are remarkably rare. The only material revision of the wording itself occurs in Act I, Scene 4, where the Doctor's anger with Wozzeck is attributed to the latter's inability to control the functions of his diaphragm rather than of his bladder. Such other changes as Berg makes in the wording are minimal indeed, and their musical and/or dramatic motivation are usually self-evident.

The libretto, although it conforms closely to a text whose overall stylistic effect is impressionistic and disjointed, conveys much of the formal strictness and symmetry of the operatic score. This transformation is achieved primarily through the reduction of Franzos's twenty-six scenes to fifteen, and to their grouping into three acts whose extrinsic interrelations are formally strict and abstract. Each act has five scenes and the three acts together, in their relative duration and complexity, form an arch, with the longer and more complex middle act bridging the symmetrically balanced outer acts.

Act I is expository, each scene relating Wozzeck to a different aspect of his environment and to another person of the drama. Scene 1 introduces the Captain, a grotesque personification of the banality of conventional notions of social propriety and morals, and shows Wozzeck in his "normal" workaday world, performing his duties as the Captain's batman. In Scene 2 we find Wozzeck with his companion, Andres, cutting kindling in an open field at sunset. It is in this scene, above all, that the "social protest" interpretation of the play is seen to be inadequate. Wozzeck's fellows may be equally poor and oppressed and misused, but they are not alienated and estranged from the world of nature about them—the ground is not hollow beneath their feet, the evening stillness is not weird to them. Scene 3 introduces Marie, first as a vital and sensuous woman admiring the soldiers on parade in the street before her house, then as a mother who finds "so much joy" in the "illegitimate face" of her infant. Wozzeck's abstracted air when he pauses at the house for a moment on his way to the barracks leaves her frightened and frustrated at the end of the scene. Scene 4 introduces the Doctor, a representative, like the Captain, of "organized society." Though he stands for its more exalted features, for its science and learning, his ideas are no less banal, even when they are uttered in Latin. Wozzeck is his human guinea pig, the subject of medical experiments through which the Doctor expects to earn undying fame. Scene 5 is the only one in the opera, aside from the epilogue after Wozzeck's death, in which Wozzeck does not appear. The new role here is that of the Drum Major, whom Marie admired as he passed by at the head of the parade at the beginning of Scene 3, and who now returns to strut and swagger before her in the street. As Knight points out:

> In no serious sense is she wicked or immoral. . . . Marie has never been promiscuous, nor even on-coming with men: the present case is an extraordinary exception. . . . Fundamentally she is deeply religious and also, in actual fact, moral and, one might say, chaste: she is sensual and passionate, naïve in this as in everything, her situation is difficult and is becoming more so all the time, not so much (though it is an important factor and one which she stresses much as Woyzeck does) because of poverty, but rather because her man is showing signs of incipient insanity; and when she lets herself be seduced by the Drum Major she simply falls for a more virile and more normal, more *cheerful,* specimen of humanity than Woyzeck, because she too is human and animal. . . . Life with Woyzeck is becoming impossible, and is, anyhow, intermittent, for he lives in barracks and can only visit her from time to time: moreover, she is becoming more and more frightened of him, and, what is perhaps worse for her, since she is a courageous, physically violent, woman, more and more *puzzled by him.* [1]

The "plot" itself, as distinguished from the exposition of characters and situations which provides its setting, commences at the very end of the act: Marie falls into the arms of the Drum Major and disappears with him into the house.

Each scene of Act 2 represents another stage in Wozzeck's gradual realization of Marie's infidelity and in the disintegration of the one human relationship upon which his manhood and his sanity depend. In the first scene Marie is seated in her room, her child on her lap. She is looking at herself in a broken piece of mirror that she holds in her hand, admiring the earrings the Drum Major has given her. When Wozzeck suddenly enters she puts her hands to

1 Knight 51, pp. 139f.

her ears. "I found them," she says. "Two at one time?" he asks, vaguely suspicious. He gives her the household money and leaves. In the following scene the Captain meets the Doctor in the street and detains him, though the Doctor is in a hurry, merely for the sake of some idle, and characteristically imbecilic, conversation. They exchange a few good-natured insults, but then the Doctor's sadistic character comes to the fore and he terrifies the Captain by prognosticating, on the basis of the Captain's physical appearance, that he will soon be a victim of apoplexy. Wozzeck comes along, and he in turn is set upon by both men, who drop vague hints about Marie's infidelity. In Scene 3 Marie cheerfully greets Wozzeck in the street before her house, but he only stares at her and asks why her sin has left no mark upon her face. She pretends not to understand and tells him that he is mad. As he grows more violent she grows more defiant, and when he raises his hand as though to strike her she cries out, "Don't touch me! Better a knife in my body than a hand upon me!" Wozzeck's suspicions of Marie's infidelity are confirmed in the next scene, when he sees her and the Drum Major dancing together among the raucous and drunken crowd of apprentices, servant girls, and soldiers in the tavern garden. In the final scene of Act II the nadir of Wozzeck's degradation is reached: the drunken Drum Major comes into the barracks late at night to boast of his conquest of Marie; he taunts Wozzeck; they fight; and Wozzeck, before the eyes of his awakened comrades, is trounced by Marie's seducer.

The first four scenes of Act III present the denouement of the drama. Scene 1: Marie in her room, remorseful, reading the Bible, tries to find comfort in the story of Jesus and the woman taken in adultery. Scene 2: Wozzeck walks with Marie along a forest path. They stop near the edge of a pond, and he suddenly draws a knife and stabs her to death. Scene 3: Wozzeck is seated at a table in a tavern, watching the girls and apprentices dance. He sings and flirts with one of the girls. She sees blood on his hand, the company crowds around him accusingly, and he runs out into the night. Scene 4: Wozzeck returns to the scene of his crime, stumbling over Marie's corpse as he searches for the murder weapon. He finds the knife and throws it into the pond, but then wades in to look for it, thinking that he hasn't thrown it far enough. He tries to wash the blood from his hands, but the water itself, reflecting the red moon, is the color of blood. Utterly deranged now, he disappears in the pond. The last scene is an epilogue whose closing curtain and curtain music recapitulate the conclusion of Act I, the point at which occurred Marie's seduction by the Drum Major, the event that initiated the movement of the drama to its predestined end. Marie's child toddles after his playmates as they go off to join the adults clustered about Marie's newly discovered corpse near the pond, and the curtain again descends upon an empty stage. The time of day, however, is morning, as it was at the beginning of the opera, rather than evening, so that a return to the "normal" workaday world of the opening scene is suggested.

The stage directions that call for these and other correspondences between different scenes are found neither in the original sources nor in the Franzos–Landau adaptation of the drama. They are Berg's own invention and must be strictly adhered to in performance, since such visual recapitulations are interrelated with musical recapitulations whose significance is obscured or even destroyed without them. These extensive cross-references generate a multiplicity of associations that are often ironic in their implications, as in the instance cited above, the recapitulation of the close of the seduction scene at the close of the epilogue, in which we see the children playing in the bright morning sunlight. Another extensive reference to the seduction scene occurs in the fight between Wozzeck and the Drum Major, where the musical setting of Marie's struggle with the Drum Major when he first attempts to embrace her is recapitulated.

In Act II, Scene 3, the dialogue between Wozzeck and Marie is an ironic paraphrase, in its visual and musical setting, of the dialogue between the Drum Major and Marie. The text is revised so as to place both scenes in the street before Marie's house; Marie pretends not to know what Wozzeck is talking about, but the music tells us that she does indeed know (and the same music returns in the following scene as part of the waltz played by the stage band in the tavern garden as Wozzeck watches Marie and the Drum Major dancing together); Wozzeck's threatening gestures become a parody, through their musical accompaniment, of the posturings of the Drum Major as he flirted with Marie. In the play Marie is given the same words when Wozzeck raises his hand to strike her that she used to rebuff the Drum Major's first attempt to embrace her: "Rühr mich nicht an!" In the context provided by Berg this exclamation becomes a verbal *Leitmotiv*, whether or not Büchner had intended it as such.

The very first word in the opera, "Slowly!", is transformed in the libretto into a large-scale referential element. In the opening lines the Captain anxiously cautions Woyzeck, who is shaving him: "Slowly, Wozzeck, slowly! One thing after the other!" Berg drops the Franzos–Landau final scene (see above, pp. 34f.), thus clarifying the epilogical character of the preceding scene, with which the libretto concludes. This is the only scene in the opera in which neither Wozzeck nor Marie, nor any other adult participant in the drama, appears. The drama proper is over, and a crushingly nihilistic "moral" is drawn, the essential meaninglessness of the tragedy, which is seen in this concluding scene as nothing but a momentary distraction in the innocently callous children's world. The tragedy proper concludes with the penultimate scene of the libretto (the antepenultimate scene of the play). In Franzos–Landau two anonymous citizens are passing near the pond as Wozzeck drowns. Frightened by the eerieness of the place, with its red moon and gray fog, and by the strange sounds, they loiter for only a moment. "Come quickly," one of them calls out, and they rush away. In the libretto the parts of the two citizens are given to the Doctor and the Captain, and it is the Captain who is given the last word, "Quickly!", just as it was the Captain, in both the play and the libretto, who was given the first word, "Slowly!" Thus, by the most economical means, Berg has provided: 1) a verbal association that has important structural significance; 2) an ironic comment on a characteristic feature of the Captain's personality and speech, for in his previous appearances in the work he had repeatedly urged first Wozzeck and later the Doctor to "take your time"; 3) a counterpart to Act II, Scene 2, the only other scene in which the Captain and the Doctor, embodying the forces of the established social order, are shown together.[2]

The Captain's cautionary words to Wozzeck in the opening lines, "Eins nach dem Andern!" ("One thing after the other!"), acquire an ironical overtone in Act II, Scene 3, when Marie, in answer to Wozzeck's accusing question, "Is this where he stood?", replies: "Many people can stand in one place, one after the other!" ("Einer nach dem Andern!"). The same phrase is Wozzeck's utterance of despair after he suffers his ultimate humiliation, his trouncing by Marie's drunken seducer. In the libretto this third and final occurrence of these words, which are now Marie's death sentence, marks the conclusion of Act II.[3] At this strategic point these words complement in a formal sense, and at the same time point up the ultimate transformation in the meaning of, the Captain's cautionary "one thing after the other" at the beginning of Act I. "Indeed," writes Knight, "if there is a moral to the story, it seems to me to be contained in a comparatively inconspicuous sentence of Woyzeck's at the end of Scene XVII [Act II, Scene 5]—'Eins nach dem andern.' One might say, with a good deal of justice, that *Woyzeck* serves to show how, for some men at least, in some circumstances, life is just 'one thing (i.e. one evil thing) after another,' and how there is nothing that can be done to alter it."[4] In the libretto this sentence is no longer "comparatively inconspicuous," for it is marked by the final curtain of Act II. Whatever "moral" these words may be said to represent, their dramatic function here is clear enough. The idea that motivates the action of Act III—the inevitability of Wozzeck's attempt to redeem his manhood by consummating the crime that Marie's own words had implanted in his mind when he had threatened to strike her ("Better a knife!")—is fixed at this point, just as the event that motivates the action of Act II—Marie's seduction—was fixed as the curtain fell upon Act I. And the earlier instances of "Eins nach dem Andern!" and "Einer nach dem Andern!" are retrospectively understood as statements of a single verbal *Leitmotiv*. In this as in other respects, the libretto in itself, independently of its musical setting, though it is one of the earliest "interpretations" of Büchner's unfinished masterpiece, anticipates the insights and discoveries of recent literary scholarship.[5]

2 Two scenes in the MSS show the Captain and the Doctor together, but these are evidently variants of a single scene.

3 At the conclusion of this scene Büchner has "Eins nach dem andern!" rather than "Einer nach dem Andern!" as in Franzos and the opera. Thus Woyzeck literally repeats the Captain's "One thing after the other!" in a new context that completely transforms the meaning of these words.

4 Knight 51, p. 139.

5 See, for example, Mautner 61, *DV*.

An outline of each scene, showing parallel segments of the libretto and of the musical design, follows.[6] Variants between the Franzos–Landau text and the libretto are pointed out, except for inessential changes made in the course of composition, such as the substitution of "sondern ein Augenblick" for "und das ist ein Augenblick," which adjusts the phrase to the metrical characteristics of the musical episode in which it occurs. Some comparisons will be made with the original text as given in Lehmann's transcription of the manuscripts. The manuscripts comprise: H-1, the first group of sketches, which carry the action through Woyzeck's return to the pond after the murder and the subsequent scene of the officials discussing the murder (see above, pp. 32ff.); H-2, the second group of sketches, consisting of supplementary scenes for the earlier part of the drama; H-4, a provisional fair copy, which includes revised versions of most of the scenes contained in H-1 and H-2 as well as several new scenes, but which breaks off before the murder scene; H-3, separate fragments, consisting of two scenes not found in the other manuscripts, one showing the Doctor lecturing to his students, the other the scene of the Idiot, the Child, and Woyzeck (see above, pp. 31ff.).[7] The two chief characters are named Louis and Margreth in H-1, Woyzeck (Franz) and Louise (Louisel) in H-2, Woyzeck and Marie in H-4.

Berg himself, in his well-known lecture on Wozzeck,[8] in the outline which he provided for Willi Reich's essay on the work,[9] and in his article, "Die Musikalischen Formen in meiner Oper 'Wozzeck,' "[10] identified all of the larger formal components and many of the smaller ones as well. Where Berg's own terms for these formal components are employed in the outline below they will be enclosed in quotation marks. The outline by Berg's pupil, Fritz Mahler, "Szenische und musikalische Übersicht der Oper 'Wozzeck' von Alban Berg," is clearly derived from the composer's own analysis of the work, and may be grouped with the three sources cited above as representing Berg's own views regarding its formal design and the terminology he employed in his description of this design.[11]

6 The Franzos-Landau text from which the libretto is derived is given in Appendix II. The English translation of the play by Theodore Hoffman 55, in Volume 1 of *The Modern Theatre*, is based on Bergemann's version, except for the scene of the children playing in the street after Wozzeck's disappearance in the pond, which is taken from Franzos. The first English translation of the play (Geoffrey Dunlop, 1928) is the only one that makes extensive use of the editions of Franzos and Landau.

7 In reference to the position of these scenes in his synoptic arrangement of the MSS, Lehmann (Büchner 67, *Textkritische Noten*, p. 55) writes: "As far as the placement of the two separate fragments, H–3: 1 and 2, is concerned, it was our intention to arrange them in such a way as not to necessitate any changes in the given ordering of H–1, H–2, and H–4." Unfortunately, he appears to be unaware of van Dam's interpretation of the scene of the Idiot, the Child, and Woyzeck, and indifferent to Martens's convincing arguments regarding the denouement of the drama: Lehmann places this scene last both in his synopsis and, even more to be regretted, in his stage version. The Lehmann reconstruction is available in an English translation (Büchner 69).

8 Reprinted in Redlich 57a and b.

9 Reich 65, p. 121.   10 Berg 24, M.

11 A facsimile of Mahler's handwritten outline was included in the original edition of the vocal score, published privately late in 1922. It was republished in *Anbruch* in February, 1930.

Act One

"Five Character Pieces"

FIRST MOVEMENT
"Suite"

"Prelude"

mm. 1–2 ♩♪

mm. ♪2–3   Curtain rises.

SCENE 1
(F. 1; L. 1) [H-4: 5][12]

Early morning. Wozzeck is shaving the
Captain.

mm. 4–29   "Slowly, Wozzeck, slowly. One thing after
the other! You're making me quite dizzy.
What am I to do with the extra ten minutes if
you finish too early today? Wozzeck, think
of it, you still have thirty good years to live.
Thirty years! That makes three hundred and
sixty months, and so many days, hours,
minutes! What are you going to do with that
monstrous stretch of time? Figure it out for
yourself, Wozzeck!" "Yes, sir, Captain."

"Pavane"

mm. 30–50   The Captain speculates on the nature of
eternity. "I get quite anxious about the
world when I think about eternity. 'Eternal,'
that's forever! You see that. But then again,
it isn't forever, it's only a moment! Wozzeck,
I shudder when I think that the world re-
volves in a single day. I can no longer look at
a mill wheel without getting melancholy."
"Yes sir, Captain."

"Cadenza" for solo viola

mm. 51–64   "Wozzeck, you always look so tense. A good
man doesn't do that. A good man, with a
good conscience, does everything slowly."
He pauses. "Say something, Wozzeck.

---

12 Berg's source in Franzos (F.) and Landau (L.) is given in parentheses; Franzos's source in
the original MSS (Lehmann, pp. 337–431) is given in brackets.

"Gigue" mm. 65–108	What's the weather like today?" "Very bad, Captain, Wind!" CAPTAIN: "I feel it, something swift out there. A wind like that reminds me of a mouse." "I think," he adds slyly, "it's blowing from the north-south." "Yes sir, Captain." The Captain laughs uproariously. "Oh, you are stupid, horribly stupid!"
"Cadenza" for double bassoon mm. 109–114	CAPTAIN, with feeling: "Wozzeck, you're a good fellow. But you have no mo-
"Gavotte" mm. 115–126	rality." The captain censures Wozzeck because he has a child that has been born out of wedlock.
mm. 127–132 ("Double I")	WOZZECK: "Sir, the good Lord's not going to look down on the poor worm, just because nobody said 'Amen' before he was made. The Lord said, 'Suffer little children to come unto me!' "
mm. 133–136 ("Double II")	CAPTAIN: "What do you mean? What kind of curious answer is that? You've got me quite confused! You have, you have indeed!"
"Air" mm. ⌐°136–153⌐	WOZZECK: "Poor folks like us! You see, Captain, money, money! If one has none! Try bringing your fellow creature into the world in a moral sort of way! One has also flesh and blood! Now, if I were a gentle-man, and had a hat, and a watch, and eye-glasses, and could speak politely, then I'd be virtuous too, It must be a fine thing to be virtuous, Captain. But I'm just a common fellow! Our kind is unlucky in this world and in the next too. I think if we got into heaven they'd make us help with the thunder!"
"Reprise" mm. °153–171	CAPTAIN: "All right, all right! You're a good fellow! A good fellow! But you think too

46

much; it wears one down. You always look
so tense. Our talk has tired me out. Go now,
and don't rush so! Take it easy down the
road, right in the middle, slow, nice and
slow!"

m. 172   Curtain.

Mm. 173–200

Berg makes a material revision in the Franzos–Landau version of this
scene only in connection with Wozzeck's Air, transposing its last two sentences
from their original position immediately following "One has also flesh and
blood!" and deleting the Captain's speech which follows these lines. In the
deleted portion of the text the Captain points out that in spite of the fact that
he too is made of "flesh and blood" he manages to remain virtuous. In deleting
the Captain's speech and in shifting the position of Wozzeck's reference to the
next world and its thunder, Berg provides an appropriate textual basis for the
musical climax of this scene (mm. 149ff.) and a striking contrast between the
conclusion of Wozzeck's speech and the Captain's reply. The Captain's last
words, in Franzos–Landau, are "Geh' Er jetzt, und renn' Er nicht so, geh' Er
langsam, hübsch langsam die Strasse hinunter, genau in der Mitte!" ("Go
now, and don't rush so! Go slowly, nice and slow down the street, right in the
middle!"). In the opera this text is slightly revised: "Geh' Er jetzt, und renn' Er
nicht so! Geh' Er langsam die Strasse hinunter, genau in der Mitte und noch-
mals, geh' Er langsam, hübsch langsam!" By transposing the Captain's key
word, "langsam" ("slowly"), so that it becomes the last as well as the first
word of the scene, Berg emphasizes the recapitulative function of the Reprise
and establishes the Captain's "langsam" as one of the verbal *Leitmotive* of the
work.

In a critical article attacking the still unperformed work,[13] Berg was taken
to task for the speciousness of the analogy with the Baroque suite implied in
the titles given to the formal components of this scene: "Apart from a few bars
in 3/8 time, consisting of chromatic wind passages ([vocal score] pp. 15–18),
which perhaps may be said to represent the gigue, a section in C [*sic*], whose
subject is morality, representing the gavotte with two doubles (pp. 19–22), and
a section in 3/2 time to which, out of goodwill, the term "air" might be applied,
I managed to discover nothing remotely resembling a suite, not to speak of the
absence of even the most obvious features that immediately differentiate the
old dance forms from one another."

One can agree with this criticism without accepting the writer's negative
conclusions in respect to the work itself. It is unlikely that anyone studying the

13 Petschnig 24, *M.*

opening scene of the opera, unaware of the titles supplied by the composer, would ever discover the analogy with the Baroque suite for himself, in view of the continuity of the overall formal design of the scene. The individual numbers are bound together by means of a *ritornello* (mm. 1–6, 24–29, 47–50, 58–64, and 153–156), recurrent motives (above all, that of Wozzeck's "Jawohl, Herr Hauptmann!"), a Cadenza that leads from the Pavane to the Gigue and (in a telescoped and transposed version) from the Gigue to the Gavotte, and the recapitulation of the first number at the conclusion of the scene. Nevertheless, within this tightly knit overall design, the individual numbers are self-contained forms. The Prelude presents the following closed symmetrical pattern:

mm. 1–6   correspond to   mm. 24–29

mm. 12–14   correspond to   mm. 22–24

mm. 16–17   correspond to   mm. 21–22

The Pavane is in a ternary form: A, mm. 30–35; B, mm. 36–40; A expanded, mm. 41–50. The same bass line, $g\flat$-f-$d\flat$, defines each statement of A. The opposition of "ewig" and "Augenblick" in the text is reflected in the bass line in the opposition between the $d\flat$ pedal of mm. 34–37 and the interrupted and unstable bass line of mm. 38–40. The Cadenza for solo viola is prefaced by a restatement of the series of dyads of m. 7 of the Prelude. The Gigue is again a *da capo* form, with mm. 97–108 corresponding to mm. 65–74. In a harmonic sense Double I of the Gavotte has the function of a "middle section," in that the harmonic material of the Gavotte proper (mm. 115–126) returns at the lower octave in the second Double (mm. 133–135) after an interpolation at the lower fifth in the first Double (mm. 127–132). The Air, a setting of Wozzeck's only extended speech in the first scene, and, indeed, in the whole opera, is set apart from the other numbers of the Suite by its lyrical character and in that it is the only one that may be said to be "through-composed." The final return of the *ritornello* in m. 153 initiates the Reprise of the first number. With the exception of the *ritornello*, the recapitulated portion of the Prelude is given in the retrograde, mm. 157–169 corresponding to mm. 14–6. The retrograde section commences immediately after the return of mm. 1–3 of the *ritornello*. (The remainder of the *ritornello*, mm. 4–6, is given in mm. 168–169 [cello] and mm. 170–171.) Many other instances of the use of retrograde motion as a means of achieving symmetry and closure are found in the works of Berg.

Specious though the implied analogy with Baroque dance forms may be, the formal designations employed by Berg correctly emphasize a significant and novel aspect of the music of *Wozzeck*—the revival, within a new musical language and in the context of large-scale motivic and structural relationships consistent with the Wagnerian heritage, of the classical concept of self-contained "numbers."

The scoring of each number of the Suite emphasizes its individuality, while the scene as a *whole* is timbrally characterized by the treatment of the orchestra as the repository of a variety of chamber ensembles. There is no orchestral *tutti*, the string section being represented much of the time by solo instruments, with *tutti* passages in the strings largely limited to *pizzicato, col legno,* or *con sordino.* A different group of instruments is assigned an *obbligato* function in each number of the Suite, with the exception of the Reprise, which recapitulates the instrumentation as well as the musical material of the Prelude. A full orchestral *tutti* occurs for the first time in the Interlude.

The latter is a complex polyphonic development of thematic material borrowed from each number of the Suite except the Prelude and Reprise. Though the Interlude is described as "Finale-Development of the Suite" in Fritz Mahler's "Übersicht," it is not, properly speaking, a component of the Suite, nor is its formal function analogous, for example, to the summary development of a Beethoven coda, as the title seems to suggest. The Interlude recapitulates the Suite in a drastically telescoped version that moves quickly to an explosive climax which is abruptly cut off by the quick curtain that rises upon Scene 2 and the sudden quiet of the muted chords with which that scene begins.

The thematic content of the Interlude is summarized in the following table:

Mm. 173–178 (three-part canon in horn, trumpet, trombone):
  "Pavane," mm. 30–33.
Mm. 177–179 (three-part canon in woodwinds and strings):
  "Gavotte," mm. 121–122.
Mm. 180–182, doublebass and tuba:
  "Gavotte," mm. 114–115, voice and trumpet.
Mm. 180–182, strings, except doublebass:
  "Gigue," mm. 86–88, oboes and clarinets.
Mm. 180–182, horns:
  "Gigue," mm. 72–75, horn.
Mm. 181–183, xylophone and oboes:
  "Gigue," mm. 83–86, voice and celesta.
Mm. 183–191, strings:
  "Gigue," mm. 65–73, flutes.
Mm. 183–191, woodwinds:
  "Air," mm. 139–141, strings.
Mm. 184–192, horns:
  "Gavotte," mm. 116–119 ♩, *Hauptstimme* in trumpet.
Mm. 191–197:
  "Air," mm. 136–138 ♩.
Mm. 192–195, flutes and clarinets:
  "Air," m. 142, flutes.
Mm. 195–200, cellos:
  "Cadenza," mm. 55–57.

Mm. 196–197, violins:
"Air," m. 151, voice.
Mm. 198–200:
"Air," m. 152.

SECOND MOVEMENT

SCENE 2
(F. 6; L. 2) [H-2: 1; H-4: 1]

An open field, the town in the distance. Late afternoon. Andres and Wozzeck are cutting kindling wood in the bushes.

"Rhapsody"

mm. 201–211

WOZZECK: "Hey, there's a curse on this place!" ANDRES: "Bah!"

"Hunting Song," Strophe I

mm. 212–222

ANDRES sings: "Now there's the life for a huntsman, shooting free for all! There's where I would be!"

"Rhapsody"

mm. 223–248

WOZZECK: "There's a curse on this place. See that bright streak over the grass there, where the toadstools are sprouting? At dusk there's a head rolls there. Fellow picked it up once, thought it was a hedgehog. Three days and three nights later he lay in a wooden box." ANDRES: "It's getting dark, that's why you're scared. Bah!"

"Hunting Song," Strophe II

mm. 249–257

He sings: "There's a hare runs by, asks if I'm a hunter. I've been a hunter, too, but don't know how to shoot!"

"Rhapsody" and "Hunting Song," Strophe III

mm. 257–270

"Quiet, Andres! It was the Freemasons! That's it, the Freemasons!" Andres continues to sing. WOZZECK: "Shh!" Andres begins to feel uneasy. "Sing along with me!" He resumes his song. Wozzeck stamps on the ground. "Hollow! All hollow! An abyss! It's trembling!" He staggers.

50   "Rhapsody"

mm. 271–285   "Do you hear? There's something under-
                   neath that's moving with us! Let's get
                   away!" ANDRES: "Hey, are you crazy?" Woz-
                   zeck stands still. "This weird quietness. It's
                   sultry. Makes you want to hold your
                   breath." ANDRES: "What?" Wozzeck stares at
                   the setting sun.

mm. 286–301   "A fire, running from the earth to the sky,
                   and a crashing noise coming down, like
                   trumpets!" ANDRES: "The sun's down.
                   There's the drum."

(mm. 302–306 ^{p})

INTERLUDE

Mm. 302–306   WOZZECK: "Still, everything still, as though
                   the world were dead." ANDRES: "Night!
                   We've got to get back!"

Mm. 307–310   Curtain, as they slowly walk off.

CHANGE OF SCENE

Mm. 311–325

Mm. 326–327[14]   The offstage military band is heard ap-
                   proaching.

Mm. 328–329   Curtain rises.

SCENE 3

Mm. 330–333

Berg makes no material revisions in the Franzos text, which brings together the two different versions of this scene that are found in the manuscripts. The condemned murderer's actual words, as recorded by Clarus, are
the basis of many of Wozzeck's lines.

The formal coherence of the Rhapsody is largely dependent upon the establishment of a focal pitch level for the series of chords upon which it is based
(Ex. 103), and upon carefully controlled digressions from that pitch level. The
basic chords at their original pitch level but in reversed order conclude the
Rhapsody (mm. 302–306 ^{p}). Whereas the interlude between the first and second
movements, framed by a quick curtain at its beginning and conclusion, coin-

---

14 The numbering given corresponds to the overlapping military music in the approaching stage band.

cides exactly with Change of Scene I/1–2, the interlude that connects Scenes 2 and 3 commences *before* the fall of the curtain and terminates *after* its rise, overlapping with the Rhapsody of Scene 2 and the Military March of Scene 3. The Military March is foreshadowed by fanfare-like motives in the horn, trumpet, and clarinet. These are followed by reminiscences of the opening figure of the Hunting Song and of the "crashing noise" motive of mm. 293ff. The latter fades away as the approaching military band is heard.

THIRD MOVEMENT
Introduction, "Military March"
(stage band)

    mm. 326–329

SCENE 3
(F. 7; L. 3) [H-4: 2; H-2: 2]

Evening. Marie is at the open window with her child.

    mm. 330–333

She mimics the cymbal and drum of the approaching band. "Do your hear, boy? Here they come!"

"Military March" (stage band)

    mm. 334–345

The band swings into view, the Drum Major at its head. Margret, in the street, talks to Marie through the open window. "What a man! Like a tree!" MARIE: "He stands on his feet like a lion." The Drum Major salutes Marie and she waves to him. MARGRET: "Such friendly glances, neighbor! We're not used to that from you."

    mm. 346–361
    ("Quasi-Trio")

MARIE sings: "The soldiers are such handsome fellows!" MARGRET: "Your eyes are shining." MARIE: "So what! It's nothing to do with you. Take yours to the Jew and have them polished. Maybe then they'll shine too, so you can sell them for two buttons." MARGRET: "Really, Mrs. Virginity! *I'm* a respectable woman, but you, everyone knows, you can stare through seven pairs of leather breeches!"

    mm. 362–363 (beginning
of the *da capo*)

MARIE: "Hussy!" She slams the window shut, cutting off the music of the band.

52   Introduction to "Cradle Song"

mm. 363–371

"Come, my child! What do people want! You're but a poor whore's child, and yet you give your mother so much joy with your illegitimate face! Hush-a-bye, baby!"

"Cradle Song"

mm. 372–387 (Strophe I)

MARIE sings: "Maiden, what are you up to? You've a child, but no husband! Oh, why mind about that! I sing the whole night long: Hush-a-bye, sweet little lad, though there's none to give us a thing.

mm. 388–416 (Strophe II)

Hansel, harness your six horses, give them their fodder again. No oats do they eat, no water do they drink, clear cool wine must it be!" The child falls asleep. Marie remains lost in thought.

Coda and transition
mm. 417–427

Through-composed episode
mm. 427–454

A knock at the window startles Marie. "Is it you, Franz? Come in!" "Can't! Must get back to the barracks." MARIE: "Have you been cutting sticks for the major?" "Yes, Marie. Ah!" "What is it, Franz? You look so upset." "Sh! I've found it out! There was a shape in the sky, and everything glowing. I've got wind of many things!" "Man!" "And now all's dark, dark. Marie, there was something again. Perhaps——Is it not written: 'And behold, the smoke rose from the land, like the smoke from a furnace'?" "Franz!" "It followed me right up to the town. What's going to happen?" Marie, trying to calm him, holds the child up to him: "Franz, your babe!" He remains engrossed in his thoughts, and absentmindedly mutters, "My babe, my babe!" Then, with the words, "I must be off now," he hastily leaves.

mm. 455–472

MARIE: "That man! So distracted! He didn't look at his child. He'll crack up with those ideas of his. Why so still, baby? Are you

frightened? It's getting so dark, it's like 53
going blind. Usually there's the street lamp
shining in. Oh, we poor folks! I can't bear it.
I'm terrified!" She rushes to the door.

m. 473ᵖ   Curtain.

CHANGE OF SCENE

mm. ⌈473–484

INTERLUDE

Mm. 484–487

M. 488ᵖ   Curtain rises.

Berg makes noteworthy revisions in Franzos's text at only two points. Since he omits from his libretto the two scenes at the fair (see below, pp. 57), he deletes Wozzeck's "See you tonight at the fair. I've a bit saved." (In Franzos, unaccountably, the fair scenes precede Wozzeck's dialogue with Marie.) In place of this line Berg interpolates an addition of his own: "My babe, my babe!" No exit is indicated for Marie at the conclusion of this scene in Franzos–Landau. In revising the text in this respect, Berg coincidently made it conform to Büchner's own version, which also calls for Marie's exit at the conclusion of this scene.

Structurally the music of Change of Scene I/2–3 is a continuation and completion of the third movement of Act I, bringing that movement to a close with a return to the pedal on *a* with which it opens. A miniature interlude overlaps with the cadential pedal-note: a reminiscence of the opening chords of the Military March;[15] the twelve-tone Passacaglia theme of the following scene; reiterations of the diminished triad with which the twelve-tone series concludes, which serve as curtain music for both the rise of the curtain at the beginning of Scene 4 and the fall of the curtain at the end of the scene.

FOURTH MOVEMENT   SCENE 4

"Passacaglia"   (F. 8; L. 4) [H-4: 8; H-2: 6]

A sunny afternoon in the Doctor's study.

"Theme," mm. ⌈488–495   DOCTOR: "What have I seen, Wozzeck? A
man of your word, eh?" "What is it, Doc-
tor?" "I saw it, Wozzeck. You coughed in
the street, barked like a dog! Is it for this I
pay you three groschen every day? Wozzeck, it's wicked!" "But Doctor, when nature
calls!"

15 See p. 139, below.

54	"Variation 1," mm. 496–502	"When nature calls! When nature calls! Superstition! Abominable superstition! Have I not proven that the diaphragm is subject to the will? Nature, Wozzeck! Man is free! In mankind individuality is transfigured into freedom. (You *had* to cough, indeed!)"
	"Variation 2," mm. 503–509	The Doctor asks Wozzeck if he is continuing to restrict himself to the prescribed diet of beans. Next week they will go on to
	"Variation 3," mm. 510–516	mutton. "There's a revolution in science. Albumen, fats, carbohydrates, and, to be sure, oxyaldehydanhydride. But, why did you have to cough!!!
	"Variation 4," mm. 517–523	No! I won't get angry, it's unhealthy, unscientific! I'm quite calm, my pulse is beating its usual sixty. Indeed, why upset oneself over a mere man! Now, if it were a lizard that had let you down! But, Wozzeck, you shouldn't have coughed!"
	"Variation 5," mm. 524–530	WOZZECK: "But look, Doctor, some people have a certain sort of character, a certain structure, but when it comes to nature, that's something else. You see, with nature, it's like this, how shall I put it——." "Wozzeck, you're philosophizing again!"
	"Variation 6," mm. 531–537	WOZZECK: "When nature gives way, when the world gets so dark that you have to grope around it with your hands, and it seems to slip away, like a spider's web. Ah, when something's there, and yet
	"Variation 7," m. 538	isn't! Ah! Ah,
	"Variation 8," mm. 539–545	Marie! When everything's dark, and only a red glow in the west, as from a furnace, what's one to
	"Variation 9," mm. 546–552	hold on to? When the sun's at midday and it seems as if the world's going up in flame,
	"Variation 10," m. 553	there's a fearful voice that's spoken to me." DOCTOR: "Wozzeck, you have an

"Variation 11," mm. 554–560	aberration." "The toadstools! Have you seen the toadstools growing in rings on the ground?
"Variation 12," m. 561	Circles, figures, if one could read them!"
"Variation 13," mm. 562–568	DOCTOR: "Wozzeck, you'll end up in the lunatic asylum. You've a fine *idée fixe*, an excellent
"Variation 14," mm. 569–575	*aberratio mentalis partialis*, second species. Very nicely developed!
"Variation 15," mm. 576–582	Wozzeck, I'll raise your wages!
"Variation 16," mm. 583–589	Are you carrying on as usual? Shaving the Captain? Catching lizards?
"Variation 17," mm. 590–596	Eating beans?" WOZZECK: "Everything regular, Doctor. The money goes to my wife for her housekeeping. That's why
"Variation 18," mm. 597–610	I do it." DOCTOR: "You're an interesting case. Keep it up! Wozzeck, you'll get more pay, another groschen. But now what must you do?" Wozzeck, not listening to the Doctor: "Ah, Marie!" "What must you do?" "Marie!" "What?" "Ah!"
"Variation 19," mm. 611–619	"Eat your beans, then mutton, no coughing, go on shaving the Captain, and in between cultivate your *idée fixe!*
"Variation 20," mm. 620–637	Oh, my theory! My fame! I shall be immortal! Immortal! Immortal!
"Variation 21"	
mm. 638–644	Immortal! Wozzeck, now let me see your tongue." Wozzeck obeys.
mm. 645–655	Curtain.

In the lines given to the Doctor, Berg departs at many points from his source. The Doctor in Franzos's version of Büchner's text says: "I saw it, Wozzeck. You p—d in the street, p—d against the wall, like a dog!" (In Büchner's own text there are no elisions.) The Doctor in the play, but not in the opera, is angry with good reason. Wozzeck, having already relieved himself, is unable to fulfill his contractual obligation, not mentioned in the opera, to provide the

Doctor with a sample of his urine. The Doctor's scientific jargon in the play refers to the bladder and the chemical constituents of urine, but Berg substituted "coughed" for "p——d" and "diaphragm" for "musculus sphincter vesicae," and he revised the terminology so that it refers to the experimental diet which the Doctor has assigned to his subject. These revisions were due not to any personal squeamishness on Berg's part but to the simple fact that retention of Büchner's original text in this scene would inevitably have precluded performance of the work on any operatic stage of the time. The probability of performance must have seemed doubtful enough, in any event, for an opera of such unprecedented difficulty by an unknown composer, and it would have been unthinkable to render the work utterly unacceptable at the outset by retaining the scatologies of the original, though one regrets the consequent weakening of sense and motivation in the operatic version of the Doctor's lines.[16]

The composer's self-identification, during the war years, with the protagonist of his opera explains other revisions of the text. In substituting "beans" for "peas" and in replacing Büchner's word for mutton, "Hammelfleisch," by the more familiar Austrian term "Schöpsenfleisch," Berg causes the text to refer to staples of his own diet as a soldier in the Austrian Army. Büchner's "Doctor" was partly a caricature of a certain Professor Wilbrand whom the author had known at Giessen, but Berg found his own living model for this role in an inhuman army doctor whom he had described in a letter to one of his pupils soon after his enlistment. In that letter Berg also spoke of his army rations: "Once or twice a week we are given mutton, which is prepared in the most disgusting manner."[17] When later, during the composition of this scene, he came upon the Doctor's line, "Next week we start on mutton," he could hardly have failed to think of himself as the Doctor's victim.

A line in which the Doctor refers to another of Wozzeck's duties is omitted by Berg: "Have you caught any frogs for me? Spawn? Fresh water polyps? Cristatellum?" The idea is retained by Berg, however, through the interpolation of the Doctor's question, "Catching lizards?," and this interpolation explains the earlier substitution, in Variation 4, of "lizard" for "Proteus." As was pointed out above (pp. 35), Wozzeck's "Ach, Marie!" (Variations 8 and 18) is not found in the authentic text. Another evident interpolation by Franzos, immediately preceding the Doctor's closing line, which assigns to Wozzeck the words, "Ja! die Marie——und der arme Wurm," was wisely omitted by the composer.

The historical Woyzeck's conversations with Hofrat Dr. Clarus as reported by the latter are the source of the fictional Wozzeck's description of his fan-

---

16 Gurlitt's *Wozzeck* omits the scene entirely. As recently as 1963 the British stage version of the play was published by Penguin Books in *Three German Plays* with the following prefatory note: "This play may only be performed in public with certain textual modifications approved by the Lord Chamberlain."

17 Blaukopf 53, *SR*; 54, *ÖM*.

tasies and hallucinations. The real Woyzeck, too, was haunted by "a fearful voice that's spoken to me." Though the fictional Wozzeck is not yet a murderer at this point in the drama, his relation to the Doctor was undoubtedly suggested by the relation between the historical Woyzeck and Dr. Clarus.

The movement as a whole falls into four large sections: Theme through Variation 4, the Doctor's monologue, marked by the recurrent motive of the Doctor's indignation with Wozzeck for coughing (Ex. 18); Variations 5 through 12, Wozzeck's monologue, incorporating musical material associated with Wozzeck in the two preceding scenes; Variations 13 through 18, the Doctor's expression of his professional interest in Wozzeck's "case," framed by a waltz episode (mm. 565–568, 600–601) that returns in II/2 when the Doctor applies his diagnostic skills to the Captain; Variations 19 through 21, *stretto* and finale, progressing from the Doctor's prosaic résumé of his instructions to Wozzeck to his exultant outburst at the thought of the immortality his scientific investigations will earn for him.

Example 18

The two scenes that follow in the Landau edition are omitted in the opera. These show Marie and Wozzeck at the fair. They enter the booth to see the performance of the calculating horse, who, though he can tell time, still retains enough of his basic animal nature to relieve himself before the eyes of his audience. Franzos has omitted the parts of a corporal and the Drum Major. Seeing Marie, they comment on her charms and follow her into the booth.

FIFTH MOVEMENT
"Andante affettuoso
(quasi-rondo)"

Section 1, mm. 656–665	**CHANGE OF SCENE**
m. 666	Curtain rises.

SCENE 5
(F. 9; L. 7) [H-4: 6]

Evening, the street before Marie's dwelling.

Section 2, mm. 667–676   Marie stands admiring the Drum Major. "Let me see you step out there. A chest like a bull and a beard like a lion. Nobody like him! I'm the proudest of women!"

58

Section 3, mm. 677–684	DRUM MAJOR: "Wait till Sunday, when I've got my plumed helmet and white gloves on. Damn! The Prince is always saying, 'Now, there's a man!'" MARIE: "Really!"
Section 4, mm. 685–693$^\flat$	She walks up to him. "Man!" "And you're a fine wench, too! We'll raise a brood of drum majors, eh?" He embraces her. MARIE: "Let go!"
Section 5, mm. $^\flat$693–698	They struggle. DRUM MAJOR: "Wild beast!" Marie pulls herself free. "Don't touch me!"
m. 699	Pause.
Section 6, mm. 700–701	The Drum Major draws himself up to his full height.
Section 7, mm. 702–709	"Is it the devil in your eyes?" He embraces her again. MARIE: "For all I care! What's the difference!"
Section 8, mm. $^{\ddot{\flat}}$709–715$^\flat$	She falls into his arms and they disappear into the house.
Section 9, mm. $^\flat$715–717	Slow curtain.

Franzos's version of this scene, which is practically identical with the text as given in Lehmann, is almost literally retained by Berg. The music of the scene as a whole may be divided into two parts, the first culminating with the struggle between Marie and the Drum Major and Marie's cry, "Don't touch me!" The music rises to a second climax in Section 8, in which the principal thematic elements are heard in *stretto*. The setting of the Drum Major's words in Section 3 is a variant of the setting of Marie's words in Section 2. The *g-d* pedal and the melodic tone center, *b*, of Section 1 are focal elements, whose emphatic return at the conclusion of the scene gives the whole a quasi-ternary character. The movement is highly rhapsodic, a polyphonic web of melodies whose rhythm and contour are constantly transformed.[18]

The scene which follows in the Landau edition is omitted by Berg. The Doctor, at his attic window, is lecturing his students in the courtyard below. He uses first a cat and then Wozzeck as the subject of some farcical demonstrations. The scene is known to be a not greatly exaggerated caricature of the lectures of the above-mentioned Professor Wilbrand.

18 Cf. the discussion of thematic procedures in the first movement of the Three Pieces for Orchestra, p. 15, above.

Act Two 59

"Symphony in Five Movements"

FIRST MOVEMENT
"Sonata"

"Introduction"

mm. 1–6

"Exposition"

Principal Section:

Theme

mm. 7–8	Curtain rises.

SCENE 1
(F. 4; L. 9) [H-4: 4]

Sunny morning in Marie's room.

mm. 9–24	Marie, the child on her lap, a piece of broken mirror in her hand, admires the earrings given to her by the Drum Major.
Transition, mm. 25–28	
Bridge Section, mm. 29–42	The child stirs and Marie admonishes him to sleep or the bogeyman will get him.

Subordinate Section:

Theme, mm. 43–48	Marie sings a "folk song": "Maiden, close up tight! Here comes a Gypsy lad, will take you by the hand,
Transition, mm. 49–54	away into Gypsyland!"
Closing Section, mm. 55–59	The frightened child, hiding his head, keeps very still.

"First Reprise"

Principal Section, mm. 60–80	Marie again looks at herself in the mirror and admires the earrings.
Bridge Section, mm. 81–89	The child sits up and Marie admonishes him to close his eyes. Still holding the mirror, she flickers its reflected light on the wall. "There's the Sandman running on the wall.

60 Subordinate Section:

Theme in diminution,
mm. 90–92

Shut your eyes, or he'll look into them and make you blind.''

Closing Section, mm. 93–95 ⌐˙

Wozzeck enters, unnoticed by Marie, who is still watching the child.

"Development"

mm. ⌐96–101 (Pr. Th.)

Startled, Marie puts her hands to her ears. WOZZECK: "What have you there?" "Nothing!" "Something's shining under your fingers." MARIE: "An earring. I found it."

mm. ⌐101–105⌐ (Cl. Th.)

WOZZECK: "I've never found anything like that, two at a time!"

mm. 105–108 (Pr. Th.)

MARIE: "Am I bad woman?" WOZZECK, soothing her: "All right, Marie, all right!"

mm. 109–112 (Br. Th.)

He turns to the child. "How the boy always sleeps! Lift his arm, the chair's hurting him. The shiny drops on his forehead! Nothing but toil under the

mm. 112–115

sun! Sweating even when we sleep! We poor!

mm. 116–123

Here's money again, Marie. My pay, and something from the Captain, and the Doctor." "God reward you, Franz!" "I've got to go, Marie. Goodbye!"

mm. 124–127 (transition)

MARIE, alone: "But I am indeed

"Second Reprise"

Principal Section:

Theme

mm. 128–139

a bad woman! I could stab myself! Oh, this world! Everything goes to the devil, man and woman and child!"

(m. 140)

Curtain.

CHANGE OF SCENE

mm. 141–149 *(stretto)*

Subordinate Section:

Theme in augmentation,
mm. 150–161

Closing Section, mm. 162–165

Final cadence, mm. 166–169

   (m. 170)   Curtain rises.

Berg makes only two noteworthy revisions in the Franzos–Landau text. There is no indication in the play that Marie's song of the Gypsy abductor has frightened the child into pretending to sleep. By adding the stage direction the composer establishes a parallel between this song and Marie's later reference to the Sandman, so that the dramatic correspondence between them is analogous to their formal correspondence in the musical design. The other change occurs at the conclusion of the scene, where Berg has added the words "and child" to Marie's exclamation, "Everything goes to the devil, man and woman!"

The climax of the scene occurs in the Development Section, mm. 112–115, with Wozzeck's words, "Nichts als Arbeit unter der Sonne, sogar Schweiss im Schlaf. Wir arme Leut!" The passage, culminating in a twelve-tone simultaneity, and in the principal *Leitmotiv* of the opera, returns in the final symphonic interlude at the conclusion of the work. The dramatic significance of the C-major triad that is sustained throughout the final episode of the Development, and that is in the sharpest possible contrast to the immediately preceding twelve-tone chord, has been much discussed, first of all by Berg himself.[19] In the prosaic relationship of Wozzeck to Marie and to their child—the "ordinary" plane of his existence, represented by this most commonplace of chords as he gives her his money and bids her adieu—there resides whatever is "sane" or "normal" in him, whatever measure he has of human dignity. This "ordinary" Wozzeck was earlier characterized musically, at the conclusion of the First Reprise, where a prosaic version of the Closing Section supplants, at Wozzeck's entrance, the version which represented the child's terror at the imagined entrance of the "Gypsy lad" and the return of which is expected as a representation of the child's terror at the imagined entrance of the "Sandman."

The change-of-scene music is simultaneously a recapitulation and a second development-section, bounded by the descending "white-note" *glissando* that accompanies the fall of the curtain and by the ascending "white-note" *glissando* that accompanies the rise of the curtain upon the following scene. Measures 141–147 develop mm. 19–20 of the Exposition in *stretto* fashion. The recapitulation of the Principal Section is completed at m. 149. In m. 148 the *Hauptstimme* of the Principal Theme commences as a countermelody in the bass line and continues throughout the recapitulation of the Subordinate Section. A final statement in augmentation of the solo violin figure (mm. 44–45) of the Subordinate Theme occurs simultaneously with the recapitulation of the Closing Section (mm. 162–165). The same figure in augmentation initiates (mm. 150–153) the recapitulation of the Subordinate Section.

19 Redlich 57b, p. 275; Redlich 52, *MR*; Keller 52, *MR*.

62   SECOND MOVEMENT   SCENE 2
               "Fantasia and Fugue"   (F. 5; L. 10) [H-2: 4; H-4: 9]

A street in the town. Day.

Part One

Invention on Subjects I and II

mm. 171–192

The Captain and the Doctor chance to meet each other. The Captain tries to detain the Doctor in idle conversation, but the Doctor is in a great hurry.

mm. 192–202

The Doctor stops. "Woman—dead in four weeks! Cancer uteri. I've already had twenty such patients. In four weeks." CAPTAIN: "Doctor, don't frighten me! People have been known to die of fright, of pure and simple fright!" DOCTOR: "In four weeks! There's an interesting prescription!"

Waltz (Aria):

Ritornello, mm. 202–207

He cold-bloodedly observes the Captain. "And what about you! Hm! Bloated,

A1, mm. 208–215

fat, thick neck, apoplectic constitution.

Ritornello, mm. 215–219

Yes, Captain, you could be getting an *apoplex-*

B, mm. 219–231

ia cerebri. But you'll probably only get it on one side. Yes! You might be paralyzed on one side, or, with good luck, only below!

Ritornello and retransition, mm. 232–238

Yes, those are just about your prospects for the next four weeks. However,

A2, mm. 238–245

I can assure you that yours will be an interesting case. And if God wills that your tongue should be partly paralyzed, we'll make some

Ritornello, mm. 245–247

immortal experiments."

Concluding Episode, mm. 248–271

The Doctor tries to go off, but the Captain restrains him. "People have been known to die of pure fright, Doctor!" His excitement brings on a fit of coughing. He recovers, and, deeply moved by the prospect of his death, imagines that he can already see the mourners at his funeral. "They'll say, 'He was a good man, a good man.'"

Part Two

Chorale Statement of Subject III, mm. ⸢·271–285

Wozzeck hastens past and salutes. DOCTOR: "Hey, Wozzeck, why do you rush by us like that? Stop a moment, Wozzeck!" CAPTAIN: "You run through the world like an open razorblade. People cut themselves on you! You run as though you had to shave all the beards in the University, and would be hanged if a single hair—

Part Three

"Fugue":

Exposition of Subject I, mm. 286–292

Right! Long beards—what was I saying?" He whistles as he reflects. "Long beards—."

Exposition of Subject II, mm. 293–297

The Doctor quotes Pliny on the subject of long beards among soldiers. The Captain strikes his forehead, and continues: "Ah, I have it—

First Development Section (Subjects I and II), mm. 298–312

long beards! How about it, Wozzeck? Haven't you found a hair from a beard in your soup plate? You know what I mean? A human hair, from a sapper's beard, or a corporal's, or a drum major's?" While the Captain speaks the Doctor hums, beating time with his cane as though it were a drum major's baton. "Hey, Wozzeck," he adds, "but you do have a good wife?"

Exposition of Subject III, mm. 313–317⸢

WOZZECK: "What do you mean to say, sir, Doctor, and you, sir, Captain?"

Second Development Section (Subjects I and III), mm. ⸢317–333

CAPTAIN: "What a face the fellow pulls! Well, perhaps not exactly in your soup, but if you hurry and run around the corner you might still find one on a pair of lips! A hair, that is! A pair of lips, too! Oh, I've also known what love is. But, fellow, you're white as chalk!" WOZZECK: "Captain, sir, I'm a poor devil! I've nothing else in the world! Captain, if you're

Third Development Section (Subjects I, II, and III), mm. 334–341

joking—?" "Joke? I? With you? Joke, fellow!" WOZZECK: "Captain, sir, to some the earth is hot as hell, hell's cold next to it." "Fellow, will you shoot yourself? You stab me with your eyes! I mean well by you, because you're a good man, Wozzeck, a good man!" The Doctor meanwhile tries to take Wozzeck's pulse and remarks on the rigidity of his features. WOZZECK, to himself: "Anything's possible. The bitch! Anything's possible."

Concluding Section (Subject III), mm. 341–345

He cries out: "God in Heaven! A man might want to hang himself! Then he would know where he stood!"

Part Four

Coda, mm. 345–362

He rushes away. CAPTAIN: "How the fellow runs, and his shadow after him!" DOCTOR: "He's a phenomenon, this Wozzeck!" CAPTAIN: "This fellow makes me quite dizzy! And despondent! I don't like it. A good man is grateful to God. A good man hasn't any courage, either! Only a cur has courage! Only a cur!"

Two versions of the first part of this scene, preceding Wozzeck's entrance, are found in H-2, and a third version in H-4. Franzos combined all three texts. The remainder of the scene exists only in H-2, in a rough sketch that remains problematical in many details. The stage direction requiring the Doctor to mark time with his cane as if it were a drum major's baton is an addition by the composer. It was apparently suggested by the Captain's line, "Don't wave your cane around in the air that way!" Addressed to the Doctor near the beginning of the scene, neither Büchner nor Franzos can have intended it as an allusion to the Drum Major.

Subject I is the Captain's *Leitmotiv*. In this scene it forms the initial segment of an extended melodic theme (Ex. 19) which first returns, at its original pitch level, in the Fugue, Exposition of Subject I, and is thereafter contrapuntally exploited in the three Development Sections. In the Coda, mm. ♪351–355♪, this theme is again recapitulated at its original pitch-level, but with octave displacements and rhythmic transformations. In the Second and Third Development Sections of the Fugue, the Captain's *Leitmotiv* and the larger melodic theme of which it is a component are employed in both prime and inversion.

Example 19

Subject II, the Doctor's *Leitmotiv* (Ex. 20), has appeared previously only as an incidental countermelody in Variation 13 of the Passacaglia (I/4). The four-bar waltz episode of this variation is quoted in the present scene at the conclusion of the A1 section of the Waltz. The transposition of the waltz tune to the bass line in the *da capo* at mm. ♪242–244 corresponds to Variation 18, mm. 599–601 of the Passacaglia. These musical parallels are suggested by a dramatic parallel: the Doctor's cold-blooded scientific interest in the respective maladies of Wozzeck and the Captain, both of whom he regards as "interesting cases," with Wozzeck already and the Captain potentially the subject of "immortal experiments." The Concluding Episode of *Part One* combines elements of the Invention and of the Waltz. Subject I returns at various pitch levels, and in rhythmic augmentation and diminution.

Example 20

The first statement of Subject III is preceded by agitated figures in the four trumpets that serve here as entrance music and at the beginning of the Coda as exit music for Wozzeck. Through the salient character of this passage, that portion of Act II, Scene 2 in which Wozzeck is present is sharply marked off from *Part One* at his entrance and *Part Four* at his exit. Subject III (Ex. 21), like Subject I, is a segment of a larger thematic idea, which consists of the

Example 21

linear components of the chorale in mm. 273–274 (Ex. 22). There is a second statement at T(11),[20] with octave displacements (mm. 276–277), and a third statement at T(1) (mm. 281–282). Each of the three linear components of the theme serves as *Hauptstimme* in turn in these three initial statements of the theme. The Exposition of Subject III in the Fugue associates Subject III with the other two linear components of the chorale theme. The Third Development Section of the Fugue is a dense polyphonic web made up of components of the *complete* theme identified with the Captain (Ex. 19), in prime and inversion, Subject II (Ex. 20), in prime and inversion, and overlapping statements of the linear components of Example 22. The Concluding Section of the Fugue is based exclusively on these last.

Example 22

In mm. 347–348 of the Coda the six chords of the first bar of Example 22 return in a version that radically distorts the original in timbre, rhythm, and register, while recapitulating the original pitch-level and vertical orderings. Elements of the Waltz return: the *ritornello* chords (mm. 349–350) and the setting of the Doctor's *"apoplexia cerebri"* to accompany the Captain's "Mir wird ganz schwindlich vor dem Menschen!" ("This fellow makes me quite dizzy!"). The movement concludes with a return to mm. 183–184 of the Invention, first at T(4) (mm. 356–358) and then in invertible counterpoint at the octave at T(0).

INTERLUDE

Mm. ♪ 362–365   Curtain.

CHANGE OF SCENE

Mm. 366–368

20 The "T"-number shows the difference in transpositional levels between corresponding statements, counting upward by semitones from the transpositional level, T(0), of the "original" or referential statement.

THIRD MOVEMENT
"Largo"

A₁ (chamber orch.)
    mm. 367–371
    m. 372 ♩ ♪

Curtain rises.

SCENE 3
(F. 11; L. 11) [H-4: 7; H-2: 8]

    mm. 372–373
    mm. 373–377

Marie stands at the door of her house. Wozzeck comes quickly on stage. "Good day, Franz!" He stares at her. "I see nothing, I see nothing. Oh, you should be able to grasp it in your fist!" "What's the matter, Franz?"

    mm. 378–387 ♩

"Is it still you, Marie? A sin, so thick and wide, its stink should be able to smoke the angels out of heaven! But you have a red mouth, a red mouth, not a blister on it?" "You're crazy, Franz! I'm frightened!" "You're beautiful as sin. But can mortal sin be so beautiful, Marie?"

B (chamber orch. and full orch.)
    mm. 387–397

"There!" he cries out, pointing toward the door. "Is that where he stood? Like this?" MARIE: "I can't order people off the street." "Devil! Is that where he stood?" MARIE: "Since the day's long and the world's old, lots of people can stand in one place, one after the other!" "I saw him!" MARIE: "You can see lots of things, if you have two eyes, and aren't blind, and the sun is shining." WOZZECK: "You beside him!" MARIE: "And if I were?" "Bitch!" he cries out, about to strike her. "Don't touch me! Better a knife in my body than a hand on me! My father didn't dare, when I was ten years old." Wozzeck stares after her as she goes into the house.

A₂ₐ (chamber orch.)
    mm. 398–402 ♩ ♪

Wozzeck, alone, repeats her words: " 'Better a knife'!" He continues, in a frightened whisper: "Man's an abyss. You get dizzy when you look down. I'm dizzy." He leaves.

68   A2$_b$ (full orch. and chamber
        orch.)

        mm.   402–405 (406)
Mm. 406–411
        INTERLUDE

                        Curtain.

    Except for the addition of a few stage directions, Berg closely follows the
Franzos text. Wozzeck's agitated entrance is marked by the same motive in the
bassoon that accompanied his knock on the window in Act I, Scene 3, and this
motive is imbedded, as it was there (mm. 425ff.), in a reminiscence of the
cadential bars of the Cradle Song, suggesting as Marie greets him that nothing
has happened to change their relationship. The rise of the curtain is preceded
by an exposition of the thematic elements specifically associated with this
movement (Ex. 23), as opposed to the extensive quotations in Section B from
Act I, Scenes 3 and 5.

Example 23

    The dramatic implications of these reminiscences were discussed above
(p. 41). The main orchestra returns, antiphonally employed against the chamber orchestra to accompany Marie's evasive replies to Wozzeck's accusing
questions. The dialogue is set against musical references to Marie's liaison with
the Drum Major. The interchange between chamber orchestra (Wozzeck) and
main orchestra (Marie) is an ironic commentary on the verbal dialogue, the
confrontation between Marie and Wozzeck parodying the earlier confrontation
between Marie and the Drum Major. When Wozzeck raises his hand to strike
Marie at the conclusion of Section B there is a return to the music that accom-

panied Marie's surrender to the Drum Major a moment before the final curtain of Act I.

This contrasting middle section of the movement is the midpoint of Act II and of the opera as a whole. The symmetry of the formal design of the movement is emphasized in the relation between the two interludes by which it is framed: the second interlude, marking the fall of the curtain, is a retrograde version of the first, which marked the fall of the curtain upon the preceding scene.

The exposition presents motives that return in conjunction with non-thematic elements in the remaining portion of A1: motive w in a rhythmic variant at T(5), m. 378, English horn; motives x and z together, mm. ♪ 376–377, with motive z at T(2); motive y in mm. ♪380–382, French horn. A *stretto* based on the opening motive (Ex. 23w) initiates the recapitulation, which is completed, after Wozzeck's exit and before the fall of the curtain upon the now empty stage, with a *fff* restatement of motives x and z.

The scene that follows in the Landau edition (F. 13; L. 12) is omitted from the opera. It shows Andres and Wozzeck together in the guard room. Andres tells Wozzeck of the dancing at the inn. Wozzeck, restless, decides he must go "to see where they're dancing."

FOURTH MOVEMENT
"Scherzo"

"Scherzo I *(Ländler)*"

CHANGE OF SCENE

A1, mm. 412–429

B, mm. 430–438

A2, mm. 439–442   Curtain rises. The stage band is heard.

SCENE 4
(F. 14; L. 13)
[H-4: 11; H-2: 4; H-1: 11; H-1: 5]

The tavern garden. Apprentices, soldiers, girls. Some are dancing.

mm. 443–447 (stage band)   Two drunken apprentices sing. Their refrain: "And my soul stinks of brandy."

Transition, mm. 447–455 (orch.)   The company leaves the dance floor. Some gather around the two apprentices.

"Trio I" (orch.)

Chorale

Strophe I, mm. 456–464   FIRST APPRENTICE: "My soul, my immortal soul, it stinks of brandy. It stinks, and I know not wherefore. Wherefore is the world so sad? Even money must turn to dust!"

Strophe II, mm. 465–480

The Second Apprentice embraces his comrade. "Forget me not! Brother! Friendship! I wish our noses were two bottles and we could pour them down each other's throats. The whole world's rosy red. Brandy, that's my life!" The First Apprentice, falling asleep: "My soul, my immortal soul, stinks. Oh, it's sad, sad, sad." The company, among them Marie and the Drum Major, returns to the dance floor.

"Scherzo II (Waltz)" (stage band)

Section 1, mm. 481–495   The dance resumes.
(mm. 495–496)   *Wozzeck rushes in.*[21]
Section 2, mm. 496–503   Marie and the Drum Major pass before him as they dance. "He! She! The devil!"
Section 3, mm. 504–513   Marie, as she dances: "On we go, on we go!" Wozzeck repeats, "On we go!" He sinks down on a bench near the dance floor.
Section 4, mm. 514–528   "Twist yourselves! Tumble about! Why does God

(mm. 517–528)   *not put the sun out? Everything rolling together in lechery, man and woman, human and beast!*
Section 5, mm. 529–538   Woman! Woman! The woman's hot, hot!
Section 6, mm. 539–545   How he paws her! On her body! And she laughs!"
Section 7, mm. 546–559   MARIE and the DRUM MAJOR: "On we go! On we go!" Wozzeck, getting more and more excited, cannot

(mm. 553–560)   *control himself any longer and is about to rush onto the dance floor.* But he desists, since the dance has ended and the dancers are leaving the floor. He sits down again.

---

21 Portions of the text shown in italics are set to interpolations by the orchestra in the pit, as indicated by the measure numbers in italics in the column at the left. The dance music of the stage band is not interrupted by these interpolations.

"Trio II"

    A₁, Hunting Chorus, mm. 561–577

        The soldiers and apprentices sing a refrain of a hunting song.

    B, Andres's song, mm. 577–580

        Andres takes the guitar from one of the musicians and accompanies himself in a solo: "O daughter, dear daughter, of what were you thinking, flirting with coachmen and carters?"

    A₂, Hunting Chorus, mm. 581–590

        The chorus repeats its refrain.

"Scherzo I (quasi-reprise of Ländler)" (stage band)

    A, mm. 592–602
      (Ostinato I, mm. 589–604)

        Andres returns the guitar and turns to Wozzeck. WOZZECK: *"What's the time?" "Eleven o'clock." "Oh? I thought it must be later. The time drags at these pastimes." "Why do you sit here by the door?" "I'm all right here. Lots of people sit by the door and don't know it, until they're carried out feet first." "You're sitting hard, there." "I'm sitting all right, and in the cool grave I'll lie even better." "Are you drunk?" "No such luck. Can't bring it off."*

    B, mm. 603–608

        Andres is bored. Whistling with the dance music, which has become audible again after having been momentarily drowned out by the main orchestra, he turns away from Wozzeck. The company leaves the dance floor and turns its attention to the First Apprentice, who is climbing onto a table.

"Trio I (quasi-reprise)"

    "Chorale variation," mm. 605–635 (stage band)

        The First Apprentice, standing on the table, delivers a mock sermon.

    Transition

      mm. 634–651 (orch.)

        There is a general uproar at the conclusion of the "sermon." The men sing a phrase of the

mm. 650–664 (stage band)

hunting song, as some of them return to the dance floor and others to the tables at the rear. The Idiot suddenly appears and approaches Wozzeck, who is still seated on the bench.

As the band retunes he draws up close to Wozzeck: "Jolly, jolly!" The players finish tuning up

mm. 665–669

and are silent as they prepare to play the Waltz again. THE IDIOT: "But it smells—" "Fool, what do you want?" "I smell, I smell blood!" WOZZECK: "Blood? Blood! Blood!"

"Scherzo II (quasi-reprise of Waltz)"

mm. 671–684 (stage band)

The apprentices, girls, and soldiers, among them Marie and the Drum Major, resume the dance.

(Ostinato II, mm. 670–684)

WOZZECK: *"Everything's turning red before my eyes. They all seem to be tumbling over one another."*

Quick curtain.

CHANGE OF SCENE

mm. 685–736 (orch.)

To the version of this scene that is found in H-4 Franzos added, with certain emendations, two "Wirtshaus" scenes found in H-1, one consisting of the dialogue between Wozzeck and Andres, the other of the dialogue between Wozzeck and the Idiot. Andres's song is taken from still another "Wirtshaus" scene (H-1: 10), where it is given to the "Barbier" (cf. pp. 33f. above). Berg's version of this song follows Witkowski rather than Franzos. The lines given to Andres in his dialogue with Wozzeck in the libretto were assigned to "A Soldier" in the Franzos edition. In this respect too Berg follows Witkowski, although he probably would have made this change in any case, since it is consistent with reassignments of minor roles that the composer made elsewhere in the work in order to reduce the number of independent roles. From a letter to his wife we know that Berg was still working on the composition of this scene as late as June of 1921.[22] His acquaintance with Witkowski's edition of 1920 is evident also in several other departures from Franzos's text, most obviously in

22 Berg 65, p. 458.

the addition of the line, "Das Weib ist heiss! ist heiss! heiss!" Except for Berg's temporary use of Witkowski's corrected spelling, "Woyzeck," there is no evidence other than what is found in this scene to indicate that he made use of any edition other than that of Franzos–Landau. There are some additional negligible revisions in the dialogue, mainly consisting of some deletions in the speeches of the Apprentices and some repetitions of words and lines for the sake of the musical design. The stage directions, here as elsewhere in the libretto, are considerably more elaborate than those given by Franzos.

Recurrent passages in Scherzo II vaguely suggest a rondo. The first two measures of the Waltz return at the conclusion of Sections 1 and 7, the latter having commenced with a varied recapitulation of the "On we go!" ("Immer zu") music of Section 3. The contrasting middle episode of Section 1 returns in the second period of Section 4. The quasi-reprise of the Waltz literally recapitulates, except for changes in scoring and dynamic level, Section 1 in the stage band, but at the point where the *da capo* had occurred earlier the main orchestra takes over the music of the dance in a violent crescendo that seems to obliterate the sound of the stage band as the curtain drops. The remainder of the reprise is at the same time a coda of the movement as a whole, a vivid musical representation of the mental state denoted by Wozzeck's last words that continues to increase in intensity to the abrupt termination of the movement. Sections 3 and 4 are simultaneously recapitulated in mm. 685ff., Section 2 in mm. 697ff., Section 6 in *stretto* in mm. 704ff., the song of the First Apprentice (mm. 456–464) simultaneously with the song of the Second Apprentice (mm. 465–471) accompanied by a tonic-dominant waltz pattern in F major in mm. 713ff., and finally Section 1 again in mm. 724ff. Only Section 5, in which the music that introduced the seduction scene of Act One is converted into a strain of the Waltz, does not return in the quasi-reprise of the Waltz.

Carefully calculated to the last detail though the scene is, "Berg really does succeed in creating the impression," as Stravinsky notes, "that the apparatus of the concertina, the band, and the soldiers' chorus has been improvised then and there for a one and only performance."[23] In his lecture Berg refers to the realistic implications of the polytonal cadences in mm. 424 and 429 of the *Ländler:*

> The antecedent of a *Ländler* in G minor—according to the rules of formal construction—either leads to the Dominant (D major) or back to the Tonic. The fact that both things happen simultaneously (who could blame the blind-fold rhapsodizings of an alcoholic band of beer fiddlers?) leads to musical chaos. . . . This chaos is prolonged when the section of the beer fiddlers which had reached the Dominant returns to the Tonic of G minor according to the rule, whereas another section—with equal justification by the laws of modulation—turns into the mediant of E-flat major.[24]

23 Stravinsky 66, p. 180.
24 Redlich 57b, p. 278. (E♭ major is the submediant key. Cf. the original text [Redlich 57a, p. 322] and Redlich's footnote to same.)

74 Since the curtain has not yet ascended, the playing of the "alcoholic band of beer fiddlers" in the passage described by Berg is represented by the orchestra. In the reprise the *Ländler* is performed by the stage band while the orchestra provides an independent musical setting for the dialogue of Wozzeck and Andres. Since the music of the stage band becomes inaudible precisely at the reprise of mm. 424–429, the "musical chaos" mentioned by the composer is not *actually* realized at this point (mm. ⌐599–602). To the dancers, of course, the stage band is still "audible" and they continue to dance in the tempo of the *Ländler*. The stage band becomes audible again with a strain (Ex. 24) that may well be an allusion to the music of the stage band in Act II of *Der Rosenkavalier*.

The music of the stage band as the curtain rises at the beginning of the scene is clearly intended as an allusion to another famous operatic stage band (Ex. 25).[25]

Example 24

Example 25

The scene that follows in both the Franzos and the Landau versions of the drama is a faithful representation of experiences that the historical Woyzeck described to his interrogator, Dr. Clarus. It is given here, in Franzos's reading, in its entirety:

25 Redlich 57a, pp. 119f.

Freies Feld

Nacht

WOZZECK

WOZZECK. Immer zu! Immer zu! Still Musik! Ha! was sagt Ihr? So—Lauter! lauter!
Jetzt hör' ich's. Stich—stich die Zickwölfin todt—Stich—stich—die—Zickwölfin todt—soll ich?—muss ich?—Ich hör's immer, immer zu—stich todt
—todt—Da unten aus dem Boden heraus spricht's, und die Pappeln
sprechen's—stich todt—stich—[26]

Though Berg omits this scene from the opera, the effect of its hallucinatory transformation of the verbal *Leitmotiv* of the Waltz, "immer zu!", is
realized in the change-of-scene music. The latter, like the omitted scene, is a
bridge from the scene in the tavern garden to the episode in the barracks that
follows the change-of-scene music in the opera and the omitted scene in the
drama.[27]

FIFTH MOVEMENT
"Introduction and Rondo"

"Introduction"

mm. 737–739	The "wordless chorus of the sleeping sol-diers" is heard through the closed curtain and continues through m. 743 $\overset{\curvearrowleft}{}$.
mm. 740–741	Curtain rises.

SCENE 5
Part One
(F. 16; L. 15) [H-4: 13; H-1: 7]
At night, in the barracks. The soldiers are
asleep on wooden beds, Andres beside
Wozzeck.

mm. 742–743 $\overset{\curvearrowleft}{}$	Wozzeck moans in his sleep.
mm. $\overset{\curvearrowright}{}$ 743–758	WOZZECK, starting up: "Andres! Andres! I can't sleep. When I shut my eyes I go on see-ing them, and I hear the fiddles, on they go, on they go! And then a voice out of the wall—don't you hear anything, Andres?

---

26   *OPEN FIELD*
    Night

WOZZECK. On they go! On they go! Stop, music! Ha! What do you say? So—louder! Louder!
Now I hear it. Stab—stab the bitch to death—stab—stab—the—bitch to death—should
I?—must I?—I hear it always, on it goes—stab to death—death—Down from under the
ground it speaks, and the poplars say it—stab to death—stab—

27 Lehmann's synopsis indicates that the placement of this scene between the scene in the
tavern garden and the scene in the barracks conforms to Büchner's intentions.

How they fiddle and dance?" ANDRES, sleep-ily: "Let them dance!" WOZZECK: "And in be-tween something flashing in front of my eyes like a knife, like a broad knife!" ANDRES: "Sleep, fool!" WOZZECK: "My Lord and God!" He prays. "And lead us not into temptation. Amen!"

mm. 759–760

The chorus of the sleeping soldiers is heard.

"Rondo marziale"

Part Two

(F. 17/12; L. 16A/16B) [H-4; H-1: 8]

A₁, mm. 761–768 ♪⁺

The drunken Drum Major blusters in. "I'm a man! I've got me a woman, I tell you, a woman! For breeding drum majors!

A₂, mm. ♪768–776

A bosom, and thighs! And all so firm! Eyes like glowing coals! A woman, I tell you!" "Who is it?" asks Andres. "Just ask Wozzeck there!"

B₁, mm. ♪776–785

He pulls a flask out of his pocket, drinks, and holds it toward Wozzeck. "Drink, fel-low! I wish the world were brandy. Man's got to drink! Drink, fellow, drink!" Wozzeck looks away and whistles.

A₃, mm. ♪785–788

DRUM MAJOR: "Fellow, do you want me to pull your tongue out of your neck and twist it around your middle?"

C, mm. 789–799

They wrestle and Wozzeck is forced to the floor. The Drum Major, choking him: "Shall I leave you enough wind for an (old woman's fart)?²⁸ Shall I—?" The Drum Major rises and takes the flask from his pock-et, as Wozzeck sinks back exhausted.

B₂, mm. 800–804

"Now let the fellow whistle! Till he's blue in the face, let him whistle!" The Drum Major whistles.

A₄, mm. 805–814

"I'm a man, I am!" He blusters out of the room. Wozzeck has in the meantime pulled himself up from the bed. "He's had it," says

---

28 The parentheses are Berg's. He also uses smaller type for "Altweiberfurz" and its vocal setting, thus implying that the word may be omitted.

	one of the soldiers, pointing to him. ANDRES: "He's bleeding." They go back to sleep. WOZZECK: "One after the other!"
Mm. 815–816, general pause	Wozzeck remains seated, staring in front of him.
Mm. 817–818 (orch. remains silent.)	Curtain.

Act II, Scene 5 commences with the text of Franzos 16 (Landau 15), continues with the first few lines of Franzos 17 (Landau 16), and concludes with almost all the text of Franzos 12 (Landau's alternative version of 16). Only the first of these three scenes is placed in the barracks in Berg's source; the second is placed in the barracks yard and the third in the tavern. The presence of "sleeping soldiers" other than Wozzeck and Andres is not mentioned in the source.

The change-of-scene music between Scenes 4 and 5 parallels that between Scenes 1 and 2 of the first act, in that it too is a final development and résumé of the musical material of the preceding scene, increasing in momentum, density, and dynamic level until it is suddenly obliterated at its climax by the music of the new scene. The resemblance lies in these extrinsic details only, not in any shared thematic ideas. The new music that suddenly interposes itself in the second instance is, on the other hand, a recapitulation of the initial bars of Scene 2 of the first act. The eerie "nature music" that is given to the orchestra there becomes the "wordless chorus of the sleeping soldiers" in Act II, Scene 5. In both instances Wozzeck is alienated and estranged from his environment, and in both his words of fear and foreboding are addressed to one who cannot comprehend them, his carefree friend Andres. The verbal *Leitmotiv* with which the scene concludes has been discussed earlier (p. 42). The Drum Major leaves, Andres and the others go back to sleep, and the music of Act II concludes with the pedal note that represents the *idée fixe* of the murder in the second scene of the following act. Wozzeck remains seated on his bunk, staring before him.

The curtain does not fall at once, though both the music and the "action" of Act II are at an end. The curtain that rises upon the remorseful Marie reading her Bible at the beginning of the next act is given the same duration of silence for its ascent as the falling final curtain of the preceding act was given for its descent, and the same duration of silence that intervened between the conclusion of the music of Act II and the falling of the curtain intervenes before the music begins after the curtain has risen upon Act III. This "delayed" fall and "premature" rise of the curtain seem to blur the distinction between the staged world and the "real" world, by prolonging beyond its conventional limits the view that the audience is given of that staged world.

Five "Inventions"[29]

M. 1 (The orch. is silent.)   Curtain rises.

SCENE I
(F. 18; L. 17) [H-4: 16]

M. 2   Marie's room, at night. She is reading the Bible by candlelight.

FIRST MOVEMENT
"Invention on a Theme"

"Theme," mm. 3–9   MARIE: "'And no guile is found in his mouth.'" She cries out, "Lord God, Lord God, Don't look upon me!

"Variation 1," mm. 10–16   'And the Pharisees brought unto him a woman taken in adultery. And Jesus said, "Neither do I condemn thee;

"Variation 2," mm. 17–18   go, and sin no more." ' Lord God!"

"Variation 3," mm. 19–25   The child cuddles up to her. "The boy stabs my heart. Be off!" She pushes him from her.

"Variation 4," mm. 26–32   "It struts in the sun!"[30] She suddenly changes her tone. "No, come, come here! Come to me!"

"Variation 5," mm. 33–39   She tells the child a fairy tale: "Once upon a time there was a poor child, had no father and no mother; everyone was dead and there was nobody left in the world, and he was hungry and wept, night and day.

"Variation 6," mm. 40–44   And since he had nobody left in the world—" She breaks off her story. "Franz hasn't come—not yesterday, not today."

"Variation 7," mm. 45–51   She hastily turns the pages of the Bible. "What does it say about Mary Magdalene?

---

29 Mahler's (Berg's) outline has the title "Six Inventions" for this movement. See p. 89, below.

30 The meaning of this expression, "Das brüst' sich in der Sonne!" is unclear. Margaret Jacobs suggests that Marie is referring to "her own sin which has been bold and evident. (She has danced with the Tambourmajor in public, and he has boasted in public of his conquest.)" Büchner (Jacobs) 54, p. 144.

"Fugue"

Exposition, Subject I, mm.
52–57 ⌐   'And kneeled down at his feet and wept,
                     and kissed his feet, and washed them with
                     her tears, and anointed them with oint-
                     ment.'

Exposition, Subject II,
mm. ⌐·57–62 ·⌐   Savior! I would anoint thy feet. Savior! Thou
                     hadst mercy upon her; have mercy upon
                     me!''

Stretto
   mm. ⌐62–64⌐   Curtain.

                        CHANGE OF SCENE

   mm. ⌐64–70

Codetta, mm. 71–72   Curtain rises.

The next three scenes in both the Franzos and the Landau editions were
omitted by Berg. The first of these shows Wozzeck purchasing the murder
weapon. In Büchner's text of the prayer scene the Idiot is also present, babbling to himself.[31] Marie calls to him and he takes the child from her. Franzos
deleted the part of the Idiot and assigned an adaptation of his lines to Marie:
"Once upon a time there was a king. The king had a golden crown and a
queen and a little boy. And what did they all eat? They all ate liverwurst." Berg
substituted for this the opening lines of the story that the old woman narrates
to the children in the street in Franzos 20 (Landau 19), the second of the three
omitted scenes. It is a tale in which the meaning that Rilke found in the play—
"the way this misused person in his stable-jacket stands in universal space,
malgré lui, in the infinite relationship of the stars"—is expressed in language
that belongs to the child's world of make-believe. By replacing Franzos's adaptation of the Idiot's lines with the beginning of the Grandmother's tale, and
breaking this off with a phrase, "And since he had nobody left in the
world—," that foreshadows the fate of her child, Berg gave to Marie's words
an extraordinary relevance and poignancy. The tale, which was evidently
invented by Büchner himself, continues as follows (in Lehmann's reading):

> And since there was nobody left in the world, he thought he'd go up to heaven,
> and the moon peeped at him so friendly, and when he came to the moon at last, it
> was a piece of rotten wood, so he went to the sun, and when he came to the sun
> it was a dried-up sunflower, and when he came to the stars they were little gold
> flies that were stuck up there the way the shrike sticks them on the blackthorn
> bush, and when he wanted to go back to the earth, the earth was an overturned
> pot, and he was all alone, and he sat down and cried, and he's still sitting there
> and is all alone.

31 See p. 33, above.

The author presumably (see above, p. 43) did not survive to revise this scene and those that follow it in the first draft of the play, H-1. Franzos departed from Büchner at the conclusion of the scene. In the original, as the Grandmother finishes her story Wozzeck suddenly appears and calls to Marie. Marie, frightened, asks, "What is it?" "Let's go, Marie," he replies. "It's time." "Where to?" she asks. "How should I know?" The murder scene follows. Franzos, however, interpolated another scene, the third of the three consecutive scenes omitted from the opera at this point, which Büchner added in the provisional fair copy, H-4, and which terminates this incomplete manuscript. To make this interpolation possible Franzos deleted the part of Wozzeck from the scene with the Grandmother. Wozzeck, in the barracks, is rummaging through his belongings. He offers Andres a jacket and shows him some family heirlooms—his sister's ring and cross and a holy picture from his mother's Bible. He pulls out a document and reads his vital statistics: "Private Johann Frank Wozzeck, soldier and rifleman, 2nd Regiment, 2nd Battalion, 4th Company, born Annunciation Day, July 20th. I'm thirty years, seven months, and twelve days old today." Andres, confused by Wozzeck's behavior, suggests that he go on sick call. "Yes, Andres," replies Wozzeck, "When the cabinetmaker puts those boards together nobody knows whose head will lie on them." Though Wozzeck's final disposition of his few worldly possessions doesn't necessarily indicate that he plans to commit suicide after the murder, it does imply that he anticipates that his life will be finished with Marie's death, and strongly supports the assumption that his death by drowning is part of Büchner's conception.

SECOND MOVEMENT

"Invention on a Note"

SCENE 2

(F. 22; L. 21) [H-1: 15]

Forest path by the pond, at dusk.

Section 1, mm. 73–76°

Marie enters with Wozzeck. MARIE: "There to the left is the town. It's still far. Hurry!" WOZZECK: "You must stay, Marie. Come, sit down." "But I must go!" "Come.

Section 2, mm. 76–80

You've gone far, Marie. You shouldn't make your feet sore, walking. It's quiet here! And so dark!

Section 3, mm. °80–85

Do you know, Marie, how long it is now, that we've known each other?" MARIE: "Three years at Pentecost." "And how long do you think it will still last?" "I must go!" "Are you frightened, Marie? But you are pious, and good, and faithful?

Section 4, mm. 86–92	"What sweet lips you have, Marie?" He kisses her. "I'd give up heaven and eternal bliss if I might go on kissing you. But I may not!	81

Section 5, mm. 92–96

"Why are you shivering?" "The night dew is falling." "When one's cold, one doesn't feel the cold any more! When the morning dew falls you won't feel the cold." "What are you saying?" "Nothing." They remain silent.

Section 6, mm. 98–108

The moon rises. MARIE: "How red the moon's rising!" WOZZECK: "Like a bloody sword!" MARIE: "Why are you shivering?" He draws a knife. "What do you want?" "Not I, Marie! And no one else either!" She screams, as Wozzeck seizes her and plunges the knife into her throat. She sinks down. Wozzeck bends over her. "Dead!" He rises anxiously, then rushes silently away.

m. 108

Curtain.

INTERLUDE   CHANGE OF SCENE

Mm. 109–121

The formal subdivisions indicated above are articulated by means of changes in tempo and in the disposition of the *ostinato b* that persists throughout the movement and that overlaps with the last two bars of the preceding movement at the rise of the curtain. The Interlude summarizes the formal basis of each of the three middle scenes of Act III: the *ostinato* pitch-class of Scene 2 in mm. 109–113 and 117–121; the *ostinato* rhythm of Scene 3 (Ex. 172) in the bass drum, mm. 114–115, and in the succession of attacks in the winds and, a beat later, in the strings, in mm. 109–113 (Ex. 171); and the *ostinato* chord of Scene 4 (Ex. 108) in m. 114.

Berg's libretto followed Franzos's version of the murder scene literally in almost every detail, but the few discrepancies are noteworthy as examples of the composer's literary sensitivity and skill. Marie's "Was zitterst?" ("Why are you shivering?") is a literal echo of the question that Wozzeck has asked Marie earlier in the scene. In Franzos's version Marie says, "Was zitterst so?" Neither Marie's question nor Wozzeck's is found in Büchner's text. In the Franzos edition Wozzeck follows his whispered statement, "When the morning dew falls you won't feel the cold," with the words, "But I? Ah, it must be!"; and at the conclusion of the scene, as he rushes away, he cries out, "Murderer! Murderer!" In both instances Berg deleted interpolations that Franzos made in the original text. However, the relation of Berg's version to that of Franzos makes it clear that in making these deletions he was not influenced by any other readings of Büchner's draft of the scene. The authentic version concludes with the stage direction, *Es kommen Leute, läuft weg. (People approach. He runs away.)* There follows a dialogue between two passersby whose coming it is, presumably, that frightens Wozzeck away. They hear, or think that they hear, sounds as of someone dying. "It's the water," says one. "It's calling. It's been a long time since anyone was drowned." Many later editors followed Franzos in transferring this episode to the conclusion of the scene in which Wozzeck, after returning to search for the knife, throws it into the water and wades in after it to throw it further. The draft of the murder scene contains no reference to the pond, but the dialogue of the two passersby seems to justify the assumption that it takes place by the pond into which Wozzeck later throws the knife. On the other hand, the manuscript has Wozzeck "at a pond" into which he throws the knife only after he has been frightened away from the place of the murder a second time by the sound of people approaching.

One of the most moving lines in the entire drama is missing in Franzos's version of the murder scene. When Wozzeck asks, "And how long do you think it will still last?" Marie evades a reply and simply says, as though nothing has happened to alter their relationship, "I must go and get supper ready."

THIRD MOVEMENT	SCENE 3
"Invention on a Rhythm"	
	(F. 23; L. 22) [H-1: 17]
	A low tavern, dimly lit.
Polka, mm. 122–145 (stage piano)	Apprentices and girls, among them Margret, are dancing to a wild polka played on an out-of-tune piano. WOZZECK, seated at a table: "Dance, all of you! Leap, sweat, and stink! The devil will get you all in the end!"
Song, mm. 145–152	He sings: "Three riders were riding along the Rhine. They stopped with a hostess for lodging. My wine is good, my beer is clear, my little daughter lies on her—"
Mm. 152–157	He interrupts his song. "Damn!" He leaps up. "Come, Margret!" He dances a few steps with her, then suddenly stops.
Mm. 158–168	"Come, sit down, Margret!" He leads her to a table and pulls her on to his lap. "Margret, you're so hot. But just wait. You'll be cold, too! Can't you sing?"

Song, mm. 169–179 (stage piano)	MARGRET sings: "To Swabia I'll not go, and long dresses I'll not wear, for long dresses, pointed shoes, don't belong to servant girls."
Mm. 180–186°	WOZZECK, flaring up: "No! No shoes! You can go to hell barefooted, too! I'd like a fight today, a fight!" MARGRET: "But what do you have there on your hand?"
Stretto, mm. ⌐186–212°	WOZZECK: "I? I?" MARGRET: "Red! Blood!" WOZZECK: "Blood? Blood?" The others gather around them. "Certainly! Blood!" "I think I must have cut myself, here, on my right hand." "Then how did it get on your elbow?" "I wiped it off there." AN APPRENTICE: "With your right hand on your right arm?" MARGRET and the others: "Phew! There's surely a stink of human blood!" WOZZECK, at the same time: "What do you want? What's it to you? Am I a murderer? Make way, or somebody's going
m. 211	to the devil!" Quick curtain, as he rushes off.

CHANGE OF SCENE

mm. 212–218

In Büchner's text the song that Wozzeck sings at the beginning of the scene is one that is given to Andres earlier, in a scene (H-1: 4 and H-4: 10) omitted from the opera (see p. 69, above). Franzos gave Wozzeck another song, one that is not found at all in the original text, evidently attributing the repetition to an oversight on the part of the author. In fact, the assignment to Wozzeck at the beginning of this scene of the song that he had heard the carefree Andres singing earlier—"Our hostess has a worthy maid, she sits in the garden night and day, she sits in the garden until the bell tolls twelve, and waits upon the soldiers"—is a dramatic stroke of marvelous subtlety and relevance. Not only does its content seem to refer to Marie's infidelity, but it also establishes the psychological keynote of the scene: Wozzeck's desperate attempt to escape from his own identity, singing another man's song and immersing himself in the crowd of merrymakers in the cheap tavern in which he finds himself after murdering Marie.[32]

32 Though Bergemann takes Franzos to task for his emendations of the original text, he too substitutes another song for the one that Büchner gives Wozzeck in H-1: 17, replacing it with one that Büchner had considered and then discarded, as the stricken-out opening line that precedes the author's final choice clearly shows.

84 Franzos's failure to understand Büchner's use of verbal *Leitmotive* is reflected also in his deletion, from the same scene, of the part of the Idiot, whose words ("Und da hat der Ries gesagt: 'ich riech, ich riech, ich riech Menschenfleisch. Puh! Das stinkt schon' "—"And then the giant said: 'I smell, I smell, I smell the flesh of a man. Puh! it stinks already' ") recall the line given to him in the version of the earlier tavern-scene that is found in the same manuscript ("Ich reich, ich reich Blut"—"I smell, I smell blood") which Franzos *did* incorporate in his text of the play. Similarly, Franzos deleted Wozzeck's words (restored in the opera), as he watches Marie dancing with the Drum Major, "Das Weib ist heiss, heiss!" ("The woman's hot, hot!"), which antici-pate his "du bist heiss!" ("You're hot!") to his dancing partner in the later scene. In restoring the antecedent phrase,[33] Berg pointed up the significance of Wozzeck's behavior as he flirts and dances with Margret after the death of Marie, reenacting, with Margret taking the place of Marie, the earlier role of the Drum Major.

Wozzeck's pathetic effort to cast himself in the role of his chief victimizer, the Drum Major, is expressed also in his sudden outburst, "Ich möcht heut raufen, raufen" ("I'd like a fight today, a fight"), and is made explicit by the composer in his setting of these words to the Drum Major's *Leitmotiv* (Ex. 55), rhythmically transformed so that it is simultaneously a statement of the rhythmic theme of the movement. But this most effective and meaningful line is not found in Büchner's text. It is an invention of Franzos's, replacing an ambiguous and seemingly unmotivated line whose connotations are very dif-ferent: "Ja wahrhaftig! ich möchte mich nicht blutig machen" ("Yes, that's right! I don't want to make myself bloody"). With the immediate repetition of the Drum Major's *Leitmotiv* as a setting for Margret's question, "Aber was hast Du an der Hand?" ("But what do you have there on your hand?") Wozzeck's attempt to assume another man's fate and character is cut short and his real and irrevocable identity is suddenly thrust upon him again.

INTERLUDE

M. 219   Curtain rises.

FOURTH MOVEMENT	SCENE 4
"Invention on a Six-Note Chord"	(F. 24; L. 23) [H-1: 19, 20, 16] The forest path by the pond. Moonlit night as before.
Part One, mm. 220–256	Wozzeck staggers in hastily, then stops to search about. "The knife? Where is the

33 See pp. 72f., above.

knife? I left it here. Nearer! Still nearer! I'm   85
terrified. Something's moving there. Silent!
Everything silent and dead!" He cries out,
"Murderer! Murderer!" He whispers: "Ah!
Someone's calling! No, I myself!" He stumbles upon the corpse. "Marie! Marie! What's
that red band around your neck? Did you
earn that red necklace, as you did the earrings, with your sins? Why does your black
hair hang so wild? Murderer! Murderer!
They will come looking for me. The knife
betrays me!" He searches about feverishly.
"Here! Here it is!

Part Two, mm. 257–284   There! Down it goes." He throws the knife
into the pond. "It dives into the dark water
like a stone." The blood-red moon breaks
through the clouds. "But the moon betrays
me. The moon is bloody. Will the whole
wide world be blabbing about it? The
knife—it's too near the edge, they'll find it
when they're bathing, or when they're div-
ing for mussels." He wades into the pond.
"I can't find it. But I must wash myself. I'm
bloody. Here's a spot, and here's another."
He wails. "Oh! Oh! I'm washing myself with
blood! The water is blood! Blood!"

Part Three, mm. 284–301   He drowns. The Doctor enters. The Captain,
following him: "Stop!" The Doctor, stop-
ping: "Do you hear? Over there!" "Christ!
What a sound!" The Doctor points to the
pond. "Yes, over there!" CAPTAIN: "It's
the water in the pond. The water's calling.
It's a long time since anyone drowned. Let's
go, Doctor! It's not good to hear." He tries to
draw the Doctor away with him. The Doctor
stands still and

Part Four, mm. 302–317   listens. "There's a groan, like someone dying. Someone's drowning there!" CAP-
TAIN: "Eerie! The moon red, and the fog
gray. Do you hear? There's that groaning
again." DOCTOR: "It's getting softer.
Now it's quite still." The Captain pulls the

86   Doctor away. "Let's go! Come quickly!" The
                                        Doctor hurries off after the Captain.

mm. 318–319   Curtain.

The dialogue between the Captain and the Doctor is given to two anonymous passersby in Franzos, as it is in Büchner. The significance of Berg's reassignment of these roles has been explained earlier (pp. 41f.). In transferring this episode from its original position in the manuscript immediately following the murder scene (see p. 82), Franzos took his cue from Büchner, who has Wozzeck running away at the sound of people approaching just after he finds the knife, and then returning to throw the knife into the pond. Berg revised the Franzos edition by deleting Wozzeck's exclamation as he discovers the knife, "Leute!—fort!" ("People!—away!") Otherwise Berg followed Franzos's text, only adding numerous stage directions. The blood-red moon breaking through the clouds and the "Unkenrufe" at mm. 227ff. and 302ff. are among these additions.[34] In interpolating sounds of nature the composer restored an element that Franzos had omitted in his version of Büchner's text. In Büchner's version of the dialogue between the two passersby, the humming of the insects "like broken bells" contributes to the eeriness of the scene.

Franzos largely rewrote the three portions of H-1 that he brought together for his twenty-fourth scene. Wozzeck's cry, "Murderer! Murderer!" is his addition, as it was at the conclusion of the murder scene. Büchner has only a single reference to the moon: as the knife that threatens to betray him disappears in the water, Wozzeck sees that the moon still calls attention to his crime and exclaims, "Der Mond ist wie ein blutig Eisen!" The same words, "like a bloody sword," were evoked by Marie's reference to the red moon and marked his drawing of the knife in the murder scene. Here, again, Franzos eliminated the verbal *Leitmotiv*, substituting for it the words, "Aber der Mond verräth mich—der Mond ist blutig." Wozzeck's last words in the libretto (and in Franzos's text), following "Here's a spot, and here's another," the last words assigned to him by Büchner, are also Franzos's invention.

What is the sound "as of someone dying" that the two passersby hear? Büchner's own version of the "Es kommen Leute" scene is as follows:

ERSTE PERSON. Halt!
ZWEITE PERSON. Hörst du! Still! Da!
ERSTE PERSON. Uu! Da! Was ein Ton.
ZWEITE PERSON. Es ist das Wasser, es ruft, schon lang ist Neimand ertrunken. Fort, s'ist nicht gut, es zu hören.
ERSTE PERSON. Uu jetzt wieder. Wie ein Mensch der stirbt.
ZWEITE PERSON. Es ist unheimlich, so dunstig, allenthalb Nebel, grau und das Summen der Käfer wie gesprungne Glocken. Fort!
ERSTE PERSON. Nein, zu deutlich, zu laut. Da hinauf. Komm mit.[35]

34 Berg's reference to the onomatopoeic effect in the orchestra as "Unkenrufe" ("croaking of toads") is found only in the piano-vocal score.
35 Büchner (Lehmann) 67, p. 428:
FIRST PERSON. Stop!
SECOND PERSON. Do you hear! Ssh! Over there!

If the scene properly belongs where it appears in the manuscript, immediately following the murder, the interpretation of Margaret Jacobs has a certain plausibility:

> [Wozzeck] is scared away by the sound of two people approaching. Hearing Marie's groans the second person thinks that the sound is made by the calling water and cries out to the first to come away from the place; but the first person refuses as the sounds are too loud and clear, and calls to the other to go with him (presumably in the direction of the groans to investigate their source). This dialogue provides a link in the action with the scenes which follow. While Woyzeck is at the inn the body is being discovered.[36]

If the scene properly follows Wozzeck's disappearance into the pond, as its content seems to suggest, the sound, "Wie ein Mensch der stirbt," presumably refers to Wozzeck's drowning. This was made more explicit by Franzos: "Someone's drowning there!" is his addition, as are the words that seem to pinpoint the moment of Wozzeck's death as the two strain to hear his dying gasps, "It's getting softer. Now it's quite still." A third interpretation, and one that seems more likely than Franzos's, since it does not involve the implausible notion that the two passersby can hear the groans of a drowning man, is that the fear that seizes them is evoked not by the fatal event that is occurring at that moment in their vicinity, but by the weirdness of the scene, and that they only *think* they hear a sound "as of someone dying." Berg's musical setting suggests that this is his interpretation. The music implies that Wozzeck's life was extinguished *before* the portion of the dialogue that commences with the line, "Das stöhnt als stürbe ein Mensch" (mm. 302ff.). The cessation of the "drowning music" and the return of the "Unkenrufe" in m. 302 seem to mark the moment of Wozzeck's death.

INTERLUDE	CHANGE OF SCENE
Mm. 320–371$^{2\cdot}$	
M. 371$^{\cdot}$	Curtain rises.
FIFTH MOVEMENT	SCENE 5
"Invention on a Continuous Eighth-Note Motion"	(F. 25; L. 24) [H-1: 18]
	Children playing and shouting in front of Marie's house on a bright, sunny morning. Among them is Marie's child, riding a hobby-horse.

FIRST PERSON. Ooh! There! What a sound!
SECOND PERSON. It's the water, it calls, it's long since anyone's drowned. Let's get away, it's not good to hear it.
FIRST PERSON. Ooh! There again! Like someone dying.
SECOND PERSON. It's weird. So foggy, mist everywhere, gray, and the humming of beetles like broken bells. Let's get out of here!
FIRST PERSON. No, it's too clear, too loud. Up that way! Come on!
36 Büchner (Jacobs) 54, pp. xxviii ff.

88	Mm. 372–374	THE CHILDREN: "Ring around a rosie—"
	Mm. 375–379	Other children, rushing in, interrupt the game: "Hey, Katie! Marie—!" "What is it?" "Haven't you heard? Everybody's out there." One of them turns to Marie's child: "Hey! Your mother's dead!"
	Mm. 380–389°	Marie's son continues to ride his hobby-horse: "Hop, hop! Hop, hop!" SECOND CHILD: "Where is she?" FIRST CHILD: "She's lying out there, on the path, near the pond." THIRD CHILD: "Come on! Let's go see!" The children run off. Marie's child continues to play: "Hop, hop! Hop, hop!" Noticing that he's alone, he hesitates a moment, then rides off on his hobby-horse after the other children.
	Mm. 389–390 ♪·	The curtain falls on the empty stage.
	Mm. ♪♪·390–392	Closed curtain.

Berg took the suggestion for the children's song, "Ringel, Ringel, Rosen-kranz," from Franzos 20, a scene omitted from the opera (see p. 79, above). The remaining dialogue closely follows Franzos's text. Marie's child is not present in Büchner's version of this scene, and from the children's conversation it seems that they do not know whose corpse it is that has been found. In the manuscript the scene is placed between the scene at the tavern and Wozzeck's return to the pond, a clearly inappropriate position which Franzos was fully justified in revising. There can be no doubt that the sequence of scenes in the final pages of the manuscript simply represents the order in which they were written, and that this corresponds only partially to their intended position in the drama.

The hobby-horse with which Marie's child is playing is an addition of Franzos's, suggested by the scene in which Wozzeck, returning to the house after the murder, gives the Idiot some money and tells him to buy the frightened child "en Reuter." Since Franzos eventually chose to omit this episode (see p. 31), the dramatic effectiveness of the introduction of the hobby-horse at this point is lost.

The symphonic interlude which precedes the last scene should, according to the composer, "be understood from the dramatist's point of view as the epilogue which follows Wozzeck's suicide; it should also be appreciated as the composer's confession, breaking through the framework of the dramatic plot and, likewise, even as an appeal to the audience, which is here meant to represent humanity itself."[37] As such it adds, at this point, an element to the drama of which there is no suggestion whatever in Büchner's version of the play. The final interlude is the only one that stands as a complete, self-contained movement. The last act may thus be said to consist of six, rather than five, movements, and the "Übersicht" does in fact describe the last act as consisting of "Six Inventions," of which the "orchestral interlude (quasi-epilogue) in D minor" is listed as No. 5 and designated by the title, "Invention on a Tonality." It is difficult to see, however, what distinctive features are to be inferred from this title that would differentiate the movement from any other tonal composition. According to Berg's lecture on the opera:[38] "The five scenes of Act III correspond with five musical forms the cohesion of which is achieved through some or other unifying principle: be it the unifying function of a musical theme, subjected to variational treatment; be it a 'note,' a 'chord,' a 'rhythm,' or an 'equalized motion' of notes." The "musical forms" based on such "unifying principles" may be either "tonal" or "atonal." The "unifying principle" implied in the term "tonality," on the other hand, belongs to another level of analytical discourse entirely.

Berg's exploitation of musical forms traditionally identified with "absolute" music in both *Wozzeck* and *Lulu*, and his evocation, in the latter, of the formal concepts of "number" opera, are indicative of an attitude toward the objective requirements of the "purely" musical component of these works that is reflected in every aspect of the musical material as well. Corresponding to the strictness of the formal design—indeed, a corollary to it—is the hierarchical ordering of the pitch levels of harmonic and thematic elements. A similarly systematic control governs temporal relationships. The discipline and order that characterize the musical component are paralleled not only in the verbal component, but also in ancillary sonorous details and in purely visual elements. The rise and fall of every curtain is "composed," in terms of extramusical as well as musical correspondences. Thus the curtains, too, are an aspect of "the formal design."

In his essay "Praktische Anweisungen zur Einstudierung des 'Wozzeck' " Berg wrote: "Knowledge of the music and of the diversity that has been sought in every respect, and which is also found in the musical language of the individual scenes, will lead in itself to a similar diversity (in every respect) in the stage design."[39] This diversity is manifested in the composer's explicit instructions regarding the curtains, as it is in every other aspect of the work. The curtain that closes the first act corresponds to that which closes the last: in both instances it falls upon an empty stage, with an identical harmonic pattern in the orchestra. On the other hand, after the final curtain that pattern persists for eleven beats, and its persistence *ad infinitum* is implied, whereas the curtain that closes the first act cuts off the music, as well as the stage. In contrast to the

37 Redlich 57b, p. 284.   38 Ibid., p. 266.
39 Reich 37, p. 169; English translation in Appendix I.

closing curtain of the first and last acts, the final curtain of Act II falls in silence, cutting the stage and its occupants off from our view *after* both action and music have come to an end, and this closing curtain is in retrograde correspondence with the opening curtain of the following act (see p. 77). The nightmarish crescendo of accusing voices at the conclusion of Act III, Scene 3 is not immediately obliterated by the closed curtain, so that again, as at the conclusion of Act II and the commencement of Act III, the conventions that separate the staged world and the "real" one are blurred.

The curtain that rises upon the last scene of Act II, like the curtain that falls upon it, is "late." The music that introduces that scene recapitulates, for dramatic reasons that have been explained above, the commencement of Act I, Scene 2 (see p. 77). But whereas an instantaneous curtain initiates both action and music in the earlier scene,[40] the action of the later scene (as represented by the "wordless chorus of the sleeping soldiers") and the musical counterpart of that scene commence three bars *before* the curtain begins its slow ascent. The curtains that rise upon Act II, Scene 2 and Act III, Scenes 2 and 5 and the curtain that falls upon Act II, Scene 1 are set to abstract and decorative musical figures, appropriate to the mechanical and decorative aspects of the means by which the stage is exposed to or removed from the view of the audience, but deliberately alien to the content of the drama and its musical setting. The third movement of Act II commences with the change of scene that follows the falling curtain of Scene 2 and terminates as the curtain falls upon Scene 3. The music that marks the latter curtain is a retrograde version of the descending passage that marks the former, and thus seems to imply a rising curtain, though in fact it again accompanies a falling one. The dramatic point here is that this closing curtain music is a transition to the *Langsamer Ländler* that commences with the change of scene between scenes 3 and 4. The dance music places us immediately among the revellers in the tavern garden at the moment that the stage of Scene 3, empty after Wozzeck's exit, is cut off from view.

Though the tempo of the passage that accompanies the first of the two falling curtains which frame the third movement of Act II is twice as slow as the tempo of the passage that accompanies the second, the durations of the two passages are practically identical. In the first instance there are nineteen eighth-notes at $\flat$ = 132–144, in the second eighteen quarter-notes at = 132–144, the slight discrepancy being made up by the *ritardando* of the last two bars of the scene to the new tempo ($\downarrow$ = 100) of the *Ländler*. An analogous relationship between music and curtain occurs between Scenes 1 and 2 of Act III: the duration of the curtain that falls upon Scene 1 is seven quarters at $\downarrow$ = 49 (= 7 × 7); the duration of the curtain that rises upon Scene 2 is six quarters at $\downarrow$ = 42 (= 6 × 7). Thus, though the tempo of the curtain music is changed, the duration, and therefore the tempo, of the moving curtain is the same in both instances, exactly 1/7 of a minute. The closing curtain of Act I,

---

40 See Appendix I, pp. 205f.

Scene 4 changes tempo as it descends, falling "at first quickly, then suddenly slowly, and at last [closing] quite gradually." It thus reflects the change in the Doctor's behavior at the conclusion of the scene, where he becomes "suddenly quite calm" as he begins his examination of Wozzeck ("Wozzeck, now let me see your tongue!") after his ecstatic outburst at the prospect of the immortal fame that his experiments will earn for him.

The "diversity that has been sought in every respect" is most ingeniously manifested in the musical episodes that coincide with the changes of scene. In only three instances (I/1–2, III/2–3, III/4–5) a musical episode that can, in terms of its formal function in the musical design, properly be called an "interlude" exactly corresponds to the change of scene. The Interlude of I/2–3 commences before the curtain falls upon Scene 2 and continues after it rises upon Scene 3. The third movement of Act I continues through most of the change of scene that follows Scene 3 and is followed by a brief interlude as the change of scene comes to an end. The remaining interludes, at the conclusions of Scenes 2 and 3 of Act II and the beginning of Scene 4 of Act III, are limited to curtain music. The change of scene coincides in some instances with the commencement of a movement (I/4–5, II/2–3, II/3–4), in others with the completion of a movement that had commenced in the preceding scene (II/1–2, III/1–2, III/3–4), and in one instance with the completion of a movement that had commenced at the beginning of the preceding change of scene (II/4–5).

The chart that follows illustrates the distribution of the formal components of the musical design in relation to the formal components of the dramatic design. The symmetrically related interludes that frame the third movement of Act II mark the symmetrical axis of the work, with seven movements and their corresponding scenes on either side of this axis.[41]

41 The remarkable diversity in the change-of-scene music and in the treatment of the curtains in *Wozzeck* may have been suggested by certain aspects of Schoenberg's *Pierrot lunaire:* "To offset the rigid uniformity of the twenty-one poems, each setting is related to the refrain pattern of the text in an individual manner. Even the pauses separating the pieces are differentiated: there are measured pauses of various durations, unmeasured pauses of various durations, conclusive pauses, anticipatory pauses, interludes, transitions" (Perle 65, p. 309).

ACT ONE

Curtain	Scene 1	Curtain	Change of Scene	Curtain	Scene 2	Curtain	Change of Scene
	First Mvt.		*Interlude*		2nd Mvt.		*Interlude*

Curtain	Scene 3	Curtain	Change of Scene	Curtain	Scene 4	Curtain	Change of Scene	Curtain	Scene 5
	Third Movement		*In- ter- lude*		4th Mvt.		Fifth Movement		Fifth Movement

ACT TWO

Curtain	Scene 1	Curtain	Change of Scene	Curtain	Scene 2	Curtain	Change of Scene
	First Movement				2nd Mvt.		Third Movement
					In- ter- lude		

Curtain	Scene 3	Curtain	Change of Scene	Curtain	Scene 4	Curtain	Change of Scene	Curtain	Scene 5
	Third Movement		Fourth Movement		Fourth Movement		5th Mvt.		5th Mvt.
	Interlude								

ACT THREE

Curtain	Scene 1	Curtain	Change of Scene	Curtain	Scene 2	Curtain	Change of Scene
	First Movement		First Movement		2nd Mvt.		Third Movement

Curtain	Scene 3	Curtain	Change of Scene	*Interlude* Curtain	Scene 4	Curtain	Change of Scene	Curtain	Scene 5
	Third Movement		*Inter- lude*		4th Mvt.		*Inter- lude*		5th Mvt.

REPRESENTATION AND SYMBOL IN
THE MUSIC OF *WOZZECK*

The problem of converting Büchner's "loosely constructed, partly fragmentary scenes" into a libretto was, according to the composer, "more musical than literary, one to be solved by the laws of musical structure rather than by the rules of dramaturgy." He regarded it as a measure of his success that

> from the moment the curtain parts until it closes for the last time, there is no one in the audience who pays any attention to the various fugues, inventions, suites, sonata movements, variations and passacaglias—no one who heeds anything but the social problems of this opera which by far transcend the personal destiny of Wozzeck.[1]

The pertinence of this assertion should not mislead one into minimizing the extent to which the "meaning" of the work is itself dependent upon the autonomy of its musical design. The musical coherence of the opera, independent of the staged events, reflects an objective order whose irrelevance to the subjective fate of Wozzeck poignantly emphasizes his total isolation in an indifferent universe. But if, as Berg said, there is "no interference by externals with [the] individual existence" of the musical entity, this is not to say that the assignment of a specific "absolute" musical form to a given scene is made without reference to dramaturgical considerations. The choice in some instances is determined by a dominant dramatic idea (for example, the *ostinato* that corresponds to Wozzeck's *idée fixe* in the murder scene), in other instances by the correspondence between a musical form and an extrinsic literary and dramatic design (for example, the Suite of I/1 and the sonata-allegro movement

1 Berg 27, *MM.*

of II/1), in yet others by the existence of traditional musical forms and styles identified with certain types of social activity depicted in the drama (the Military March, the dance music of II/4 and III/3, the "folk songs"), and in at least one instance by the symbolic meaning that may be associated with a given musical form (the Passacaglia to which the scene in the Doctor's study is set).

Though *Leitmotive* play an enormously important role in *Wozzeck*, they do not pervade the musical and dramatic texture of the work. There are recurrent verbal expressions, verbal *Leitmotive*, that are not associated with specific recurrent musical figures. The Captain's "Eins nach dem Andern" at the beginning of Act I, Marie's "Einer nach dem Andern" in Scene 3 of Act II, and Wozzeck's "Einer nach dem Andern" at the conclusion of Act II are melodically similar in that each is sung to a descending scale-segment, but these segments are dissimilar in rhythm and intervallic pattern. The Captain's "Ein guter Mensch" in mm. 55 and 155–156 of Act I and mm. 270–271 of Act II are similar in rhythm and melodic direction, but greatly dissimilar otherwise; his "Ein guter Mensch" in mm. 355–356 of Act II is sung to a completely different melodic figure, but one that is rhythmically similar to "Ein guter Mensch" in mm. 153–154 of Act I and mm. 268–269 of Act II. There are also numerous significant visual correspondences—lightings, stage settings, curtains, the red moon that is a witness both to the murder of Marie and to the drowning of Wozzeck—which are not marked by musical figures that one can classify as *Leitmotive*. Stravinsky's criticism of Wagner's "system" of *Leitmotive*, "the monumental absurdity which consists of bestowing on every accessory, as well as on every feeling and every character of the lyrical drama, a sort of check-room number,"[2] cannot be levelled against Berg. Moreover, the *Leitmotiv* in Wagner's operas serves two essential *musical* purposes that it is not required to serve in *Wozzeck*: the recurrence of the same salient musical details throughout a work plays a significant role in its overall unity and coherence; contrapuntal elaboration of *Leitmotive* is the compositional technique on which the extensive through-composed sections are based. In freeing the *Leitmotiv* from the *necessity* of performing these musical tasks, Berg enhanced, rather than lessened, its usefulness as a dramatic device.

We will classify as a *Leitmotiv* any characteristic musical idea that occurs in more than one scene and that acquires an explicit referential function in the drama through its consistent association with an extra-musical element. In obeying "the necessity of giving each scene and each accompanying interlude an unmistakable aspect, a rounded-off and finished character," Berg depended not only on self-contained and clearly differentiated forms but also on special motives restricted to a single scene. We will not include these in our list of *Leitmotive*, even where such a motive is consistently linked with a specific verbal or dramatic detail, such as, for example, Wozzeck's "Jawohl, Herr Hauptmann!" in Act I, Scene 1.

2 Stravinsky 47, p. 79.

Many dramatic details in *Wozzeck* are linked through musical cross-references that are not *Leitmotive*. The figure that accompanies Wozzeck's entrance in Scene 1 of Act II (Ex. 26) is associated in timbre and pitch content (a segment of the whole-tone scale) with the subject that represents him in the triple fugue of the following scene (Ex. 27).[3] The single pitch class that symbolizes Wozzeck's *idée fixe* in the murder scene is first asserted in this connection as the final note of Act II, at the precise moment when this *idée fixe* is

Example 26

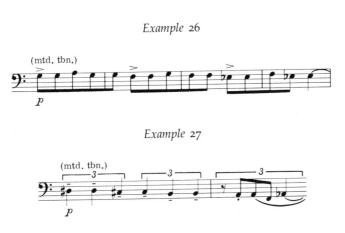

Example 27

irrevocably established in his mind. The subject of the "Invention on a Rhythm" of Act III, Scene 3, obsessively reiterated as Wozzeck's drinking companions question him about the blood on his arm, returns at one point in Scene 4 as he searches for the knife: "Sie werden nach mir suchen. Das Messer verrät mich!" ("They will come looking for me. The knife betrays me!"). There are relatively extensive recapitulations, such as the return, at the tritone transposition, of the opening bars of I/2 at the beginning of II/5—a device comparable to the return at the conclusion of *Tristan und Isolde* of the final episode of the love duet of Act II. Here the referential function is assigned to the total musical complex rather than to a motive. (Such a referential episode will be designated by the term *Leitsektion*.)

There are also a few minimal referential figures whose musical and dramatic implications do not seem sufficiently extensive to merit their inclusion in a list of *Leitmotive*. The "immer zu" figure of the scene in the tavern garden (mm. 504ff. and 546ff.), which Wozzeck, unable to sleep, recalls in the barracks scene (mm. 747f.), is an example. Another is Wozzeck's "Das Messer!" ("The knife!") in Act III, Scene 4, mm. 222 and 270, and "Ich find's nicht" ("I can't find it"), m. 274 of the same scene, a figure which may be intended to recall Marie's "Was zitterst?" ("Why do you tremble?") and Wozzeck's drawing of the knife in the murder scene.

Each *Leitmotiv* is listed below in the order of its initial occurrence in the

3 See pp. 157f., below.

opera. As can be inferred from the above discussion, the list is not a definitive one. The following are minimal, not exclusive, criteria for inclusion:

1. The motive must be clearly linked to some specific dramatic detail and must recur in association with, or in allusion to, that detail.
2. The motive must appear in more than one scene, exclusive of the final symphonic interlude.

Obviously, it is impossible to establish any hard-and-fast rules on the basis of which one can invariably differentiate unambiguously between *Leitmotive* and other dramatically significant referential musical ideas.

The descriptive title assigned to a *Leitmotiv* is not necessarily appropriate to every statement of that *Leitmotiv*, since a *Leitmotiv* may have several important significations, but the one that is denoted by the title will be found to have precedence over the others. In some instances the primary signification is clearly established at the initial statement of the *Leitmotiv*; in other instances it can only be deduced from the various contexts in which the *Leitmotiv* occurs. For example, the title "the child rebuffed" for *Leitmotiv* No. 16 is suggested by the fact that Marie's admonition to the child to sleep, associated with this *Leitmotiv* in the bridge section of the sonata-allegro movement of Act II (mm. 29ff. and 81ff.), is motivated by her wish not to be distracted by her restless child from the self-image that the Drum Major's flattering attentions to her have awakened. The same *Leitmotiv* returns in the development section of the sonata-allegro movement, as Wozzeck observes the sleeping child, though his words express only solicitude. "The child rebuffed" nevertheless remains a more appropriate general designation for this *Leitmotiv* than, for example, "the child asleep," for it is associated at its previous appearances with the child's restlessness and with Marie's impatient attempts to persuade the child to sleep, and at its return at the beginning of Variation 3 of III/1 its explicit and exclusive signification is that of "the child rebuffed."

Leitmotiv No. 1: The Captain (I/1; II/2; Change of Scene III/4–5, mm. 347–351).

Example 28

Though *Leitmotiv* No. 1 makes only a few appearances (always at the same pitch level) in Act I, Scene 1, it plays a leading role in the pitch organization and design of the scene (cf. Chapter Five, pp. 131f.). *Leitmotiv* No. 1 is developed for the first time, in conjunction with *Leitmotiv* No. 12, when the Captain and the Doctor meet in the street at the beginning of the second scene of Act II (cf. the discussion of *Leitmotiv* No. 12, below).

Leitmotiv No. 2: "Wir arme Leut!" (I/1; II/1, m. 114; II/5, mm. 776ff.; Change of Scene I/1–2, mm. 191f., 198–200; Change of Scene III/4–5, mm. ♪361f.).

Example 29

The primary role assigned to this *Leitmotiv* in the opera as a whole is unmistakably implied in its initial statement as the salient opening figure of Wozzeck's aria in I/1. Both here and at the climax of the development section of II/1 it is the vehicle of Wozzeck's utterance of the verbal keynote of the work, "We poor people!" The *Leitmotiv* first occurs as a component of the larger melodic theme with which Wozzeck's aria commences (Ex. 30). This initial statement is fully recapitulated in the orchestra a number of times: at the midpoint of Wozzeck's aria; in the following change of scene; at the climax of the development section of II/1 (the sonata-allegro movement), where it appears in canon against a twelve-tone chord generated by the piling up of three discrete diminished-seventh chords (mm. 114f.); and finally at the climax of the concluding symphonic interlude, which literally recapitulates, except for the scoring, the climactic statement of this theme in II/1.

Example 30

Though it makes only a single appearance in II/1, the "Wir arme Leut!" *Leitmotiv* is an integral structural element of the sonata-allegro movement. The formal components of II/1 are based on characteristic harmonic cells, the principal one of which is a four-note collection equivalent in content to an augmented triad with conjunct superimposed semitone (*c♯-f-a-b♭* at its primary pitch-level). The "Wir arme Leut!" *Leitmotiv* is a linearization of this collection.[4] This derivation is made explicit in II/5 when Wozzeck, overcome in his fight with the Drum Major, sinks exhausted to the floor (Ex. 31). The verticalized statement of the *Leitmotiv* is sustained in the orchestra as the Drum Major taunts his victim, and then converges through semitonal inflection upon a second chord, a harmonic pattern that is identical with the *ostinato* figure of mm. 670ff. of the preceding scene (Ex. 32).[5] The first occurrence of the *Leitmotiv* in

4 See pp. 145ff., below.   5 See pp. 170f., below.

Example 31

II/5 is as an accompaniment to the Drum Major's reply when Andres asks him to name the woman of whose favors he is boasting: "Frag' Er den Wozzeck da!" ("Just ask Wozzeck there!"). A rhythmic variant of the same *Leitmotiv* is then taken up by the Drum Major as he urges Wozzeck to drink with him (Ex. 33).

Example 32   *Example 33*

Leitmotiv No. 3: Folk Song (I/2, mm. 249ff.; III/5. Cf. *Leitmotiv* No. 8).

Example 34

Leitmotiv No. 3 is a component of the *Leitmotiv* of the Cradle Song (No. 8) and as such becomes a prominent detail in other "folk songs." Example 35 illustrates its employment in the second strophe of Andres's Hunting Song.

Example 35

As Lindenberger points out,[6] the many folk songs that are found in Büchner's play "create effects both of amplification and of ironic commentary" and at the same time "serve to assert the folk-like character of the play, to remind us that the work is rooted 'in the life of the very humblest person,' as Büchner, by way of his character Lenz, had attempted to define the duty of the serious artist." Some of the songs tell, in poignant contrast to the world of the common folk who sing these songs, of an ideal world where men spend their time hunting, women wear pointed shoes and long dresses, young girls are in danger of being abducted by romantic Gypsy lads, and even the horses drink "clear, cool wine" instead of water. Other folk songs, down-to-earth drinking songs with vulgar references to the easy virtue of peasant girls, serve as persistent reminders of Marie's infidelity:

> Nowhere in Büchner's work do songs appear with such profusion as in *Woyzeck*: fragments of thirteen different songs occur within the twenty-five pages which the text covers in the standard German edition. Indeed, as G.-L. Fink has pointed out in his exhaustive study of Büchner's songs, no serious German drama before *Woyzeck* shows them with such frequency. . . .[7] If the songs which fill the play serve in one sense to render that "fullness of life" which Büchner so evidently prizes, through the irony they express they work no less to evaluate and define the life which he attempted to record in the play.[8]

In an opera "songs" must be differentiated in some way from the musical language that is its conventional mode of expression and communication. An "atonal" opera presents special problems in this respect. In his lecture of 1929 Berg explained how he

> coped with the necessity of including music of a "folky" and singable character, i.e., with the necessity to establish an appreciable relationship between art-music and folk-music in this opera—a matter of course in a tonally conceived work. It was by no means easy to express their differentiation of levels in so-called atonal harmony. I believe I have succeeded by composing all sections requiring the atmosphere of *Volkstümlichkeit* in a primitive manner which applies equally to the style of Atonality. That particular manner favours a symmetrical arrangement of periods and sections, it utilizes harmonies in thirds and especially in fourths and a type of melody in which whole-tone scales and perfect fourths play an integral part, in contrast with the diminished and augmented intervals which usually dominate the atonal music of the "Vienna School." Also the so-called polytonality may be counted among the devices of a more primitive brand of harmony. We find a popular element in them in the Military March (with its intentionally "wrong basses")[9] and in Marie's Lullaby (with its harmonies in fourths).[10]

Leitmotiv No. 4 is a quotation from the *Marsch* of Berg's Three Pieces for Orchestra, mm. 8off.[11] At its first appearance (I/2: "Hörst Du, es wandert was mit uns da unten!" ["Do you hear? There's something following us down under!"]) the quoted passage is given in its original harmonic context, but is

---

6 Lindenberger 64, p. 90.   7 Fink 61, *DV*.   8 Lindenberger 64, p. 90.
9 Cf. pp. 73f., above.   10 Redlich 57b, p. 271.   11 See pp. 18f., above.

radically modified in rhythm and orchestration.[12] The second statement of the *Leitmotiv* (I/3: "Es ist hinter mir hergegangen bis vor die Stadt" ["It followed me right up to the town"]) gives only the principal voice and *ostinato* bass figure of the original passage, in a new rhythmic variant and transposed down a semitone. The final statement (II/5: "Und dann spricht's aus der Wand heraus. Hörst Du nix, Andres? Wie das geigt und spricht?!" ["And then a voice out of the wall—don't you hear anything, Andres? How they fiddle and dance?"]) recapitulates the first in rhythmic diminution.

Leitmotiv No. 4: Wozzeck's Hallucination (I-2, mm. 275–278; I/3, mm. 448f.; II/4, mm. 748f.).

Example 36

Leitmotiv No. 5: Fanfare (I/3, mm. 328–331, 419–420; I/4, mm. 528–529; II/3, m. 373; Change of Scene I/3–4, mm. ♪ 483–484 ♩.).

Example 37

Leitmotiv No. 5 is first heard in the distant strains of the approaching military band as the curtain rises upon Scene 3 of Act I. Marie stands with her child at the window, waiting for the band to come into view. The *Leitmotiv* foreshadows her first glimpse of the Drum Major. As the band nears, the melodic figure is converted into the first of the two chords of the *ostinato* pattern that introduces the March (Ex. 38).

Example 38

The *Leitmotiv* returns at the conclusion of the Cradle Song "as from afar," a reminiscence of the military music against the sustained cadential chord of

12 The eighth tone of the original melodic pattern is changed from c♯ to d♯. Otherwise the succession of intervals is the same in the two versions.

the Cradle Song. (The passage, according to Berg, is expressive of Marie's "aimless and indefinable attitude of waiting.")[13] It recurs in Scene 3 of Act II, in conjunction with the closing fifths of the Cradle Song (*Leitmotiv* No. 9), as the curtain rises upon Marie standing outside the door of her house, just before Wozzeck abruptly appears to confront her after his conversation with the Captain and the Doctor, from whose taunting remarks he has learned of Marie's infidelity. The same combination of *Leitmotive* Nos. 9 and 5 is heard earlier in the scene in the Doctor's study (I/4), where it anticipates Wozzeck's sudden cry, "Ach, Marie!"—a seemingly unmotivated interpolation as he describes his neurotic fantasies to the Doctor.

Leitmotiv No. 6: Military March (I/3; I/5, mm. 669f.; II/3, m. 387; III/2, mm. ⌈104–105⌉).

Example 39

    Leitmotiv No. 6 is the first measure of the principal theme of the Military March, to the strains of which the Drum Major appears for the first time, at the head of the military band. Like *Leitmotiv* No. 5, it returns later in the same scene as a reminiscence of the military music during Marie's reverie at the conclusion of the Cradle Song. It is heard again at the beginning of the seduction scene as the Drum Major struts before Marie in response to her request, "Geh' einmal vor Dich hin!" When Wozzeck confronts Marie in II/3 it returns as an ironic comment upon Wozzeck's accusing cry, "Da! Hat er da gestanden?" ("There! Is that where he stood?"). At its final appearance in III/2 it is one of an aggregate of *Leitmotive* associated with Marie that are recalled at the moment of her death.

Leitmotiv No. 7: Marie as Mother (I/3, mm. 363–364, 467; I/4, mm. 539–541, 606–610; II/1, mm. ⌈78–80; III/2, mm. 105f.; III/5; Change of Scene I/3–4).

Example 40

I, mm. 363f.

---

13 Redlich 57b, p. 272.

The basic melodic cell and harmonic progression (Ex. 41) of *Leitmotiv* No. 7 are incorporated in the *Leitmotiv* of the Cradle Song (Ex. 47).

Example 41

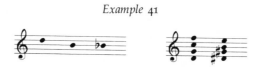

In the change-of-scene music that follows I/3 a variant of the complete *Leitmotiv* (the relative pitch-level of the initial segment is a whole step higher) appears in three-part canonic imitation (Ex. 42). The melodic cell in its inverted form, which first occurs as a component of this canonic episode, is given to Marie at the beginning of the bridge section of the First Reprise of the sonata-allegro movement (II/1), immediately following a rhythmic variant of the complete *Leitmotiv* in the orchestra (Ex. 43). The melodic cell occurs also in the retrograde, and, especially, the retrograde inversion. The latter transformation is already implied in the fourth to sixth notes of the original melodic line. (Such literal transformations of *Leitmotive,* though extensively employed in the fugue of II/2, are not a characteristic feature of the work as a whole.) The content of the inverted melodic cell is comprised in the harmonic cell on which the bridge section of the first exposition of II/1 is based (Ex. 44).[14] It is at this point, upon the initial statement of *Leitmotiv* No. 16, that Marie turns to the child, his restlessness distracting her from thoughts of the Drum Major. The same harmonic cell is an important element of the final scene.

Example 42

The melodic line of *Leitmotiv* No. 7, both in its original form and in the variant employed in the canonic episode, and other concatenations of the basic melodic cell are found in the final scene (Ex. 45). The children's song with which the scene commences incorporates the basic melodic cell of *Leitmotiv* No.

14 See p. 145, below.

7 as well as *Leitmotiv* No. 3 (Ex. 46). As an important component of the musical setting for the games and conversation of the children in the final scene, *Leitmotiv* No. 7 becomes a poignant reminder of the dead woman.

Example 43

Example 44

Example 45

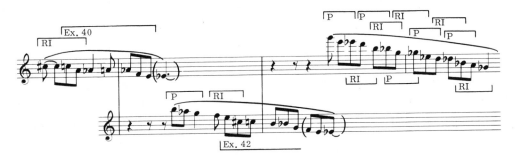

Example 46

It is *Leitmotiv* No. 7 rather than No. 2 that serves as the vehicle for Marie's single utterance of the phrase "Wir arme Leut" in Scene 3 of Act I. Here we have a superb example of the complexity and subtlety of Berg's use of *Leitmotive,* and of the concrete, rather than abstract, connotations that he assigned to them. Had Marie's exclamation at this point recapitulated the figure to which these words are set in Wozzeck's aria in the opening scene, and that is the principal thematic element of that aria, it would have emphasized her tie to Wozzeck rather than the desperate need for release that is expressed in her very next words, "I can't bear it!", and in her sudden rush to the door to escape from the house as the curtain falls, a need that is again expressed when we next see her, in her readiness to accept the attentions of the Drum Major. The climactic development of *Leitmotiv* No. 7 in the change-of-scene music that follows Marie's despairing cry, "Wir arme Leut!", re-echoes that cry. The sense of "Wir arme Leut!" remains implicitly identified with this *Leitmotiv* at the moment of Marie's death (III/2, mm. 105f.), according to Berg's own interpretation. In his list of the *Leitmotive* that at the moment of her death "pass through her consciousness with lightning speed and in a macabre grimace, like the real characters which had permeated her life," the composer describes this *Leitmotiv* as "the motif of Marie bemoaning her wretched life."[15] And, indeed, though Marie's "Come, my child!" indelibly stamps the basic melodic cell of the *Leitmotiv*, there is a reference to her poverty in I/3, within the context dominated by the *Leitmotiv* at its first appearance ("Bist nur ein arm Hurenkind" ["You're but a poor whore's child"]) and again at its return (Ex. 43) in II/1 ("Ich bin nur ein armes Weibsbild" ["I'm only a poor wench"]).

Leitmotiv No. 8: Cradle Song (I/3; II/1, mm. 43–48, 90f.; III/2, m. 104; III/3, mm. 145f.; III/5, mm. 386–388; Change of Scene II/1–2, mm. 151–160 *passim*).

Example 47

The connection of this *Leitmotiv* with *Leitmotive* Nos. 3 and 7 has been pointed out above. Its initial chord is the basic harmonic cell of the subordinate section of the sonata-allegro movement,[16] in which Marie tries to frighten her restless child into going to sleep. Wozzeck's only "folk song," in the tavern to which he goes immediately after the murder, employs the *Leitmotiv* of the Cradle Song in its entirety, at its original pitch level (Ex. 48), not merely the "folk song" figure, *Leitmotiv* No. 3. At the conclusion of the opera quasi-sequential variants of *Leitmotiv* No. 8 in the perpetual eighth-note motion of the final "invention" lead into the closing curtain music (Ex. 49).

15 Redlich 57b, p. 280.

Example 48

III, mm. 145f.

WOZZECK

Es rit - ten drei Rei – ter wohl___ an den Rhein, Bei

Example 49

III, mm. 386ff.

Leitmotiv No. 9: Marie's Aimless Waiting[17] (I/3, mm. 415f., 425–427, 455; I/4, m. 528;[18] II/3, mm. 372f.;[19] III/2, mm. 106f.; III/3, mm. 152f.; III/5, mm. 379f.).

Example 50

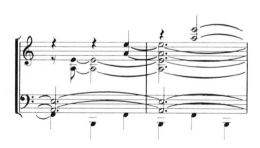

Example 50 illustrates the form in which *Leitmotiv* No. 9 appears at its second statement. Ten bars earlier it served as the closing cadence of the Cradle Song, with the pedal *f-c* instead of *f-b*. The replacement of *c* by *b* as Marie

16 See p. 146, below.   17 Redlich 57b, p. 272.
    18 *Leitmotiv* No. 9 here foreshadows Wozzeck's "Ach, Marie!" a few bars later. Cf. p. 35, above.
    19 See p. 68, above.

remains "lost in thought" converts the bass figure into the dyadic tone-center of the opera and is an intimation of Wozzeck's approach.[20] The recapitulation of this *Leitmotiv* at Wozzeck's exit (m. 455) is an adumbration of his final leavetaking from Marie in the murder scene (III/2, mm. 106f.). In Berg's words, "her aimless and indefinable attitude of waiting . . . finds its final solution only in death." In the tavern scene that follows there is a reference to the same music (mm. 152f.), now representing the sudden obtrusion of thoughts which Wozzeck has come here to escape. The rhythmic pattern of the reiterated open fifths and of the pedal on *b-f* is here converted into the *ostinato* rhythm that governs this scene. A last reminiscence of the *Leitmotiv* is heard in the concluding scene, when one of the children calls out to Marie's child, "You! Your mother's dead!" Through its original connection with the Cradle Song, *Leitmotiv* No. 9 shares some of the dramatic implications of *Leitmotiv* Nos. 7 and 8. Like these, in the final scene No. 9 is a reminiscence of Marie as the mother of the orphaned child.

Leitmotiv No. 10: Wozzeck's Entrance and Exit (I/3, mm. 427f., 454; I/4, mm. 524–525, 528, 530ff.; II/3, mm. 373f.; II/4, m. 495; III/1, mm. 44f.; III/2, mm. 101, 107; Change of Scene III/4–5, mm. 343–345).

Example 51

Marie's reverie at the conclusion of the Cradle Song is cut short by Wozzeck's knock at the window and the interjection of *Leitmotiv* No. 10a against the sustained fifths of *Leitmotiv* No. 9. Wozzeck is represented as the haunted victim of neurotic fantasies, a "distracted" man who may "crack up with those ideas," and who "didn't even look at his child," as Marie says immediately after his exit, marked by *Leitmotiv* No. 10b. In Act II, Scene 1 we see another side of Wozzeck, that of the prosaic family man bringing Marie her household money and expressing his solicitude for the child. *Leitmotiv* No. 10 does not appear in connection with his entrance and exit in this scene. Specifically, No. 10 represents the "distracted" Wozzeck entering or leaving Marie's presence. The employment of *Leitmotiv* No. 10a in I/4 is exceptional, in that Marie is not physically present in that scene. However, three other *Leitmotive*—Nos. 5, 7, and 9—that are explicitly identified with Marie occur in the same context, and

20 See pp. 135f., below.

her presence in Wozzeck's thoughts is expressly indicated when he suddenly cries out her name in the midst of relating his neurotic fantasies to the doctor. The appearance of *Leitmotiv* No. 10a at the conclusion of Variation 6 of III/1 is more obviously relevant, for Marie refers specifically to the thought of Wozzeck's *entrance* when she breaks off her narration of the fairy tale to the child and exclaims, "Der Franz ist nit kommen, gestern nit, heut' nit" ("Franz hasn't come, not yesterday, not today").

Leitmotiv No. 11: Marie's Fear (I/3, mm. 462, 467f.; III/2, m. 103; Change of Scene I/3-4, mm. 473-476).

Example 52

The inclusion of the above figure among the others, all of them important *Leitmotive*, that are heard at the moment of Marie's death would seem to justify its listing as a *Leitmotiv*, though it is found elsewhere only at the conclusion of I/3, after Wozzeck's brief visit with Marie and his hasty departure for the barracks. His strangeness has left her puzzled and worried and her uneasiness grows more and more extreme. She looks at the sleeping child:

> Was bist so still, Bub. Fürch'st Dich? Es wird so dunkel, man meint, man wird blind; sonst scheint doch die Latern' herein! Ach! Wir arme Leut. Ich halt's nit aus. Es schauert mich.

She rushes to the door as the curtain quickly falls. At "Fürch'st Dich?" there is a *pianissimo* statement of *Leitmotiv* No. 11. A second statement *forte* occurs in conjunction with her sudden outburst, "Wir arme Leut," and *Leitmotiv* No. 7. A variant of *Leitmotiv* No. 11 (Ex. 53) is developed in *stretto* as Marie rushes out into the street. It is precisely Marie's puzzlement and fright as described by Knight[21] that are represented by *Leitmotiv* No. 11. This does not appear in II/3 because the puzzlement that Marie expresses at Wozzeck's accusations is feigned, and his threats, since she understands them, do not frighten her, but rather inspire in her a "courageous, physically violent" response.

Example 53

21 See p. 39, above.

Leitmotiv No. 12: The Doctor (I/4, mm. 562–564; II/2; Change of Scene III/4–5, mm. 345–349).

Example 54

Leitmotiv No. 12 appears briefly in Variation 13 of I/4. The entire scene concerns itself with the Doctor, and no special musical or dramatic associative properties are conferred upon this motive as compared with others. In Act II, Scene 2, the *Leitmotive* of the Captain and the Doctor are Subjects I and II of the Fantasia and Fugue (II/2). Their sadistic persecution of Wozzeck, when Wozzeck comes upon them in the street, is climaxed in their hints of Marie's infidelity. The theme that represents Wozzeck in II/2 is Subject III (Ex. 21) of the Fugue.

Leitmotiv No. 13: The Drum Major Posturing before Marie (I/5, mm. 666–668, 676, 693–696, ⌐714–715⌐; II/3, mm. 388, 392; II/4, mm. 509, 543f.; II/5, mm. 761–805 *passim*; III/2, m. 104; III/3, mm. 183–186; III/4, m. 243; Change of Scene II/4–5, m. 690; Change of Scene III/4–5, mm. 357–358).

Example 55

The initial statement of *Leitmotiv* No. 13 is heard as the curtain rises upon I/3. The Drum Major stands ostentatiously before the admiring eyes of Marie as the *Leitmotiv* is twice repeated. It returns in II/3 as Wozzeck strikes a pose, mimicking the Drum Major. "Hat er da gestanden, so, so?" he asks. The place is again the street before Marie's house. In the tavern scene after the murder of Marie, Wozzeck, asking for a fight, again assumes the role of the Drum Major, not ironically this time but in an unconscious attempt to reassert his manhood, of which the Drum Major's seduction of Marie and trouncing of Wozzeck before the eyes of his comrades had deprived him and which his act of vengeance has momentarily redeemed for him. Wozzeck's assumption of the Drum Major's manner is again marked by *Leitmotiv* No. 13, transformed by the fatal *ostinato* rhythmic theme of the scene (Ex. 56).

Example 56

15. Erich Kleiber, *Generalmusikdirektor*, Staatsoper, Berlin, 1925.

Staats-Theater

Opernhaus
Unter den Linden.

Anfang 7 Montag, den 14. Dezember 1925. **Anfang 7**
14. Karten-Reservesatz.
(Außer Abonnement.)

Uraufführung:
Georg Büchners

Wozzeck

Oper in drei Akten (15 Szenen) von Alban Berg.
Musikal. Leitung: General-Musikdirektor Erich Kleiber.
In Szene gesetzt von Franz Ludwig Hörth.

Wozzeck	Leo Schützendorf
Tambourmajor	Fritz Soot
Andres	Gerhard Witting
Hauptmann	Waldemar Henke
Doktor	Martin Abendroth
1. Handwerksbursch	Ernst Osterkamp
2. Handwerksbursch	Alfred Borchardt
Der Narr	Marcel Noë
Marie	Sigrid Johanson
Margret	Jessyka Koettrik
Mariens Knabe	Ruth Iris Witting
Soldat	Leonhard Kern

Soldaten und Burschen, Mägde und Dirnen, Kinder.

Gesamtausstattung: P. Aravantinos.

Technische Einrichtung: Georg Linnebach.

Nach dem zweiten Akt findet eine längere Pause statt.

Kein Vorspiel.

Anfang 7 Uhr.   **Ende nach 9 Uhr.**

Den Besuchern der heutigen Vorstellung wird das neu
erschienene Heft der „Blätter der Staatsoper"
unentgeltlich verabfolgt.

Oper
Am Königsplatz.

Anfang 7½ Montag, den 14. Dezember 1925. **Anfang 7½**
280. Abonnements-Vorstellung.

Tosca

Musikdrama in drei Akten von V. Sardou — L.
Illica — G. Giacosa. Deutsch von Max Kalbeck
Musik von Giacomo Puccini.
Musikalische Leitung: Selmar Meyrowitz
Spielleitung: Josef Höpfl.

Floria Tosca, berühmte Sängerin	Mafalda Salvatini
Mario Cavaradossi, Maler	Alexander Kirchner
Baron Scarpia, Chef der Polizei	Theodor Scheidl
Cesare Angelotti	Eduard Habich
Der Mesner	Heinrich Schultz
Spoletta, Agent der Polizei	Emil Lücke
Sciarrone, Gendarm	Rudolf Krasa
Ein Hirt	Trude Conrad
Ein Schließer	Rudolf Watzke
Zwei Häscher	Bernhard Sperber
	Albert Wehrle
Roberti, Gerichtsbüttel	Alfred Kunze

Ein Kardinal. Ein Offizier. Ein Sergeant.
Soldaten. Damen. Herren. Bürger. Volk usw.

Dekorationen nach Entwürfen von P. Aravantinos in den
Werkstätten der Staats-Theater angefertigt. Technische
Einrichtung: Georg Linnebach.

Nach dem 1. und 2. Akt je 15 Minuten Pause.
Die Pausen werden durch ein rotes Lichtzeichen zu beiden
Seiten der Bühne bekanntgegeben.

Anfang 7½ Uhr.   **Ende gegen 10 Uhr.**

In dem Eintrittspreise ist die Garderobeablagegebühr von 50 Pfg.,
die Sozialabgabe von 10 Pfg., die Garderobe-Versicherungsgebühr
von 30 Pfg. mit enthalten.
Garderobehaftung nur bis 150 Mk.; höhere Versicherungen nur
auf etwaigen Wunsch. (Siehe Aushang im Theater).

Wochenspielplan für:

	Opernhaus Unter den Linden.	Oper am Königsplatz.
Dienstag, 15. Dez.	279. Ab.-Vorst. 7½ Uhr La Traviata.	251. Ab.-Vorst. 7½ Uhr: Mignon.
Mittwoch, 16. „	250. Ab.-Vorst. 8 „ Fidelio.	252. Ab.-Vorst. 7½ „ Die Fledermaus.
Donnerstag, 17. „	251. Ab.-Vorst. 6½ „ Die Meistersinger.	253. Ab.-Vorst. 8 „ Das Christelflein.
Freitag, 18. „	12 Uhr: Sinfonie-Mittags-Konzert. Abends 7½ Uhr: 5 Sinfonie-Konzert	254. Ab.-Vorst. 7½ „ Hänsel und Gretel. Klein Idas Blumen
Sonnabend, 19. „	252. Ab.-Vorst. 8 Uhr: Wozzeck	255. Ab.-Vorst. 7½ „ Rigoletto.
Sonntag, 20. „	253. Ab.-Vorst. 7 „ Hänsel und Gretel. Klein Idas Blumen	256. Ab.-Vorst. 7 „ Bohème.
Montag, 21. „	254. Ab.-Vorst. 7½ „ Tanzabend. Erstaufführung. Renaissance. Pulcinella. Erstaufführung: Spielzeug	257. Ab.-Vorst. 7½ „ Der Evangelimann.

Preise

im Opernhause am:	15.—21.	14.	Sinfonie-Mittags-Konzert	in der Oper a K. am:	14.	15.—21.
Fremden- u. Orch.-Loge	17.— Mk.	19.— Mk.	8.50 Mk.	1. Parkett (1.— 9 M.)	10.— Mk.	20.— Mk.
1. Rang u. 1. Parkett	15.50	17.50	7.25	2. Parkett (10.—19. M.)	2.—	
2. Parkett	12.50	14.50	6.25	3. Parkett (19.—26 M.)	5.—	
2. Rang	9.50		4.75	Vorpl. u. 2. R u. Loge	10.—	
3. Rang	2.50	9.50		3. Rang (4.—6. M.)	2.—	
3. Rang Stehplatz	4.—			4. Parkett (3. M.)	1.—	
4. Rang Stehplatz				4. Rang (4. M.)		

... nach dem Theater täglich in Betrieb

16. Advance announcement of the world première of *Wozzeck* at the
Berlin Staatsoper, December 14, 1925.

17. The Doctor's study (Act I, Scene 4). Sketch by Panos Aravantinos
for the first Berlin production

18. The Doctor's study as designed by Robert Edmond Jones for the
American première by the Philadelphia Grand Opera Company,
March 19, 1931. The conductor was Leopold Stokowski.

19. Marie's house as designed by Stefano Pekary for the Italian première of *Wozzeck* at the Teatro Reale dell' Opera, Rome, November 3, 1942. Political tyranny and war had brought to a sudden halt the extraordinarily successful career of the opera initiated by the Berlin première on December 14, 1925. Between the London première in a concert version on March 14, 1934, and the first post-war revival in Dusseldorf on June 30, 1948, there was but a single production. It is remarkable that that one production should have taken place in Rome at the height of the war and in spite of the pressure and influence of Mussolini's wartime ally, the German Nazi regime. The work was conducted by Tullio Serafin, with Tito Gobbi in the title role. The performance was repeated on November 7 and 11.

20. An autographed excerpt from Act II, Scene 1, of *Wozzeck*, with photograph of the composer.

21. A picture-postcard view of the Berghof.

Wozzeck's struggle with the Drum Major in II/5 is represented in the or- 109
chestra by the same four-part canon on *Leitmotiv* No. 13 that accompanied
Marie's struggle with the Drum Major in the seduction scene. This *Leitmotiv*
and other quotations from the seduction scene are incorporated into the dance
scene of the stage band in II/4, and the *Leitmotiv* is also recalled in a quotation
from the dance music when Wozzeck stumbles upon Marie's corpse in III/4.
The first half, employed in both its prime and inverted forms (Ex. 57), is a
principal figure in II/5, together with the Drum Major's variant of the "Wir
arme Leut" *Leitmotiv*. The same figure is suggested at the moment of Marie's
death, where it is conjoined (Ex. 62) with *Leitmotiv* No. 14.

Example 57

Leitmotiv No. 14: Seduction (I/5, mm. 673, 677, 679, 681; II/4, mm. 510f.; II/5,
mm. 806f.; III/2, m. 104; Change of Scene II/4–5, mm. 691f.).

Example 58

The upward leaps, repeated notes, and equal time-values of Example 58
characterize much of the melodic material of the concluding movement of Act
I. Its special significance as a *Leitmotiv* that epitomizes this material emerges in
II/4, where the accordion and clarinet of the stage band present this *Leitmotiv* in
mm. 510f. in the form illustrated below (Ex. 59a), recalling the opening figure of
the change-of-scene music that introduces the seduction scene (Ex. 59b) and
foreshadowing the *Leitsektion* based on this music that is given to the stage
band in mm. 529ff.

Example 59

Leitmotiv No. 14 and related melodic details of the fifth movement of Act I
are presaged in the Fanfare *Leitmotiv* that ushers in the military band, with the
Drum Major at its head, in I/3 (Ex. 37). The *Leitmotiv* itself is embedded in the
initial exchange between Marie and the Drum Major (Ex. 60), and it returns at
the drunken Drum Major's concluding words as he blusters out of the barracks

after trouncing Wozzeck in II/5 (Ex. 61). A figure (Ex. 62) found in the convergence of *Leitmotive* that occurs at the moment of Marie's death combines the drunken Drum Major's segment of *Leitmotiv* No. 13 (the xylophone, to which this segment is repeatedly assigned in II/5, supports this identification) with a variant of *Leitmotiv* No. 14 (the tritone replacing the perfect fourth as the concluding interval). The latter variant of *Leitmotiv* No. 14 is linked, through common harmonic material and through overlapping, with *Leitmotiv* No. 13 in Change of Scene II/4–5, mm. 690–692 (Ex. 63). This linking of the two *Leitmotive* in the preceding music of the stage orchestra, mm. 509–511 (Ex. 64), is a reminiscence of the juxtaposed statements of these *Leitmotive* in I/5, mm. 676f.

Example 60

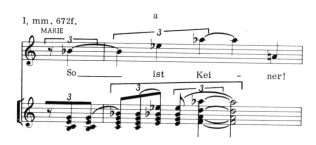

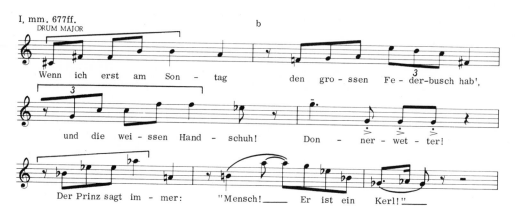

Example 61

Example 62

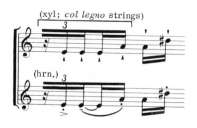

Example 63

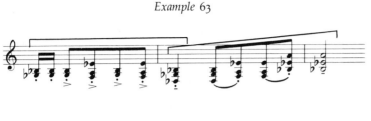

Example 64

Leitmotiv No. 15: The Earrings[22] (II/1; III/2, m. 𝄞 104; Change of Scene II/1–2, mm. 148–151).

Example 65

Leitmotiv No. 15 is the initial phrase of the principal theme of the sonata-allegro movement (II/1). It is heard, in one form or another, at the commencement of each of the four sections of the movement (exposition, reprise, development, recapitulation). The only explicit statement of this *Leitmotiv* in another scene occurs in III/2, at the moment of Marie's death. If the earrings are a symbol of Marie's womanly pride, they are also a symbol of her sin and guilt. This double significance of the Drum Major's gift to Marie is affirmed in the relationship between *Leitmotive* Nos. 15 and 17. The same relative pitch-class content (Ex. 66) that generates, in one linear permutation, *Leitmotiv* No. 15, representing Marie admiring the earrings, generates in another permutation *Leitmotiv* No. 17, representing her guilt.

Example 66

22 The importance of this *Leitmotiv* in II/1 is indicated by Berg's own title for the scene, "Schmuck-Szene," in his lecture on *Wozzeck*. Redlich 57b, p. 280, translates this as "trinket-scene."

Leitmotiv No. 16: The Child Rebuffed (II/1; III/1, mm. 19–22; III/5, mm. 372f.).

Example 67

Leitmotiv No. 16 is the theme of the bridge section of the sonata-allegro movement. The child's restlessness disturbs Marie as she admires herself in the glass; her admonition to the child to sleep (II/1, mm. 29ff., 37ff., 81ff.) is an unconscious expression of rejection of those aspects of her life of which the child's presence is the constant sign and from which the attentions of the Drum Major have given her a brief respite. The *Leitmotiv* is heard again when the child distracts her from reading the Bible in III/1. Here the child is an insupportable reminder to the remorseful woman of her guilt, and this time her rebuff is a conscious act, explicitly expressed in her words, "Der Bub gibt mir einen Stich in's Herz. Fort!" ("The child stabs my heart. Be off!").

Like *Leitmotiv* No. 7, No. 16 is employed in both its prime and inverted forms. The basic harmonic cell of the bridge section of II/1 incorporates the reiterated minor seconds of the *Leitmotiv*. In the opening bars of the final scene a last suggestion of *Leitmotiv* No. 16 occurs in the form of three statements of that cell (Ex. 68). The various statements of *Leitmotiv* No. 16 are assigned to similar timbres: *pizzicato* strings and xylophone (II/1, mm. 29ff.), *col legno* strings and timpani (II/1, mm. 37ff. and 81ff.), celesta (II/1, mm. 109ff.; III/1, mm. 19ff.; III/5, mm. 372f.).

Example 68

Leitmotiv No. 17: Guilt (II/1, mm. 105f., 126–128; III/3, mm. 206–207; III/4, mm. 244–246).

Example 69

The *Leitmotiv* that represents Marie's guilt and the *Leitmotiv* that represents the earrings are both, as we have seen, linearizations of the same relative pitch-class collection. Thus Marie's guilt, a token of which is her possession of the earrings, is implied in her defensive reply to Wozzeck, "Bin ich ein schlecht Mensch?" ("Am I a bad woman?"), when he hints that he suspects the veracity of her claim of having found them. Conscience-stricken upon Wozzeck's departure, Marie affirms her guilt in a retrograde statement of the same *Leitmotiv* (Ex. 70).

Example 70

Wozzeck's sudden cry, "Bin ich ein Mörder?" ("Am I a murderer?"), as the company in the tavern accusingly gathers round him after Margret observes the blood on his hand, is an echo of Marie's question, "Bin ich ein schlecht Mensch?" (cf. Exx. 69 and 71). In the following scene the inverted form of *Leitmotiv* No. 17 is heard when Wozzeck, stumbling upon the corpse, is reminded of the earrings by the "red necklace" of blood, "earned, like the earrings, by your sin!" (Ex. 72). In this form the *Leitmotiv* of guilt recalls the concluding melodic phrase of the Cradle Song, identified with the other side of Marie, that of the tender and devoted mother (Ex. 73)—a phrase that becomes a *Leitmotiv* of expiation when it recurs in the final scene, accompanying the spoken words of one of the children to Marie's little boy: "Du! Dein Mutter ist tot!"

Example 71

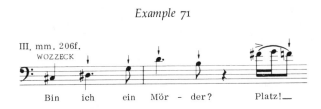

Example 72

Example 73

Leitmotiv No. 18: The Knife (II/3, mm. 395f., 398; II/4, mm. 599–602; II/5, m. 752; III/2, mm. ʃ77, 100; III/4, mm. 222–225, 270–274).

Example 74

Example 74 illustrates the musical figure that accompanies Marie's words as Wozzeck raises his hand to strike her in II/3: "Better a knife in my body than a hand on me!" This is the first intimation, except for Marie's conscience-stricken "I could stab myself" after Wozzeck's departure at the conclusion of II/1, of the deed and the weapon that are destined to bring Marie's life to its violent end. Wozzeck, staring after her as she goes into the house, repeats, "Better a knife," against another version of *Leitmotiv* No. 18 (Ex. 75). The descending component of this version of the *Leitmotiv* is extended through four bars in the next scene, at Wozzeck's ominous concluding words in his reply to Andres's question, "Why do you sit here by the door?" Though Wozzeck explicitly refers only to his own death, *Leitmotiv* No. 18 and another motive (Ex. 23w) that figures importantly in the preceding scene immediately after Wozzeck's repetition of Marie's words, "Leiber ein Messer," point to Marie (Ex. 76).

Example 75

Example 76

In the concluding scene of Act II another version of *Leitmotiv* No. 18 represents the knife that Wozzeck imagines flashing before his eyes as he recalls Marie and the Drum Major dancing together (Ex. 77). In the murder scene a transposition of the descending component of this version of the *Leitmotiv* accompanies Wozzeck's response to Marie's remark on the redness of the rising moon and is the cue for his drawing of the weapon (Ex. 78). Chromatically descending minor ninths symbolize the knife that Wozzeck searches for when he later returns to the scene of the crime (III/4, mm. 222ff.). *Leitmotiv* No. 18 is heard again when Wozzeck, after finding the knife and throwing it into the pond, realizes that he hasn't thrown it far enough to prevent its discovery. This

Example 77

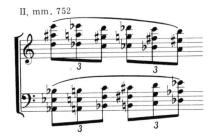

final statement of the *Leitmotiv* is in the form of converging semitonal progressions of the vertical set on which the movement is based (Ex. 79).[23]

Example 78

Example 79

Leitmotiv No. 18 is associated not with the knife itself but with allusions to the knife. Thus in III/4 it is heard when Wozzeck searches, or thinks of searching, for the knife, not when he finds it, and in III/2 it marks the moment that Marie's comment on the red moon reminds him of his fatal task, but terminates at the moment that he draws the weapon. Near the beginning of the murder scene an ominous undertone is given to his remark, "Sollst Dir die Füsse nicht mehr wund laufen" ("You shouldn't go on making your feet sore, walking"), by the chromatically descending chords that introduce these words.

Leitmotiv No. 19: *Ländler* (II/4; II/5, mm. 744–747; III/3, mm. 167 f., 180–181).

Example 80

Example 80 is the headmotive of the *Ländler* of II/4. In the recapitulation of Scherzo I (mm. 592ff.) the *Ländler* is assigned to the stage band against reiterated statements of the *Leitmotiv* in the pit orchestra (Ex. 161). The dialogue between Andres and Wozzeck which is set against this music incorporates this

23 See p. 142, below.

Leitmotiv (Ex. 164). The *Ländler* is recalled in III/3, when Wozzeck asks Margret
to sing, and again in the comment with which he interrupts her song (Ex. 163).
Leitmotiv No. 20: Drunkenness (II/4, mm. 445–447, 633f.; II/5, mm. 784–785,
♪ 802–804).

Example 81

Und mei - ne See - le stinkt nach Bran - te - wein.

Berg's stage directions don't explicitly say so, but the musical references
make it unmistakably clear that the scene of the sleeping soldiers in the barracks marks the close of the same night that had earlier given us their revels in
the tavern garden. The return to the tune of the drunken apprentices as Wozzeck declines the Drum Major's offer of a drink is an example.

The mainspring of the tragedy is neither Marie's treachery nor the degradation to which Wozzeck is condemned by the callous and banal agents of the
established order, but rather the impact of this treachery and degradation upon
a fear-haunted and alienated individual. The mental condition that sets Wozzeck apart from his fellows—the latter represented by Wozzeck's "normal" and
prosaic companion, Andres—is set forth in the scene of Wozzeck and Andres
in the open field. This, the second scene in the edition on which the opera is
based, was intended by Büchner to open the play. Its quality and meaning are
well summed up by Margaret Jacobs:

> In constructing Woyzeck's visionary experience Büchner has elaborated the real
> Woyzeck's fear of the freemasons and his fiery visions into something more
> haunted, mysterious and elemental. Büchner does not intend us to consider
> Woyzeck as insane, or even primarily as a pathological case; he has drawn him as
> an ill and anxiety-ridden human being with taut nerves, wrought up to a pitch of
> hypersensitiveness, where sounds and colours are magnified to abnormal propor-
> tions. Nature for him holds a terror and a mystery, and he is held fascinated in an
> elemental world whose meaning he cannot fathom, but which speaks to him au-
> dibly. Out in the toadstool-ridden fields there are signs and strange sounds. The
> fire and thunder of the storm brings to his mind the images of the Apocalypse and
> of the divine acts of judgment—fire from heaven, thunder like angels' trumpets,
> voices and the smoke of ruined cities. His hallucinations have all the terror and
> ecstasy of weird folk-superstition, and in his inarticulateness before the Doctor he
> can only give to all these unintelligible, irrational and fearful things the name,
> "die doppelte Natur." The mysteriousness of it comes across with magnificent
> effect because Woyzeck's words are tersely allusive, not explanatory: "Es geht
> hinter mir, unter mir. (Stampft auf den Boden:) Hohl, hörst du? alles hohl da
> unten!" "Andres! wie hell! Über der Stadt ist alles Glut! Ein Feuer fährt um den
> Himmel und ein Getös herunter wie Posaunen. Wie's heraufzieht!—Fort! Sieh
> nicht hinter dich!"[24]

24 Büchner (Jacobs) 54, p. xxiv. See also Treitler 76, *SM*.

The psychological condition that makes Wozzeck react as he does to the mistreatment he suffers is repeatedly reasserted in Acts I and II of the opera, but not in Act III, where he is no longer the passive victim and where his mental breakdown, when it comes, is total and irremediable.

Though only Nos. 3 and 4 of the *Leitmotive* listed above are introduced in the second scene, the music of this scene is more extensively recapitulated than that of any other. The chordal progression on which the scene is based (Ex. 103) returns in the dialogue between Marie and Wozzeck in the following scene.

Recapitulations of passages from the earlier scene are interspersed among new variations on the basic chords. The music of the fiery sunset, mm. 289–293, returns at mm. 435–437 in reference to Wozzeck's "Es war ein Gebild am Himmel, und Alles in Glut!" ("There was a shape in the sky, and everything glowing!") and recurs in a more literal restatement in II/4, mm. 517–522, as Wozzeck, watching Marie and the Drum Major among the dancers in the tavern garden, cries out, "Warum löscht Gott die Sonne nicht aus?" ("Why doesn't God put out the sun?"). The canonic episode that commences at m. 238 in the second scene, associated at this, its first appearance, with Wozzeck's superstitious faith in signs and omens, returns as the setting of his quotation from the Bible in the dialogue with Marie: "Steht nicht geschrieben: 'Und sieh, es ging der Rauch auf vom Land, wie ein Rauch vom Ofen'?" ("Is it not written: 'And behold, the smoke rose from the land, like the smoke from a furnace'?"). This direct reference to the judgment of God on Sodom and Gomorrah suggests that the image of the fiery sunset alludes to the same theme and foreshadows Wozzeck's call upon the judgment of God in Scene 4 of Act II, with its simultaneous musical reference to that image in the pit orchestra.

The basic chord of the Cradle Song is combined with the climactic third chord of the chord series on which the second scene is based when Marie tries to calm Wozzeck in I/3 by drawing his attention to the child (cf. Ex. 82 with Exx. 47 and 103). As he hurries off to the barracks, unmoved by the sight of his child, the exit music of the preceding scene (mm. 302ff.) is recapitulated in abbreviated form (m. 453). At the conclusion of the third movement of Act I there is a brief restatement of the basic chord-series of I/2, restored to its primary pitch-level and order (Ex. 83).

Example 82

I, mm. 449–453

Example 83

When Wozzeck relates his hallucinatory fears to the Doctor in Variations 9–12 of I/4, the chord series (Ex. 103) of the second scene is combined with the twelve-tone theme of the Passacaglia. The reference to the toadstools in I/4 (mm. 554–561?) recapitulates the musical setting of "Siehst Du den lichten Streif da über das Gras hin, wo die Schwämme so nachwachsen?" ("Do you see that bright streak over the grass there, where the toadstools are sprouting?") in the second scene. Wozzeck's inarticulate first attempt to describe to the Doctor the irrational fantasies evoked by the natural phenomena of I/2 recapitulates in mm. 533–537 a passage associated with his relation of these fantasies to Marie in I/3, mm. 440–443. Both passages are a prolongation of the chordal trill that introduces the initial statement of the canonic episode associated with Wozzeck's superstitious piety (I/2, mm. 237f.). The third and last statement of this canonic episode is the musical setting of Wozzeck's prayer in the first part of the barracks scene and is a component of a more extensive recapitulation from the scene in the open field (cf. I/2, mm. 237–244 with II/5, mm. ⌐752–757). The visions that the sleepless Wozzeck describes to Andres are associated through their musical setting with the images that had terrified him in the earlier scene with Andres. Wozzeck's estrangement from his human environment—the sleeping soldiers (an addition of Berg's to the corresponding scene of the drama)—is paralleled, through the music, with his estrangement from the natural environment of the second scene, whose eerie opening bars return at the beginning and close of the first part of the barracks scene (mm. 737–743, 759–760). The "hallucination" Leitmotiv returns (mm. 748–750) in the rhythmic, harmonic, and textural context of its initial statement in I/2 (mm. 275–280).

Other Leitsektionen originate in the remaining scenes of Act I. The return, as Wozzeck wrestles with the Drum Major in the final scene of Act II, of the musical setting of Marie's struggle to free herself from the Drum Major's embrace in I/5 has already been cited (p. 41). The Doctor's "diagnosis" of Wozzeck in I/4, "You've a fine idée fixe, an excellent aberratio mentalis partialis, second species," and his expression of satisfaction with his subject, "You're an interesting case," are given a cheerful waltz-like setting (mm. ⌐564–572, 599–601) which is recapitulated for the Doctor's "diagnosis" of the Captain in II/2 (mm. 212–217, 242–244). The musical setting of Marie's evasive replies to Wozzeck's accusations in II/3 affirms the guilt that her words seem to deny. The "quasi-trio" of the Military March, Marie's song of the fine-looking soldier lads, is recapitulated in mm. ♪·392–394. The opening section of the fifth movement of Act I, preceding the curtain that rises upon the seduction scene, is recapitulated, minus the important melodic theme in the top line of the first three bars, in mm. ♭388–392 ♪♪ (cf. I/4–5, mm. 656–659, ♪661–666). The same *Leitsektion* is converted into a waltz episode by the stage band in the following scene (mm. 529–538), as Wozzeck watches Marie and the Drum Major dancing together. When to Wozzeck's accusation in II/3, "Du bei ihm!" ("You beside him!"), Marie boldly replies, "Und wenn auch!" ("And if I were?"), the music refers to her words at the close of Act I, as she surrendered to the Drum Major's advances: "Es ist Alles eins!" ("What's the difference!") (cf. I/5, mm. ♪♪708–710 ♪ with II/3, mm. ♪♪394–395♪).

As a purely musical summation of the drama the final interlude has an affinity with the romantic "tone poem," and even with the traditional "overture," though it comments upon a drama on which the curtain has fallen, rather than upon one on which the curtain is about to rise. Between the two presentations—in the opening bars and at the conclusion—of a special theme that appears only in this movement, musical ideas that have been given explicit dramatic content in the course of the opera are developed contrapuntally. Since the interludes, unlike the individual scenes, are nowhere else given independent thematic material, this final interlude is the only one that claims for itself, from its very opening, a formal status comparable to that of the scenes themselves.

Through a prominent melodic fragment that they have in common, the principal theme, at m. 339, merges with the initial motive of Andres's Hunting Song from Act I, Scene 2 (Ex. 84). The motive is assigned to two muted horns in unison, sounding "as from afar," just as it was in the transition between the scene of Wozzeck and Andres in the open field and the Military March of the following scene. Overlapping with this motive is a suggestion of the music that accompanies the concluding exchange between Wozzeck and Andres in I/2 (cf. p. 118 above): "Still, alles still, als wäre die Welt tot." "Nacht! Wir müssen heim!" (Ex. 85).

Example 84

III, mm. 338ff.

Example 85

III, mm. 340f.

Leitmotiv No. 10, the figure that accompanies the exit and entrance of the "distracted" Wozzeck, is heard in mm. 342–345, reiterated in increasingly shorter durational values and greater dynamic intensity. The *Leitmotiv* of the Doctor (No. 12) enters on the upbeat to m. 346, and is repeated against the *Leitmotiv* of the Captain. The twelve-tone Passacaglia theme of the scene in the Doctor's study (p. 165, below) occurs simultaneously with a three-part canon on the *Leitmotiv* of the Captain in mm. 349–351.

The seduction scene is recalled in mm. 352–357, in a passage cited earlier as a *Leitsektion*—the opening bars (mm. 656–660) of the final movement of Act I. This, its third and final recapitulation, is the only one which includes the prominent melodic line that appears in the original statement of this passage, assigned in both instances to unison clarinets—a melodic line whose contour is an elusive but persistent thematic component of the seduction scene. The *Leitmotiv* of the Drum Major (No. 13) in mm. 357–358 overlaps with the last bar of the seduction music and the first bar of a restatement (mm. 358–364) of the climactic episode of the development section of II/1 (mm. 111–115), in which Wozzeck, gazing upon his sleeping child, says to Marie, "The shiny drops on his forehead! Nothing but toil under the sun, sweating even when we sleep! We poor people!" The twelve-tone chord with which the canon on the "Wir arme Leut" *Leitmotiv* culminates resolves into the D-minor keynote and tonic sonority (Ex. 86) of the movement. The final component of the musical résumé of the drama is a *fortissimo* statement (mm. 365–366) of the subject assigned to Wozzeck in the triple fugue of II/2 (Ex. 27).

Example 86

III, mm. 364f.

Berg describes the final interlude as "a thematic development-section, utilizing all the important musical characters related to Wozzeck."[25] There is, however, no *direct* reference to Marie, as there is to every one of the other chief characters: Andres, the Doctor, the Captain, the Drum Major, and, of course, Wozzeck. The seduction scene is recalled in mm. 352–357, but her three important *Leitmotive*—No. 7, Marie as Mother; No. 8, the Cradle Song; No. 9, Marie's Aimless Waiting—do not appear. In the final interlude Berg speaks only of Wozzeck's suffering, and in doing so intensifies and transforms the earlier musical references to Wozzeck's humiliations and torments by making them the vehicle of a profoundly passionate commentary upon this suffering. Marie's tragedy is poignantly, if distantly, recalled in the music of the epilogue that follows. The brevity of this last scene, which is only about half as long as the preceding interlude, is at one with the clarity and calmness of its music and with the casual inquisitiveness that induces the children to interrupt their play when they learn of Marie's death. We are left with an ironic comment on the insignificance, in a world of man and nature that remains oblivious and unaffected, of the tragic fate of Wozzeck and Marie.

The dramatic significance of *Leitmotive* and *Leitsektionen* is primarily dependent not upon their intrinsic musical properties but upon extra-musical elements—words, actions, things seen—that convey a meaning which attaches itself to them through association. This is not to say that the assignment of a given meaning to a given musical idea is entirely arbitrary. Though there is nothing in the musical quality of *Leitmotiv* No. 12, for example, that makes it more suitable as a representation of the Doctor than of the Captain, it is obviously *not* suitable as a representation of "Marie as Mother." Though one may not be able to say what a given motive "means" in itself, it can mean enough, as Schoenberg has pointed out, to tell us that King Mark's words, "This, Tristan, to me?" are not expressed in appreciation for a Christmas gift. It is, nevertheless, obvious that if *Leitmotiv* No. 7 unmistakably suggests Marie as mother it is because Berg has, among other things, conjoined to the memorable initial statement of a suitable musical idea Marie's words, "Come, my child," and employed the melodic and harmonic components of this idea significantly in the Cradle Song, and not because of its inherent musical character.

At the same time, Berg—like other composers, and perhaps more than most—delighted in more obscure cross-references, discoverable only by the patient analyst. A characteristic example is found at the Captain's comment on the departing Wozzeck near the end of II/2: "Mir wird ganz schwindlich vor dem Menschen!" ("This fellow makes me quite dizzy!"). A meaning other than the one intended by the speaker is implied for the word "schwindlich" in the accompanying tuba part (mm. 350–352), which repeats a melodic line that had earlier (mm. 219–221) been the vehicle of the Doctor's prognosis that the Captain might shortly be struck down by *apoplexia cerebri*. This signification and those of the *Leitmotive* and *Leitsektionen* depend upon primary contexts that are

25 Redlich 57b, p. 284.

entirely contained within the work itself. There are others that depend upon prior associations originating outside the work. As the curtain rises upon the stage band in II/4, for example, Berg—in what is in effect a musical aside to the audience—recalls the stage musicians in the finale of Act I of *Don Giovanni* (Ex. 25). A more esoteric allusion is found in the preceding scene, where Berg pays his respects to his teacher by employing, in antiphony with the main orchestra, a chamber ensemble consisting of the instruments of Schoenberg's Chamber Symphony, a work which had had an important influence upon him. The sustained chord that marks the Doctor's reference to the regularity of his pulse in I/4 (m. 520) may likewise be intended as an allusion to the master: it is identical with the basic chord of the third movement of Schoenberg's Five Pieces for Orchestra.[26] A personal and private signification, not, to my knowledge, ever explained, may also be the ground for Berg's use of a quotation from his own Three Pieces for Orchestra as the *Leitmotiv* (No. 4) of Wozzeck's hallucination.

"Descriptive" music derives its meaning not from its prior conjunction with a specific verbal text or other extra-musical detail but from a direct correspondence between an intrinsic feature of the music and an aspect of the intended signification. Perhaps the most remarkable example to be found in the entire literature is the "drowning music" of *Wozzeck.* Here the correspondence is not based on an external and objective aspect of the drowning man's experience but, rather, on his subjective impression of the water rising around him, an impression whose gradual obliteration as he loses consciousness is represented by the successively narrower compass and longer durational values assigned to each of the overlapping chromatically ascending progressions of the single chord on which the movement is based. An example of supremely effective and dramatically apposite "tone-painting" achieved by the most daringly simple means, the only antecedent to it that comes to mind is the Prelude to the first act of *Das Rheingold,* with its 136 bars on the tonic chord of E♭-major.

The cessation of the chromatically ascending progressions at m. 302 and the return of the "nature music" of the first part of the movement (mm. ♭226ff.), representing the croaking of the toads, marks the ultimate extinction of Wozzeck's life. This music and the world of nature that it symbolizes, in which Wozzeck's death is only an organic phenomenon devoid of "meaning" or "significance," is in sardonic contrast to the apprehensive utterances of the Captain and the Doctor, who, happening to pass as Wozzeck drowns, hear, or imagine that they hear, a moaning from the pond. The eerie and inhuman quality of the natural environment moves even this pair to transcend, for a moment, the smug and banal attitudes that govern their lives. The "drowning music" ceases; Wozzeck is dead; only the croaking of the toads is to be heard, but the passersby continue to "hear" the groans of a dying man and hastily depart, for "it's not good to hear." Through his musical settings of the scene the composer draws complex and profound implications from the verbal text, implications that only a most masterful stage director could conceivably have

---

26 The quotation (assuming it to be such and not a coincidence), which was brought to my attention by Mark DeVoto, may have been suggested by the rhythmic character of the opening sections of that movement.

discovered, but that even he could hardly have projected as effectively in the spoken drama.

The special music accompanying the falling curtain that closes II/1 and the rising curtains that open II/2 and III/5 is, in a sense, "descriptive," but it is descriptive merely of the moving curtain. The musical figures, given to the harp in Act II and to the harp and celesta in Act III, are as irrelevant to the staged events as is the architectural ornament that decorates the proscenium. The irony of this irrelevance is particularly forceful in the curtain music at the conclusion of Change of Scene III/1–2. This music marks the end of the closing fugue of the Bible-reading scene. The fateful *ostinato* that represents the *idée fixe* of the murder scene which follows is heard in the bass against tinkling arabesque-like figures in harp and celesta as the curtain ascends. There is even a touch of humor in the unexpected flourish with which these instruments bring the curtain music to an end in m. 72. At the conclusion of the final interlude the ascending sweep of harp, celesta, and clarinets seems to brush aside the tragedy and to set us at once among the carefree children playing in the bright morning sunlight of the epilogue.

It is hardly necessary to call attention to the more traditional examples of tone-painting that are found in this work: the music that "describes" the blessedness of virtue in Wozzeck's aria of I/1; the rising of the moon in III/2; the sinking of the knife into the water in III/4. Verbal locutions that suggest upward or downward motion are likely to be set to musical figures whose "direction" is consistent with that suggestion, in *Wozzeck* as in other works. Though the concept of "up" and "down" can be applied to music only metaphorically, it is a concept that is universally so applied, at least within the musical culture of which *Wozzeck* forms a part. There are other musical metaphors in *Wozzeck* that are *not* based on any generally shared musical conceptions, but that are, rather, personal and individual conceits, such as one finds in the music of Josquin Des Prez, Lassus, Bach, and many other masters—a *musica reservata* of negligible practical influence upon the musical and dramatic character of the work, but nevertheless meaningful to the composer and to those whom special knowledge and interest have initiated into its secrets.

In the third scene of Act II the passage given in Example 87 occurs. A glance at the words (shown below in italics) marked by this passage suggests that we have here a conventional programmatic device: Wozzeck, staring at Marie, says, "Eine Sünde, so dick und breit—das müsst' stinken, dass man die *Engel zum Himmel hinausräuchern könnt*" ("A sin, so thick and wide—it must stink enough to smoke the angels out of heaven"). But a closer inspection of the passage will reveal a more subtle analogy between music and words than the conventional one that associates the idea of ascension with rising musical patterns. Ignoring for the moment the solo violin part, we note that each of the remaining instruments fills the span between the first and last notes of the figure assigned to it with successions of a single interval—of 1, 2, 3, and 4 semitones, respectively. The simultaneities are likewise uni-intervallic structures, successively generated by intervals of 0, 1, 2, 3, 4, 5, 6, and 7 semitones.

Example 87

Thus, commencing from the unison, each instrument progresses in a straight and "perfect" line to the final simultaneity, a four-note segment of the circle of perfect fifths. The solo violin part, representing the odor of Marie's sin rising to heaven, spoils this otherwise "perfect" design in its weaving and irregular ascent and in its interpolation of a "wrong" note into each of the simultaneities after the initial unison. In a letter to Schoenberg dated July 27, 1920,[27] Berg completes his symmetrical partitioning of musical space by the addition of eight more lines, one for each of the remaining intervals, and by a continuation of the progression to the point where all twelve lines simultaneously restate the initial pitch-class, which occurs at twelve different octave-positions as opposed to the initial unison. In the text of this letter Berg makes no reference whatever to *Wozzeck*, accompanying his example merely by a terse statement that describes it as a "theoretical trifle" he has come upon by chance.

A segment of the endless series of perfect fifths symbolizes "eternity" in the opening scene, where the Captain says to Wozzeck: "Es wird mir ganz angst um die Welt, wenn ich an die Ewigkeit denk" ("I get quite anxious about the world, when I think about eternity"). Here, too, the musical figure simultaneously offers a more obvious analogy with the verbal text, its straightforward descent to the most profound depths of musical space mocking the supposed profundity of the Captain's reflection: " 'Ewig,' das ist ewig!" (" 'Eternal,' that's forever!").

27 Reprinted in facsimile in Perle 77a, *MQ*. I am grateful to Wayne D. Shirley, Reference Librarian of the Music Division, The Library of Congress, for bringing this letter to my attention.

The passacaglia, as a "learned" and "academic" musical form, was chosen by Berg for the fourth movement of Act I as an appropriate musical setting for the scene in the Doctor's study, though his altogether unconventional treatment of the form seems rather to defeat his presumed purpose in making this choice. Apart from the formal design of the movement as a whole, there are a number of specific musical references to the Doctor's scientific pretensions. A remarkable example of Berg's "secret art" is found in mm. 503–515, where the Doctor, after having angrily scolded Wozzeck for disobeying his instructions not to cough and for his "superstitious" surrender to the call of Nature in spite of the Doctor's proof that the diaphragm is controlled by the will, adopts a more sober and objective manner in keeping with his scientific calling as he shifts his attention to the dietary experiments to which he is subjecting Wozzeck. The vocal line reflects the "learned" character of the verbal text, consisting as it does entirely of symmetrical segments—segments, that is to say, each of which may be inverted without revision of its pitch content (Ex. 88).[28] The inversionally complementary pitch-relations in each melodic segment are indicated in the example. A particularly amusing touch is the literal musical symbolism of the phrase, "Es gibt eine Revolution." These words, and the pseudo-scientific expressions with which the Doctor concludes this episode of the Passacaglia, are set to musical patterns whose symmetry of content is made explicit in the ordering of the notes, as indicated by the brackets marked "P = RI" in the example.

Recalling Wozzeck's failure to regulate the action of his diaphragm in accordance with his instructions, the Doctor again loses his temper. But it suddenly occurs to him (Variation 4) that anger is unwholesome and unscientific and he checks his outburst. The success of this exercise in self-control is expressed in the orchestra, with its representation of his pulse, whose "customary sixty" is confirmed in the metronome marking at mm. 520ff.

Toward the end of the scene (Variation 19), the Doctor reviews Wozzeck's duties: "Bohnen essen, dann Schöpsenfleisch essen, nicht husten, seinen Hauptmann rasieren" ("Eat beans, then mutton, don't cough, shave the Captain"). Each of these instructions is again set to a symmetrical pitch-class collection. The three-part canon on an *ostinato* motive that accompanies these words refers not only to the Doctor's "science," but also, more specifically, to the new task assigned by the Doctor to Wozzeck as he concludes his enumeration of Wozzeck's duties: "Dazwischen die *fixe Idée* pflegen" ("Meanwhile, cultivate your obsession"). This music, and that which follows as the Doctor suddenly exclaims in exultation, "Oh! meine Theorie!"—a six-part canon on chromati-

28 Every collection of fewer than three or more than nine pitch-classes is self-invertible. Of the remaining collections, the proportions of those that are self-invertible are: 26 6/19 percent for collections of three or nine pitch-classes, 34 38/43 percent for collections of four or eight pitch-classes, 15 5/33 percent for collections of five or seven pitch-classes, and 25 percent for collections of six pitch-classes. Where the segments are of varied intervallic content, as in the example, and not largely restricted to the familiar symmetrical collections—diminished and augmented triads, diminished-seventh chords, whole-tone scales—it is altogether exceptional to find an extended passage that may be entirely partitioned into self-invertible collections, such as is illustrated in the example.

Example 88

cally descending segments of the whole-tone scale, with the successive entries a major third apart so that they twice outline an augmented triad, culminating in a verticalized segment of the cycle of perfect fourths—tells us that the Doctor himself is passionately cultivating an obsession. The penultimate variation continues with the Doctor's ecstatic vision of the fame and immortality that his experiments will earn for him, his "science" symbolized in the orchestra by a climactic harmonic progression whose outer voices are inversionally symmetrical to one another.

In Variation 12 inversional symmetry between paired voices—celesta and harp, first and second cellos, first and second violins—is assigned a literal rather than a metaphoric signification: the mysterious omens, "could one but read them," of which Wozzeck speaks to the Doctor, the circles marked out on the ground by the growing toadstools, are suggested not only aurally but also graphically, through the musical notation itself.

Musical metaphors based on inversionally symmetrical pitch collections and progressions, equal partitionings of the octave, and cycles of perfect fifths or fourths are not instances of "descriptive" music, for the analogies upon which their meanings depend are indirect, referring to some intermediate concept that is itself a symbol. The cycle of fifths may represent the notion of eternity but it cannot suggest eternity through imitation, as the "nature music" of the drowning scene suggests the croaking of the toads. It can serve as a symbol for eternity only for the informed musician who observes that a verbal reference to this concept is joined to a series of fifths, and who is led by this conjunction to associate the concept of eternity with a musical concept that can "stand" for it. (A series of fifths, or fourths, since it is generated by a single interval, can also "stand," as we have seen, for the Doctor's monomaniacal obsession.)

Finally, there is Berg's well-known preoccupation with the symbolism of numbers, which led him to attribute a special significance to certain integers and to represent these in some way in his compositions—particularly in the works that follow *Wozzeck*, but to some extent in *Wozzeck* as well. Whatever authentic "meaning" is to be discovered in these artifices is related to the composer personally rather than to some objective element in the content of the opera. Perhaps Berg took the numerical artifices of Schoenberg's *Pierrot lunaire* as a precedent, but Schoenberg's artifices are in keeping with the deliberate artificiality of language and form of Albert Giraud's cycle of poems, and thus are in a sense part of the "idea" of the work.[29] The opus number assigned to *Pierrot lunaire* is 21, and this number coincides with the number of poems out of Giraud's cycle of fifty that Schoenberg selected for his song cycle. The twenty-one songs are arranged in three groups of seven each, and all three numbers are referred to on the title page: "*Dreimal sieben Gedichte aus Albert Girauds Pierrot lunaire . . . Op. 21.*" Berg's representations of the number 7 in III/1 of *Wozzeck* have no such quasi-programmatic connotations, and he makes no reference to any in his own comment on these representations:

> The principle of scene I is a theme, subjected to variational treatment. The strictness of architecture (I use this term deliberately) is responsible for the fact that this dual theme, with its antecedent and consequent, consists of seven bars, that it returns in sevenfold variation, and that the double fugue, consisting of two subjects in accordance with the dualism inherent in the original theme, is based on a theme consisting of seven notes.[30]

The composer does not call attention to the fact that the number of beats in each variation and the metronome markings are also multiples of 7. Whatever Berg's motivation may have been in basing so many aspects of the music of III/1

29 See Perle 65.   30 Redlich 57b, pp. 279f. For "notes" read "pitch classes."

on representations of the number 7, "strictness of architecture" seems to have had little to do with it.[31]

A less pervasive role is assigned to the number 7 in the Passacaglia, the seven-bar theme of which is followed by twenty-one (i.e., 7 × 3) variations. Fourteen (i.e., 7 × 2) variations consist of seven bars each. Of the remaining *seven* variations, the dimensions of four refer to the integer 7 in some way (Nos. 7, 10, and 12 each consist of a single bar in 7/4 time, and No. 18 consists of 7 × 2 bars). The number of bars in each of the last *three* variations is 9 (i.e., 3 × 3) or a multiple thereof. It is a comment upon the nature of the subject itself that speculation along these lines unavoidably tends to be questionable in its methods, trivial in its results, and tendentious in its arguments. The following observations on Bartók's use of the golden section as a basis for the determination of formal proportions in his Fifth Quartet are apropos:

> For Bartók, as for some other composers, the predetermination of certain fixed spatial relations acts as a catalyst for creative inspiration. "My freedom," writes Stravinsky in *The Poetics of Music*, "will be so much the greater and more meaningful the more narrowly I limit my field of action and the more I surround myself with obstacles." The number of measures contained in each of the six movements of Alban Berg's *Lyric Suite*, as well as every one of its numerous metronome markings, is a multiple of either 23 or 50—numbers of entirely private significance for Berg. As a general *a priori* principle for determining the number of measures to be contained in a given formal component of a piece of music the golden section is probably no less irrelevant. It is only the explicit musical content with which Berg and Bartók have filled the supposedly perfect proportions of their preconceived formal designs that establishes the ideality, for this explicit content, of these proportions.[32]

"There is a bit of me in his character," Berg wrote to his wife during his military service in 1918, identifying himself with the protagonist of his opera. "I have been spending these war years just as dependent on people I hate, have been in chains, sick, captive, resigned, in fact, humiliated."[33] In the scene in the Doctor's study Berg revises the original text so that the Doctor's references to Wozzeck's diet name the staples of the composer's own fare as a soldier in the Austrian army. Perhaps an unconscious(?) affinity between the composer and his subject is reflected in the same scene, in the parallel between Berg's preoccupation with the symbolism of numbers and Wozzeck's preoccupation with the symbolism of the geometrical patterns made by "the toadstools growing in rings on the ground."

31 See p. 90, above.   32 Perle 67a [77].   33 Berg 71.

5

THE MUSICAL LANGUAGE OF *WOZZECK*

Pitch Organization

In the present chapter we turn our attention from the thematic material and formal design of *Wozzeck* to those elements of pitch organization that generate the context within which themes and motives operate—that determine, in other words, the various pitch-levels at which themes and motives are stated and the type and scope of modifications to which they are subjected—and that provide a basis for harmonic continuity and contrast. A description of these elements in the domain of the traditional tonal system may be reduced to a statement of the fundamental assumptions of that system: the triad as the sole criterion of harmonic stability, and the complex of functional relationships postulated in the concept of a "key center." No comparable generalizations regarding the musical language of *Wozzeck* are offered here, but a first attempt is made to describe certain means of integration and differentiation that are characteristic features of that language. Thematic and formal aspects of the work will be discussed only to the extent—in some instances considerable— that an elucidation of the central topic demands.

TONE CENTERS

Though one notes the occasional presence of tonic functionality in this otherwise "atonal" work (explicitly only in III/1 and in the symphonic interlude between the last two scenes, but also more or less vaguely and transiently elsewhere, as in the *Ländler* of Act II and in the "folk song" episodes), the centricity of a given pitch or collection of pitches is no less unmistakable in many of the "atonal" sections of *Wozzeck*. In attempting to resolve the semantic contradictions that arise from an admission of the presence of "tone centers" in "atonal" music, I cannot hope to improve upon the introductory remarks of Arthur Berger's article, "Problems of Pitch Organization in Stravinsky."[1] Though Berger's observations refer to his ensuing discussion of Stravinsky's "pre-twelve-tone" works, the following quotations are explicitly relevant to the present study:

> There are other means besides functional ones for asserting pitch-class priority; from which it follows that pitch-class priority per se: 1) is not a sufficient condition of that music which is tonal, and 2) is compatible with music that is not tonally functional.

> For purposes of non-tonal centric music it might be a good idea to have the term "tone center" refer to the more general class of which "tonics" (or tone centers in tonal contexts) could be regarded as a sub-class.

In the first scene of the opera, $c\#/d\flat$ is unequivocally established as a tone center by "other means besides functional ones." The first musical statement after the curtain is raised is the unaccompanied *Leitmotiv* of the Captain (Ex. 89). Within this context, the priority of $c\#/d\flat$ is established by its exposed position in the melodic contour (highest and lowest note), its exposed temporal position (last note), repetition (not only is it the only reiterated pitch class but also the only one which appears in more than one octave-position), and durational preponderance. The priority of $c\#/d\flat$ is extended through Scene 1 as a whole by analogous means within the larger context. Throughout this scene, $c\#/d\flat$ recurs as a spatial and temporal boundary and as an *ostinato* in inner and outer voices. The *Leitmotiv* of the Captain, at its primary pitch-level, is a salient component of the formal design. The repeated $d\flat$ of bars 5–6 becomes the recurrent monotone motive of Wozzeck's "Jawohl, Herr Hauptmann!" (mm. 25–26, 67–69, 76–79, 87–89, 90–96, 136–137, 151). The series of perfect fourths that marks the Captain's ruminations on eternity descends to $d\flat_1$, the lowest note of Scene 1.[2] Wozzeck's pensive reflection on virtue ("Es muss was

1 Berger 63, *PNM.*
2 The subscript refers to octave register, with each octave assumed to begin on c and with "middle c" represented as c_4.

Example 89

Schönes sein um die Tugend") is accompanied by a passage in the solo violin that ascends to $c\sharp_8$, the registral climax of the second half of Scene 1.

The presence of more or less traditional functional relations in "atonal" and "twelve-tone" music has been asserted by some theorists. The basis for this claim is probably to be found in a tendency noted by Roger Sessions:

> The intervals, and their effects, remain precisely the same; two notes a fifth apart still produce the effect of the fifth, and in whatever degree the context permits, will convey a sensation similar to that of a root and its fifth, or of a tonic and its dominant. A rising interval of a semitone will produce somewhat the effect of a "leading tone," principal or secondary, and so on.[3]

There is no question that an "atonal" melodic line, "in whatever degree the context permits," or in isolation from its context, will present a complex interplay of tensions and resolutions that are to some extent analogous to characteristic elements of melodic motion in tonal music. But it is precisely the fact that the intervallic "effects" to which Sessions calls attention generate a tone center in certain contexts but not in others that justifies the theorist in distinguishing between "tonality" and "atonality." The means by which $c\sharp/d\flat$ is made to function as a tone center in Act I, Scene 1 of *Wozzeck* do not depend upon criteria of the sort mentioned by Sessions. An unwarranted projection of these criteria, supplemented by imaginary implied notes, has led other writers to attribute tonic functionality to "atonal" motives. The *Leitmotiv* of the Captain can imply not only a tonic of *b*, as has been conjectured, but also, with as much (or as little) justification, a tonic of *f♯*, *a*, or *e* (Ex. 90). (The assumption of tonic centricity requires that the composer's notated *d♭* in mm. 5–6 be replaced by *c♯*.)

3 Sessions 51, p. 407.

Example 90

The moment this music is considered in its vertical aspects, the distinction between centricity in an "atonal" and in a tonal context becomes doubly clear. Any inferences of tonic functionality that a tonally oriented ear may make will be dispelled by the dyads, *f-b* and *g-d*, that accompany the reiterated *d♭* of m. 6. These are again associated with the linear tone-center *c♯/d♭* at salient cadential points of Scene 1. The dyad *f-b* is sustained throughout the first return of the *Leitmotiv* of the Captain at the conclusion of the first number of Scene 1 (mm. 26–30). Here the addition of a second tritone, *a-e♭*, produces, in conjunction with *f-b* and *d♭*, a five-note segment of the whole-tone scale (whose significance in the total context of the work will be discussed below). The tone *e♭* as upper neighbor to the tone center introduces the second number (mm. 30ff.), at the conclusion of which both dyads of bar 6 are sustained against the final note of the *Leitmotiv* (Ex. 91).

At the conclusion of Scene 1 (mm. 170f.), *a* is added to this collection to form a simultaneity that serves as the principal referential chord of the work as a whole (Ex. 92). This final cadential chord of Scene 1 subsequently demarcates only the largest formal divisions, the three acts. The slow descent of the curtain at the conclusion of Act I and of Act III is in each case accompanied by a pedal on *g-d* and a *tremolo* figure of two chords, the second of which consists of the remaining notes of Example 92 (Ex. 93).

Example 91

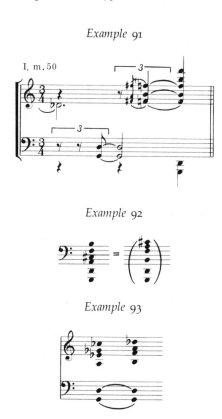

Example 92

Example 93

The prelude to Act II opens with an arpeggiated version of Example 92 leading into the same *tremolo* figure (Ex. 94). At the conclusion of Act II, the cadential figure (Ex. 93) is dissipated by the elimination of one note at a time, with the curtain falling in the ensuing bars of silence (Ex. 95). The final act commences with silence of the same duration as that which marked the conclusion of the preceding act, followed by a melodic figure whose initial notes, *g-d*, are those of the sustained dyad of Example 93.

The concept of "centricity" in the context of the present discussion must be broad enough to encompass the priority in Scene 1 of *c♯/d♭* and the priority in the work as a whole of the chord illustrated in Example 92, and even of that chord plus its neighbor (Ex. 93), with which it is invariably associated except in Scene 1. We shall designate a chord that is stabilized at a specific pitch-level and that functions significantly as a referential detail by the term "compound tone-center," as opposed to a "simple tone-center" such as the *c♯/d♭* of Scene 1. The term "tone center" is not intended to suggest any parallel with what is understood by "tonic" in the major-minor system, other than the quality of centricity within a given context.[4] In the traditional tonal system, centricity is asserted not only by the tonic and by the tonic triad but also by the dominant, which acts as a focal element in its own right in a definite functional relationship with the tonic. Various kinds of centricity may also be asserted in non-tonal music. The simple tone-center *c♯/d♭* is the primary linear focal element of Scene 1 only, its priority expressed through repetition, durational preponder-

4 I have borrowed the term "priority" from Berger, who, however, employs it only in reference to "simple tone-centers." I use the term "chord" rather than "simultaneity" designedly, in the paragraph above and elsewhere, in reference to recurrent, stable, or referential vertical structures. Such a structure is still a "chord" even when it is not a "simultaneity," that is, when it is a "broken chord."

Example 94

Example 95

ance, and prominence at registral and temporal boundaries. The primary compound tone-center (Ex. 92), although it asserts its priority in terms of the largest formal components of the work, does not display, as a tone center, the variety of functions of the simple tone-center of Scene 1. One of the dyadic constituents of this primary compound tone-center, *b-f*, functions as a tone center in the context of *both* the largest and the smallest dimensions of the work.

By means of the dyadic tone-center *b-f*, a referential pitch-level is established for some of the principal *Leitmotive* whose intervallic content includes a tritone. Throughout Scene 1, the *Leitmotiv* of the Captain is stated at the pitch that will generate the adjacency *b-f*. A *Leitmotiv* associated with the Doctor, first heard at the Doctor's words, "Wozzeck, Er kommt in's Narrenhaus," I/4 (mm. 562–564), returns at the beginning of II/2, transposed so as to unfold the same adjacency, *b-f*, that defines the "home key" of the *Leitmotiv* of the Captain, and stated concurrently with the latter (Ex. 96). At m. 286 a triple fugue begins, with the initial entry of each subject presenting the same fixed dyad. The first subject, the *Leitmotiv* of the Captain, enters at m. 286, the second, the *Leitmotiv* of the Doctor, at the upbeat to m. 293. The third subject, representing Wozzeck, contains no tritone among its adjacencies, but its entrance at m. 313 (Ex. 27) is at a pitch level that generates the notes *b-f* as prominent components of the pitch content of this subject. The initial appearance of this motive occurs near the conclusion of the preceding "Fantasia" (Ex. 22).

The priority of *b-f* (or *f-b*) is established in the first number of I/1 (mm. 1–29). In the first three bars this dyad appears only as an incidental detail, first as one of the linear intervals between the two chords with which the opera opens, and then as a vertical interval of the final chord of m. 3, which marks the conclusion of the curtain music. Thereafter it rises to prominence very quickly (mm. 4, 6, 10–11, 26–29; note also that each of the first four vocal passages begins or ends on *b* or *f*). The importance of this dyad at certain cadential points of Scene 1 was discussed above. The tones *b* and *f* frequently mark the outer limits of salient simultaneities, as at mm. 32–33, 59–60, and the *ostinato* passage for four trumpets at mm. 93–96.

The priority of *b-f* is asserted again and again throughout the work, often as a means of reaffirming the dramatic, as well as the musical, "keynote" of the opera. The most striking instance is at the conclusion of the Cradle Song in I/3.

Example 96

Before the appearance of *b-f*, Marie is *in Gedanken versunken* as the orchestra plays the cadential chords of this number (Ex. 97).[5] The open fifths express, according to Berg, Marie's "aimless and indefinable attitude of waiting."[6] The pitch content of mm. 412–416 is sustained to m. 423, where *c* is replaced by *b*. The concluding bars of the Cradle Song (mm. 415–416) return at mm. 425–426 (Ex. 98), but with the earlier pedal, *f-c*, converted into the basic dyad, *f-b*, a musical intimation of Wozzeck's approach. Marie's reverie is interrupted when Wozzeck knocks at the window, at the 32nd-note figure in m. 427 (Ex. 98). Mm. 425–426 are recapitulated at the same pitch-level at Wozzeck's exit (m. 455).

The primary dyad *b-f* is frequently associated with the rise or fall of the curtain. As a component of Example 93, *b-f* is part of the curtain music at the end of each act. Its inclusion in the chord that marks the rise of the first curtain at the conclusion of m. 3 was mentioned above. It returns at the fall of the first curtain as part of the final chord of the first scene (Ex. 92). As a component of the Fanfare motive (Ex. 99), it is the first linear adjacency of I/3. The quick

5 Cf. p. 105, above.   6 Redlich 57b, p. 272.

Example 97

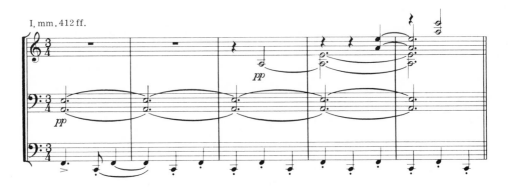

Example 98

curtain that opens the final scene of Act I is accompanied by the inversion of the same dyad (Ex. 100).

The concluding melodic interval of II/1 is *b-f* (Ex. 101). The same two notes mark the extremes of the "white-note" collection in the orchestra at this point. A "white-note" *glissando* from b_6 to b_1 accompanies the quick curtain in the following bar. The importance of the basic dyad at the beginning of the next scene has already been pointed out (Ex. 96).

In the first bar of III/2 a sustained *f* joins the pedal *b* upon which the curtain rises (Ex. 102). When the curtain falls upon this scene, the repeated linear adjacency in the pedal, *f-b,* comes to rest upon its final note. In III/4, *b* and *f* are components of the reiterated chord that accompanies the rising of the curtain.

Example 99

Example 100

Example 101

Example 102

Not only the means but also the degree of centricity varies throughout the work. There are extensive sections whose special character seems to reside in the *absence* of tone centers. Even so, most themes and motives, including those not clearly oriented around a tone center, are stabilized at times at particular transpositions that have priority among the various pitch-levels at which these themes and motives appear.

Scene 2 of Act I commences with a series of three chords which, at various transpositions, generates most of the tonal material of the scene. Although centricity (in the sense in which this term has been used above) is not unambiguously present, the lowest note of the first chord of the series as initially given asserts some degree of priority in the scene as a whole, in consequence of the treatment of the bass line. With each return of the series of chords to its original pitch-level (Ex. 103), c is heard as the lowest note and point of departure in the bass line. In its principal thematic statement at T(o), the succession of chords—XYX, XYZYXYX—gives priority to chord X, which serves not only as point of departure but also as destination. Thus, c functions as a goal of motion as well. At mm. 269–275 c_1 is reiterated as the lowest note of the scene, and c_4 is the point of departure for a chromatic descent of the bass line to f_3 at mm. 252–256, leading to a new permutation of the series: ZXYZ (mm. 257f.).

Example 103

As a whole the following scene, I/3, more or less suggests a as its tone center. The curtain rises upon a sustained chord whose lowest notes are the open octave on a; the Cradle Song begins with a neighbor-note motion from and to a chord whose lowest note is a (mm. 372–373); the repeated open fifth in the cadential bars of the Cradle Song, twice recapitulated in the same scene, is a-e (Exx. 97 and 98); at the conclusion of the orchestral transition that follows this scene, a is sustained for seven bars, into the curtain music of Scene 4.

The principal tone center of Scene 4 is $e\flat/d\sharp$. This scene commences and concludes on an $e\flat$ pedal. The same pitch class also acquires a certain measure of prominence through its position as the first note of the twelve-tone Passacaglia theme on which each variation is based, and it repeatedly occurs as an exposed element in the upper range of the Doctor's vocal line, culminating in the ecstatic solo with which the scene concludes (mm. 620ff.): "Oh! meine Theorie! Oh mein Ruhm! Ich werde unsterblich! Unsterblich!" (Ex. 137c). At m. 636, the bass line begins a chromatic descent from $e\flat$ to the $d\sharp$ pedal that accompanies the fall of the curtain. The transition to the final scene of Act I opens with a pedal on *g-d,* in preparation for the pedal on the same notes in the concluding bars of the same scene (Ex. 93).

Though the dyadic tone-center *b-f* far transcends in importance the simple tone-centers whose priority is asserted only within the limited context of a scene, or merely part of a scene, within that limited context the dyadic tone-center is often subordinate as a referential element. In I/4, for example, the dyad is referentially significant only in association with musical reminiscences of earlier scenes. The twelve-tone theme of the Passacaglia (which, as a unit, is never transposed, though segments are elaborated at various pitch-levels against the *ostinato* theme) comprises four tritones among its adjacencies, but none of them is *b-f*. The first statement of the twelve-tone series (in the two bars preceding the rise of the curtain upon this scene) is immediately anticipated by a passage which is rhythmically identical with that statement, and which, except at three points, duplicates the pitch succession as well. This is a linearization of the symmetrical progression that introduces the Military March at the beginning of I/3. (Compare the solo viola passage in Example 104 with the last two chords of m. 333 and the first chord of m. 334.) The revised re-statement of this pattern expunges a *b-f* adjacency and eliminates a second occurrence of each of these notes to convert it into a twelve-tone series.

Example 104

The ultimate dramatic implications of the basic dyad are realized in the Invention on a Note (III/2), in which an *ostinato b,* symbolizing Wozzeck's obsession with the murder of Marie, is maintained in one form or another, culminating in the two crescendi on *b* in the orchestral interlude which follows. At the conclusion of Act II *b* had been charged with this meaning; there it appeared as the last element of the gradually dissipated cadential figure (cf. p. 134, above). Throughout the murder scene (III/2), *f* is employed as a complementary tone-center: as the upper limit of the first sustained simultaneity in the orchestra (Ex. 102); as a recurrent goal of motion (Ex. 105); as the highest note or boundary note of segments of the vocal line (Ex. 106).

The death of Marie (III/2) and the death of Wozzeck (III/4) are complementary climaxes of the opera. The principal *Leitmotive* linking the two scenes are visual: the locale, the murder weapon, and, above all, the red moon, which

Example 105

III, mm. 80 f.

Example 106

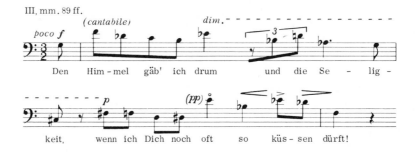

III, mm. 89 ff.

(cantabile)   dim. - - - - - - - - - - -

poco f

Den   Him – mel   gäb' ich drum   und   die   Se   –   lig –

p   (pp)

keit,   wenn ich Dich noch   oft   so   küs – sen   dürft!

triggers both catastrophes, first rising "wie ein blutig Eisen" as the immediate incitement to the crime and later breaking through the clouds as witness and betrayer, its blood-red reflection in the pond as Wozzeck attempts to cleanse himself of the blood inducing his ultimate irremediable derangement.

The musical links between the two scenes do not depend on motivic connections, but rather on the complementary relationship of the two members of the basic dyad. Compare, for example, the linear juxtaposition of the two tone-centers at the moment of the murder (Ex. 107a) with the setting of the words "todt" and "Mörder" at Wozzeck's return to the scene of the crime (Ex. 107b). The reiterated or sustained f in the top line of the orchestral part at salient moments in the formal design of III/4, as well as the prominence of f elsewhere in the scene, parallels the reiterated or sustained b of the earlier scene, and just as f played a subsidiary but complementary role within that scene, so b does within the later scene.

In Variations 5 and 6 of III/1, the presence of a conventional key-signature explicitly confirms the tonality of F minor. The interval f-c expresses a tonic-dominant relation in mm. 33–36 and 40–41; at the same time, in its reference to the opening bars of the Theme, f-c must be understood as the T(10) transposition of g-d, the motivic interval at its primary pitch-level. In Example 95 we showed how the cadential chord that punctuates the largest dimensions of the work is gradually dissipated by the elimination of one note at a time in the final bars of Act II. The initial bars of Act III, in restoring the g-d component of the cadential chord, are harmonically tied to the conclusion of the preceding act. (In Examples 93 and 94 we showed how the same chord established a harmonic

Example 107   141

connection between the conclusion of Act I and the beginning of Act II.) Only the initial segment of the Theme of III/1 is tonal in any traditional sense, but the six-note simultaneity upon which the quasi-canonic entries converge (Ex. 146)—implying a conjunction of two triads, VI⁶ and V of G minor—remains unresolved, and eventually becomes a referential chord of the movement as a whole. Together with other components of the Theme, it is transposed to T(11) in Variation 3 (m. 22), and to T(10) in Variations 5 and 6 (mm. 37 and 42). The return to T(0) is established in the first seven bars of the Fugue, through the pitch levels assigned to the successive entries of the individual parts. The initial note of each entering voice is an element of the referential chord: these are, for the successive statements of Subject I, *g*, *e♭*, *g*, *b♭*, *d*. The entrance of an accompanying voice in the third bar of the Fugue is on *f♯*, one of the two remaining notes of the referential chord; the first statement of Subject II begins on *a*, the sole remaining note of the chord. (The harmonic significance of the whole-tone simultaneity which brings the exposition of Subject I to a close in m. 57 is explained below, pp. 155ff.). The music for the rising curtain of the murder scene is simultaneously a final cadential statement of the referential chord of the first movement of Act III (cf. p. 123, above).

VERTICAL SETS

The term "vertical set" as employed here will mean a collection of pitch classes that is defined solely in terms of its unordered content, of which any simultaneity within a given musical complex will represent an equivalent or transposed statement. To whatever extent horizontal details are generated by the linearization—rather than the juxtaposition—of such simultaneities, the set is the sole determinant of horizontal, as well as vertical, association. Such vertical sets were consistently employed by Scriabin as early as 1911.

The chord on which III/4, "Invention on a Six-Note Chord," is based (Ex. 108) conforms to the above definition of a vertical set. Aside from a single exceptional statement, this set is exploited only in III/4. In the orchestral interlude that follows the murder of Marie (III/2), Scene 4 is foreshadowed in the *fortissimo* chord that simultaneously marks the conclusion of the sustained unison on *b* and the inception of the bass-drum statement of the thematic rhythm of III/3. This interlude thus gives us what one might call the *Urform* of each of the three *idées fixes* that respectively govern Scenes 2, 3, and 4 of the final act.

The principal form of this set (Ex. 108) is defined by its pitch level, S(0),[7] and by the vertical disposition of its components. Scene 4 of Act III opens with reiterated statements of this "thematic" or "referential" version of the set (mm. 220–222). The first section of the scene is bounded by these opening bars and their recapitulation, two octaves lower, at the midpoint of the scene (mm. 257ff.). Within this section, the set is employed exclusively at its original pitch-level, but in various vertical permutations and linearizations, and with octave displacements of segments of the set.

Example 108

Almost all pitch-elements through m. 266 are to be explained as components of S(0). The only exceptions are a few passing notes, a quotation of several motives from II/4 (at Wozzeck's words, "Hast Dir das rote Halsband verdient, wie die Ohrringlein, mit Deiner Sünde!"), a few passages in the vocal part, and a tone cluster (trumpets and trombones, m. 251) consisting of the notes that are not contained in S(0). At m. 267 the set is transposed to S(3), and following this there are overlapping set-statements at various pitch-levels. The "drowning music" that begins at m. 284 returns to the primary vertical pattern and uses this form of the set exclusively, but transposes the set repeatedly along the twelve degrees of the semitonal scale.

The final section commences at m. 302 with a return to the initial sonority, transposed one octave down and sustained to the end of the scene. Against this final statement of S(0) as a pedal, two passages that had appeared earlier in S(0), the "toad music" of mm. 226ff. and the "moon music" of mm. 262ff., are recapitulated in S(7), a version of the set that is maximally invariant with

7 Cf. Chapter Three; fn. 20.

S(0).[8] In the sixth bar before the end of the scene, S(7) is retired, so that the conclusion recapitulates the beginning of the scene in its exclusive use of the primary form of S(0).

CHORD SERIES

A series of chords which generates the principal material of I/2 was illustrated at T(0) in Example 103. In its formal design, this scene gives expression to two alternating ideas: Wozzeck's superstitious dread of the "accursed place" and Andres's lightheartedness, the former represented in the episodes based on Example 103 (mm. 201–212, 223–245, 257–263, 266–309), the latter in the intervening "folk song" episodes. It is noteworthy that two of the three basic chords contain, at T(0), the primary dyad, *b-f*. There is a curious "rightness" about the progression, possibly as a result of the linear connections between chords X and Y—dyads moving in parallel motion against a semitonal inflection—and the pitch classes held in common by chords Y and Z (Ex. 109).

Example 109

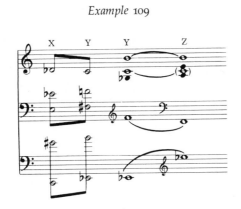

The thematic version of the chord series is defined not only by the initial pitch-level and initial vertical ordering of each chord as illustrated in Example 103, but also in the overall succession of the three chords as presented in the first eight bars of the scene (cf. p. 138). As the scene progresses, new material is derived from vertical permutations, transpositions, temporal displacements of chordal segments, and revisions of the thematic statement. As a source of pitch relations the chord series does not play the almost exclusive role of the set on which III/4 is based. Notes that are not components of the basic chords appear in association with these chords throughout the scene. The initial thematic statement of the basic chords, representing Wozzeck's estrangement

---

8 I.e., no transposition of S(0) duplicates more of the pitch content of S(0) than does S(7). The number of pitch classes common to S(x) and S(x + y) is the same as the number of pitch classes that are common to S(x) and S(x − y). Thus, except where the maximally invariant transposition is at the tritone of S(x), there must be at least two maximally invariant transpositions. In the present instance these are S(7) and S(5).

from his physical environment in I/2, returns at the beginning of the barracks scene (II/5) in reference to his estrangement from his social environment. Other reminiscences and quotations from I/2 are found in this scene as well as in I/3 (mm. 431–454), where Wozzeck, stopping to greet Marie on his way to the barracks, persists in his obsessions of the preceding scene, and in I/4 (mm. 546–561), where he reveals his "aberration" to the Doctor.

The Trio of the *Langsamer Ländler* of II/4 (mm. 456–480), is based, in the orchestra, upon a more extensive chord-series (Ex. 110), the ordering of which remains inviolate except for certain modifications where one statement of the series is linked to the next. Within each restatement the chords retain the relative octave-position and vertical structure of the original statement of the series in the bridge section between the *Ländler* and the Trio (mm. 447–455). The Trio comprises two restatements of the series, the first at T(0), the second at T(1). In the former a single rhythmic pattern is reiterated eight times, with the chord changes occurring at irregular points within this pattern (Ex. 111). In the second variation (mm. 465–480) passing chords are interpolated to fill in the missing semitonal degrees between the linear adjacencies of the series. At the conclusion of this variation the concluding chords (mm. 454–455) of the bridge section return in the retrograde of the rhythmic pattern of the first variation. The reiteration of a single chordal pattern is evidently intended as a reference to the chordal texture and strophic form of a chorale, in analogy with the grotesque employment of religious verbal motives in the text. Segments of the chord series return in the Chorale of the stage orchestra at mm. 605–633, the original chords being broken to form a *cantus firmus* against material not derived from the series. The Chorale is followed by a retrograde version of the series, with mm. ⌐641–649 corresponding to mm. 455♩-⌐ ♩447.

Example 110

Example 111

I have cited examples of extensive sections whose tone material is entirely, or largely, derived from a single vertical formation or a series of such formations. A greater complexity and subtlety in the structural use of vertical formations are occasioned by the imposition of the formal design of the traditional sonata-form in the opening scene of Act II. The formal components of this scene are characterized and coordinated by means that are in certain respects analogous to those provided in the traditional tonal system. A prerequisite is the possibility of defining and interrelating different harmonic areas. The latter are established, in the sonata movement of *Wozzeck*, by means of characteristic harmonic cells and aggregates of such cells. Harmonic areas may be differentiated in two ways: as to type, or "mode," dependent upon the intervallic structure of the basic cell; or, within a given "mode," as to pitch level, or "key," as indicated by the transposition numbers assigned to the basic cells and aggregates. Though the basic cell occasionally generates the totality of pitch components within a certain limited context (as in the Bridge Section of the First Exposition), this is not its function in general. It is therefore not to be confused with what was designated above by the term "vertical set." The vertical set of III/4 generates the complex of pitch components of that scene; the basic cells and aggregates of II/1 are characteristic harmonic details and focal elements *within* a given complex of pitch components.

As always with Berg, the text is arranged to delineate a formal design that parallels, in dramatic terms, the formal design of the music.[9] Corresponding sections of the libretto and the musical design are shown in Chapter Three, pp. 59ff., to which reference is assumed in the following analysis.

The Principal Section, Bridge Section, Subordinate Section, and Closing Section are each characterized by a special harmonic cell, and the movement as a whole is based on aggregates of the different cells. This dependence on a special cell is most obvious in the Bridge Section of the Exposition. The cell, at the pitch level assigned to it at its initial appearance in the Bridge Section, is anticipated, before the rise of the curtain, in the Introduction (Ex. 112). This cell, a diminished triad with conjunct semitone superimposed, will be designated as "cell B." The first six bars of the Bridge Section comprise four statements of cell B, in the order shown in Example 113. In mm. 34–36 two new

9 See Berg's own commentary on this scene: Redlich 57b, pp. 274f. The reader may be interested in comparing the following analysis with that which is given in Schweizer 70.

Example 112

II, mm. 4 f.

(trumpets)

notes are joined to the cell (Ex. 114). The resulting hexad, marking the median cadence of the Bridge Section, is an aggregate of the four basic cells of the movement (Ex. 115). The transposition number assigned to Example 115 is T(10), for reasons that are explained below.[10]

In the second half of the Bridge Section the order of transpositions is inverted, with the fourth statement of the cell converted, as before, into the hexad illustrated in Example 114, now at T(9) (cf. Examples 113 and 114 with Example 116). A symmetrical inflection of a four-note segment of the concluding chord of the Bridge Section generates the initial chord and special cell (cell C) of the Subordinate Section (Ex. 117). In content, the concluding chord of the

10 Cell A (the harmonic cell of the Principal Section) is contained in the aggregate hexad at two different pitch-levels. Each cell is shown in a characteristic vertical permutation. Cells and sets are primarily defined by their relative pitch-content, however, and are cited in various vertical permutations in the examples.

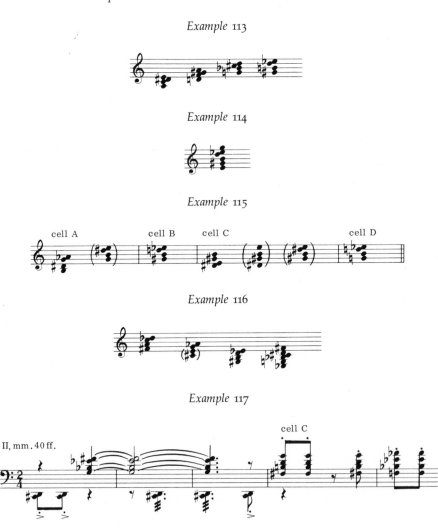

Example 113

Example 114

Example 115

Example 116

Example 117

Bridge Section points toward the Closing Section of the Exposition (given in its entirety in Example 118). Four notes of the aggregate collection of mm. 40–42 are redistributed to form cell D, and the two remaining notes, *g* and *e*♭, outline the melodic component of the Closing Section.

The basic aggregate of the movement is the five-note collection that initiates the Closing Section (Ex. 118, m. 55). This basic pentad may be regarded as a diminished triad with conjunct semitone not only superimposed (cell B) but also subimposed, or it may be regarded, more relevantly in terms of the movement as a whole, as an augmented and a diminished triad sharing a common central tone. The basic pentad in its "home key," T(0), and its three component cells are illustrated in Example 119. (The criteria that determine which pitch level represents the "home key" of the basic pentad have been established earlier in the Principal Section of the movement and will be discussed below.)

Example 118

Example 119

The expository statement and first reprise of the subordinate theme conclude with ascending semitonal transpositions of the basic pentad from T(7) to T(11) (Ex. 120). In the Recapitulation, the same progression (mm. 160–161) rises by another semitone into the final statement of the Closing Section, the latter thus commencing with the basic pentad at T(0) (Ex. 121). The movement concludes with a restatement of the basic pentad at T(0), with cell C—the only cell not contained in the basic pentad (cf. Example 119)—incorporated into the fi-

Example 120

148   nal aggregate through the addition of one new element to the basic pentad (Ex. 122).

The relevance of this or any other collection cannot be evaluated without some comprehension of the tonal resources from which it is selected. In terms of absolute pitch-content, there are 924 different hexads comprised within the material of the semitonal scale.[11] The basic pentad at T(o) is a component of seven of these, of which only the hexads shown in Example 123 can be construed as aggregates of all four basic cells.

Let us assume an additional requirement for the final chord, predicated on the fact that the irreducible referential sonority of the movement is the augmented triad on $c\sharp$, f, or a, the overriding importance of which will become clear when we consider the principal theme of the movement. Only the first

11 See Perle 77a, pp. 106ff. With the exclusion of transpositions, the number of hexads is reduced to the 80 non-equivalent six-note segments of Hauer's 44 tropes (see Perle 77b, pp. 1–3, and 77a, pp. 109, 153–155.)

Example 121

Example 122

Example 123

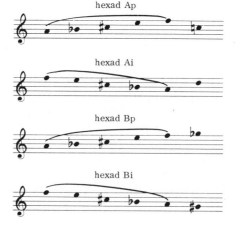

and second hexads can give special emphasis to this component, by the containment of each within the minor sixth, the boundary interval of the augmented triad. Berg chose the first of these for the final chord of the movement (Ex. 122). The same chord, in an arpeggiated version in oboes, trumpets, and harp, returns at the instant of the murder and Marie's death-cry (III/2, m. 103). Had the composer chosen the second hexad in Example 123, the aggregate of basic cells would have been the same except for cell C, which would have appeared as shown in Example 124. In the preceding bar, cell C appears at precisely this pitch level, as the climax of the final statement of the Closing Section (Ex. 125).

Example 124

Example 125

The hexads illustrated in Example 123 represent four out of eighty possible collections in terms of their *relative* pitch-content—that is, with each hexad taken as a representation of the pitch content of any one of its twelve transpositions. If it is assumed that any two hexads that can be transformed into one another through inversion are to be regarded as representations of the same set, the total number of possible hexads is reduced to fifty. Of these, only the two whose mutually invertible forms are illustrated in Example 123 can represent aggregates of the four basic cells. The digression from the "home key" of the principal theme in the Bridge Section of the exposition is expressed through hexad B_p at T(10) (Ex. 114) and T(9) (Ex. 116). Thus, hexads A and B are both significantly exploited in the movement. Berg's compositional procedures in *Wozzeck*, however, do not appear to require, or to justify, the evaluation of complementary forms of a hexad as representations of a single set.[12] It would seem to be appropriate, in the present context, to regard Example 123 as illustrating four nonequivalent sets.

12 The inversional forms of the basic cells play a subordinate role, however. Where the aspect—prime or inversion—of the latter is not specified by a subscript "p" or "i," the name assigned to a cell is understood to refer to the prime, unless the context indicates that in the given instance it is to be understood as referring equally to either of the complementary forms.

The fact that cell C, where it is stated as the climactic chord of the final Closing Section (Ex. 125), coincides in absolute pitch-content with cell C as a component of hexad A_i encourages one to speculate that this pitch content may be structurally significant and that hexad A_i may be present as an aggregate. Cell C at the given pitch-level (Ex. 125) is found to be maximally related in pitch content with cell A at T(0) (Ex. 119), the compound tone-center of the principal theme, the latter restored as a component of the basic pentad at T(0) with which the final statement of the Closing Section commences (Ex. 121). The total tone-material in the climactic bar of the final section (Ex. 126) may be construed as comprising: 126a, a linearization of the basic pentad at T(2); 126b, a series of passing chords; and 126c, hexad A_i.

Example 126

The basic cell of the principal theme, and indeed of the movement, is cell A, which may be conveniently defined as an augmented triad plus a conjunct semitone superimposed upon any one of its constituent notes. The three forms thus generated are equivalent to transpositions of a single collection (Ex. 127). The basic pentad, equivalent in content to an augmented and a diminished triad conjoined through a common central tone, shares cell A with the prime form of another pentad, equivalent in content to an augmented and a diminished triad conjoined through a common boundary-tone. The complementary forms of this pentad will be identified as x_p and x_i. (The basic pentad is a symmetrical, that is, self-complementary, set, the same pitch-content repre-

Example 127

senting both prime and inversion.) Pentads x_p and x_i and the basic pentad, at their respective primary pitch-levels, incorporate the complementary forms of cell A as illustrated in Example 128.

The augmented triad $c\sharp$-f-a is a pivotal harmonic center whose absolute pitch-content is repeated at three different levels—T(0), T(4), T(8)—of cell A, pentad x, the basic pentad, and the aggregate hexads. The same augmented triad is a component of the primary referential chord (Ex. 92) of the opera as a whole. As such it is prominently exposed in the Prelude to Act II and serves to introduce the "tonality" of the principal theme of the sonata movement. (The anticipation of the beginning of the Bridge Section in mm. 4–5 of the Prelude was pointed out above, Ex. 112.) In fact, the characteristic pentad of the principal theme is completely contained, at T(4), in the principal compound tone-center of the opera, and is thus an important component of the beginning and conclusion of the Prelude (Ex. 129).

Example 128

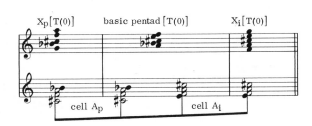

Example 129

That the chord on the initial downbeat of the Principal Section (m. 7) is to be interpreted as pentad x_p at T(0) with $c\sharp$ displaced by an *appoggiatura* may seem conjectural, but a comparison with the corresponding measures of the First Reprise and with the transition into the Second Reprise confirms this interpretation (Ex. 130).

The harmonic material of the Principal Section is far more elaborately organized and diversified than that of the other sections. The augmented triad emerges as the most consistent harmonic feature of the principal theme, within a complex which also includes pentad x and the prime and inversion of cells A and B. (The inversion of cell A is equivalent in content to cell D [Ex. 131], but in

Example 130

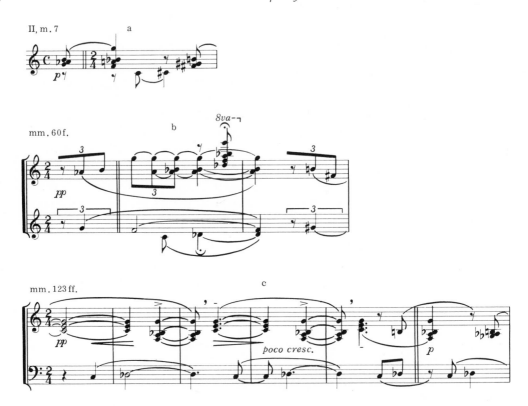

Example 131

view of the harmonic character of the principal theme, it is more appropriate to refer to this collection in terms that stress the presence of the augmented triad.) These harmonic entities overlap with themselves and with other elements, some of which are of sufficient general importance to require discussion below.[13] Though pentad x is a characteristic feature of the principal theme, within which the basic pentad plays no explicit role whatsoever, the former is, within the movement, clearly subordinate to the latter. Whereas the basic pentad may be construed as an aggregate of the prime and inverted forms of both cells A and B, pentad x_p and pentad x_i each incorporate one form of cell A only (Ex. 128). Moreover, the basic pentad, but not pentad x, is contained in the aggregate hexads whose all-important structural functions have been discussed above.

[13] These other elements are discussed under "Scale Segments" and "Symmetrical Formations," without special reference to II/i.

The structural role of the augmented triad in the principal theme of the Sonata is made clear in Example 132. Statements of the augmented triad are shown extracted from the simultaneities in which they appear and in their closest linear juxtapositions. Wherever the augmented triad occurs at its principal pitch level, T(0), T(4), or T(8), the basic cell or pentad of which it is a component is indicated. Each of these points represents a salient moment in the formal design of the principal theme. Measures 7–8 mark the beginning of the first period, m. 16 the parallel beginning of the second period, m. 22 the climax, and m. 24 the conclusion.

Example 132

$X_p[T(0)]$ $A[T(0)]$ $X_p[T(0)]$ $X_p[T(8)]$ $A[T(8)]$

It is the augmented triad above all that differentiates the principal theme from the other formal components of the Sonata. The augmented triad does not appear elsewhere in the Exposition until the Closing Section (where it is a component of cell D), except as a component of an aggregate collection of basic cells (mm. 34–36, 41–42, 48).

In the concluding bars of the recapitulation of the principal theme, immediately after the curtain falls, the harmonic material is greatly simplified and the basic harmonic ideas clearly and emphatically exposed. Parallel lines generating successive statements of the augmented triad (mm. 145–146) or of the basic cells (mm. 147–149) supplant the various types of simultaneities that are found in the expository statements of the principal theme.

In the light of the present analysis of II/1 it can be demonstrated that the C-major triad in the concluding bars of the Development is not only uniquely appropriate as a dramatic device,[14] but that it is also an integral element in the purely musical context of the movement. The most characteristic triadic components of the Sonata are the augmented triad (principal theme), diminished triad (Bridge Section), and major triad (Subordinate and Closing Sections). In the concluding bars of the Development (Ex. 133) the major triad is sustained in the orchestra as the vocal line unfolds a diminished triad (m. 117), an augmented triad (mm. 120–121), and cell B (mm. ⸢121–123). Voice and orchestra together present cell C (m. 118) and cell D (mm. 120–121). In the transitional bars that lead into the Second Reprise, pentad x_p returns at T(0) (m. 124) and is reiterated against a linear version of pentad x_i at T(0) (mm. 126–128).

The stability acquired by the note *c* as a pedal in mm. 116–127 and the transformation of this note into an *appoggiatura* in the first bar of the Second

14 See p. 61, above.

Example 133

Reprise parallel the structural employment of *c* in the Prelude to Act II (Ex. 152) and its transformation into an *appoggiatura* in the first bar of the Sonata. Finally, the C-major scale, upon which the curtain of II/2 rises, associates itself with these elements of the Sonata, as well as with the "white-note" collection that accompanied the fall of the curtain at the conclusion of the preceding scene.

Examples of linearized basic cells and pentads that appear at formally strategic moments of II/1, other than those which were discussed in connection with Example 133, are shown in Example 134: 134a, the beginning of the *Hauptstimme* of the principal theme; 134b, the beginning of the subordinate theme; 134c and 134d, two salient points in the Development. The musical and dramatic elements of II/1 pervade the opera as a whole, principally through the

Example 134

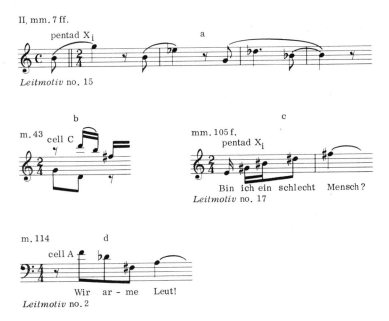

II, mm. 7 ff.

pentad X_i

a

Leitmotiv no. 15

b

m. 43 cell C

c

mm. 105 f.

pentad X_i

Bin ich ein schlecht Mensch?

Leitmotiv no. 17

m. 114

d

cell A

Wir ar - me Leut!

Leitmotiv no. 2

connection of cell A with *Leitmotiv* No. 2, of cell C with *Leitmotive* Nos. 7 and 8, and of pentad x_i with *Leitmotive* Nos. 15 and 17.

SCALE SEGMENTS

The tonal material of numerous passages throughout the work may be defined in terms of three types of scale—the whole-tone, the semitonal, and the diatonic. Associated with the last are collections that are reducible (as is the diatonic scale) to segments of the cycle of fifths. In Example 135 characteristic instances of each type are quoted from the first sixteen bars of the opera: 135a, a recurrent figure of I/1, which incorporates a permuted five-note segment (g-a-b-$c\sharp$-$d\sharp$) of the whole-tone scale; 135b, the basic dyad (b-f) encompassing a permuted segment of the semitonal scale; 135c, overlapping "white-note" and "one-sharp" diatonic collections.[15] Collections derived from the three types of scale segment are qualitatively distinct sonorities, easily differentiated from elements not so derived. The quotations cited above in isolation from their original context define distinct harmonic planes within that context.

Example 136 illustrates a passage in which the complete gamut of twelve pitch classes is generated from the two distinct whole-tone scales. Whole-tone formations are more significantly represented in mixed collections consisting of

15 If one could divorce such terms from extraneous associations, it might not be implausible, in view of the actual distribution of notes in Example 135c and considering the passage in isolation from its context, to describe it as "Phrygian-Aeolian." It is usually more convenient to refer such passages to the cycle of fifths, of which every diatonic collection is a reordered segment. The overlapping "white-note" and "one-sharp" diatonic collections of Example 135c are equivalent in content to the following segment of the cycle of fifths: f-c-g-d-a-e-b-$f\sharp$. See Perle 77a, *MQ*, pp. 10f.

The Musical Language

156

Example 135

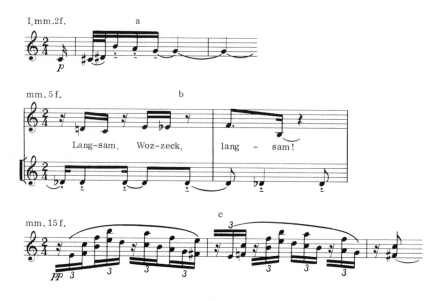

Example 136

a five-note segment of the whole-tone scale preceded or followed by a single note that is not a component of that scale. Prominent melodic motives of this type that are found in Act I are illustrated in Example 137: 137a, the first linear motive of the opera and a prominent melodic idea of Scene 1; 137b, the initial motive of Andres's first "folk song" in Scene 2; 137c, the initial melodic phrase of the Doctor's ecstatic solo, the culminating and concluding episode of Scene 4; 137d, a prominent melodic idea with which the interlude between Scenes 4 and 5 begins, and which is literally recapitulated in the final symphonic interlude of Act III. The same collection of pitch classes (g-a-b-$c\sharp$-$d\sharp$) is shared by these most important self-contained melodic motives based on whole-tone segments in Act I.

One of the principal motives of Scene 5 commences with another five-note whole-tone collection (Ex. 138). At the climax of the movement—at the moment that Marie and the Drum Major enter the house together just before the curtain falls on an empty stage—a final statement of the same motive ap-

Example 137

Example 138

pears, revised as Example 139 shows. This version of the motive restores the fixed collection of Example 137 and at the same time recalls a salient motive from Scene 1 (Ex. 140), a variant of the first motivic element, Example 137a.

An important motive of Act II, based, at T(0), on another five-note segment of the whole-tone scale, is first heard at Wozzeck's entrance in II/2 (Ex. 21). This motive clearly associates itself with the whole-tone motive that accompanied Wozzeck's entrance in the preceding scene (Ex. 26).

Of the two discrete whole-tone scales that together generate the twelve pitch classes, one (Ex. 141) has distinct priority over the other throughout the work. Each of the mixed collections illustrated in Examples 137–140 and Example 27 comprises one or another five-note segment of this scale. The fact that the primary compound tone-center of the opera (Ex. 92) is such a collection

Example 139

Example 140

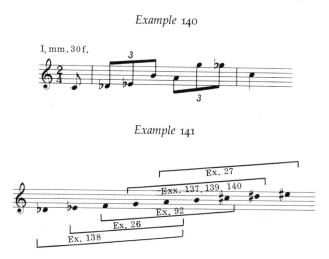

Example 141

Example 142

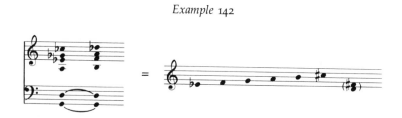

suggests the significance that must be ascribed to this scale in the work as a whole. Outside of I/1, this chord invariably appears in the context of a cadential figure (Ex. 93) which comprises, within a totality of eight pitch classes, the collective content of these whole-tone segments—the principal whole-tone scale of the work (Ex. 142).

The most extensive exploitation of whole-tone formations occurs in the final symphonic interlude of the last act: the two whole-tone collections are explicitly unfolded in scale passages; segments of one or the other whole-tone collection are verticalized at a number of rhythmically stressed points, and the *total* content of the principal whole-tone collection is verticalized on the downbeat of m. 335; included among the motives that are recapitulated from earlier scenes are those illustrated above in Examples 137b, 137d, and 21; and the initial phrase of the special theme of the interlude presents a mixed collection (a♭-b♭-c-d-e plus a) of the type discussed above. The whole-tone segment of the last is, however, derived from the subordinate rather than the principal whole-tone scale. Unlike the earlier examples of these mixed collections, it is employed in a tonally functional context. In the closing bars of the interlude (Ex. 143), an explicit linear statement of the principal whole-tone scale, in the top line, is heard against the recapitulated opening phrase of the special theme.

If the final symphonic interlude is a culminating episode in its explicit employment of whole-tone formations, so is, in respect to the semitonal scale,

Example 143

the scene that precedes this interlude. Registral transfers effected by means of semitonal-scale passages are so common throughout the opera that it is hardly necessary to cite specific instances. Where such passages occur simultaneously with other types of motion, they are heard on a separate plane, as in I/2, in which semitonal-scale segments are juxtaposed against the series of chords (Ex. 103) that generates the principal thematic material of the scene.

Explicit semitonal progressions are extensively employed to direct the motion of the bass line toward a specific goal. The semitonal descent of the bass line in Act I (mm. 252–256) was cited earlier (p. 138). Coinciding with this bass line is a soprano line, marked *Hauptstimme,* that is reducible to its symmetrical inversion (Ex. 144).

Two focal elements outline the semitonal bass-progression of the last thirty-three bars of I/4 (Ex. 145): the *e♭* tone-center of this scene and the *g-d* pedal of the orchestral interlude which follows (cf. pp. 138f., above). The descent from *g* to *e♭* in mm. 623–636 is symmetrically inverted in the ascent from

Example 144

Example 145

$g\flat$ to $b\flat$ in the top line. The semitonal scale (mm. 638–642), by means of which the $e\flat$ in the bass of mm. 636–637 is transferred to the lower octave, is aligned note-for-note with the final statement, in the top line, of the twelve-tone Passacaglia theme.

The music of the orchestral interlude that begins at m. 656 of Act I is transformed into a waltz for the stage orchestra in II/4. In this version it is introduced by a descending semitonal scale to the pedal tone g (mm. 521–529).

The use of explicit semitonal-scale segments to fill in the intervals between linear adjacencies of a chordal pattern in II/4 was cited above (p. 144). The filling-in of a boundary interval with the *reordered* content of such a segment, rather than with the explicit segment itself, was illustrated in Example 135b. This is the principle that determines the modifications to which the initial motive of III/1 is subjected in the quasi-canonic opening bars (Ex. 146). The initial motive is twice approximately imitated, the three statements together outlining a G-minor triad in root position, with the root doubled in the soprano in the octave above and the span between fifth and octave melodically filled in by semitonal inflections of the initial motive. A telescoped version of the opening bars occurs at the beginning of the Second Variation (Ex. 147a) and another telescoped version forms the subject of the closing fugue (Ex. 147b).

Movement by semitonal inflection permeates the texture of the entire work, generating elements that range in scope from neighbor notes and neighbor chords (Ex. 148) to the harmonic basis of an entire scene (Ex. 149).

Example 146

Example 147

Example 148

I, mm. 372 f.

Example 149

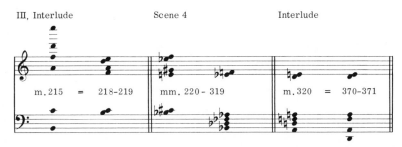

III, Interlude   Scene 4   Interlude

m. 215   =   218–219   mm. 220 – 319   m. 320   =   370–371

      A number of passages are based on special orderings of the total content of the semitonal scale. Berg thus foreshadowed a concept that was subsequently generalized in the twelve-tone system. Examples of such passages include: the two whole-tone collections into which the semitonal scale is divided in Example 136; the three simultaneous diminished-seventh chords associated with *Leitmotiv* No. 2 in Act I, mm. 136–137, Act II, m. 115, and Act III, m. 364 (Ex. 150); the twelve-tone Passacaglia theme of I/4; the twelve-tone series that forms a segment of the Theme of III/1 (Ex. 157); the eleven-tone series against a sustained *b* that accompanies the rising of the moon in III/2 (mm. 97–100); a statement of the basic set of III/4, simultaneously with a tone cluster comprising the notes not contained in that set (Ex. 151).

      Tonic functionality is more or less consistently expressed in III/1 (G minor), and in the final symphonic interlude (D minor). (Key centers are explicitly represented by key signatures only in the latter and in the F-minor episode, mm. 33–41, of the former.) In neither section is tonic functionality associated with the employment of diatonic collections. Conversely, diatonic

Example 150

Example 151

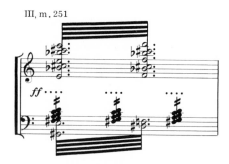

III, m. 251

collections are found that do not, in their context, imply tonic functionality. An example is the "white-note" collection of Act I, mm. 45–46.

Directed motion in the bass line sometimes proceeds along a series of perfect fifths, rather than along a series of semitones as illustrated in Examples 144–145. The structural use of successive fifths in the bass line of the Prelude to Act II is shown in Example 152. The final cadential chord of this passage comprises a seven-note segment of the cycle of fifths plus one "odd" note (Ex. 153a). Verticalized series of fifths occur at other important points: the vertical set on which III/4 is based consists of a five-note segment of the cycle of fifths plus one "odd" note (Ex. 153b); the cadential chord of the preceding interlude consists of a six-note diatonic segment, equivalent to a gapped seven-note segment of the cycle of fifths (Ex. 153c); and the concluding chord (m. 379) of the first section of the Cradle Song of I/3 consists of a seven-note segment of the cycle of fifths (Ex. 153d).

Example 152

Example 153

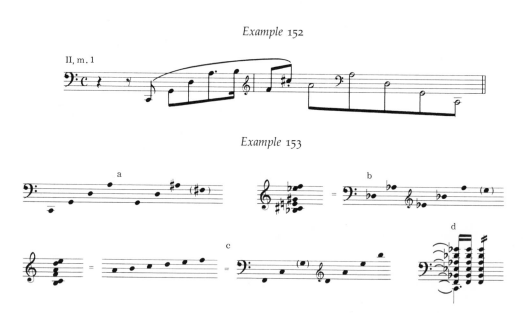

The polarity of outer voices that is found in much of *Wozzeck* is a traditional textural feature, the absence of which in other "atonal" music is one of the revolutionary characteristics of that music. A striking instance of this polarity is found in I/2. A series of fifths and a series of semitones are here simultaneously aligned in the outer voices (Ex. 154). The total simultaneous content is given at three points in the example, where vertical statements of whole-tone segments appear.

SYMMETRICAL FORMATIONS

Simultaneous voices moving by semitonal inflection are often symmetrically related to each other, as in Examples 144, 145, and 148. In Examples 144 and 145 this type of progression is presented in the outer voices only. In Example 148 *all* the parts are symmetrically disposed around the same axis, so that they are paired in parallel and contrary motion.[16] Such symmetrical formations often occur together with non-symmetrical elements, as in Example 155. (The symmetrical components are given in the two outer staves. The first and sec-

16 In Act II, mm. 42ff., a transposition of this symmetrical progression is enlarged to include three chordal components (cf. Ex. 117).

Example 154

Example 155

ond chords, in conjunction with the vocal line, are each a five-note segment of a whole-tone scale.)

OSTINATI

The most primitive means of achieving musical coherence is simple reiteration. As Ernst Kurth points out in his *Musikpsychologie:* "Through repetition an entire melodic unit becomes stable, in spite of its own movement. . . . That is, it acts in principle no differently from one repeated tone."[17] In much of the music of the early decades of this century, the *ostinato* is a primary structural device, occasioned by the increasing ambiguity of the articulative means provided by a disintegrating tonal system. The surface reiteration that is characteristic of certain works of Stravinsky, Bartók, Varèse, and other composers is relatively rare in the music of the atonal school, but the most extreme development of the *ostinato* principle is nevertheless to be found in the evolution of this school. In the twelve-tone system of Schoenberg, a serial permutation of the semitonal scale is the ever-present groundwork of each composition. The *ostinato* concept is represented here only in the assumed succession of pitch classes, not in their relative octave-positions and durations.

The basic principles of the twelve-tone system were formulated by Schoenberg between 1920 and 1923 in the Five Piano Pieces, Opus 23, the Serenade, Opus 24, and the Piano Suite, Opus 25. By the summer of 1919 Berg had already completed, in short score, the first act of *Wozzeck*. The *ostinato* theme of the Passacaglia, Scene 4, anticipates Schoenberg's "tone row" in that it is a fixed serial ordering of the twelve pitch classes. If Schoenberg's Opus 25 and the last movement of Opus 23 are to be given priority as examples of twelve-tone music, it is because they are the first in which *every* note is a component of one or another statement of the twelve-tone set. This concept is foreshadowed in the "vertical set" of *Wozzeck,* III/4 (see pp. 141f., above), not to speak of still earlier examples—the Seventh Sonata and other works by Scriabin—in which all pitch-relations are referable to an unordered collection of pitch classes and to transpositions of this collection; but in each of these instances the set, being unordered, can comprise only a partial selection of the twelve pitch classes.[18]

The function of the tone row in the Passacaglia movement of *Wozzeck* is not comparable to that of the Schoenbergian twelve-tone row. The series in question is, rather, a special sort of *theme:* special in that, like the tone-row, it is defined by a specific ordering of the twelve pitch classes, independently of other features that traditionally characterize a melodic theme—rhythm, contour, tonal functions. Within this special theme are recurrent rhythmic and melodic motives, but none of these is sufficiently associated with the invariant

17 Quoted from Fox 48.

18 A totally unordered twelve-tone set is simply equivalent to the semitonal scale. A twelve-tone set may be defined either by partitioning its otherwise unordered content (Hauer) or by specifying the order of pitch classes (Schoenberg).

pitch-class succession to function as a defining element of the *ostinato* theme in general. In this respect the Passacaglia theme of *Wozzeck* has more in common with the Schoenbergian twelve-tone row than does its precedent in the *Altenberg Lieder*. A twelve-tone series is only one of several *ostinato* themes in the Passacaglia movement of the *Altenberg Lieder*, and the thematic character of this series resides in its contour and rhythm as well as in the pitch-class succession.

Since the twelve-tone theme of I/4 is a series of pitch classes, it is appropriate to illustrate that theme with a series of letter-names rather than in ordinary pitch-notation:

$$\overline{\text{E}\flat\ \text{B}\ \underline{\text{G}\ \text{C}\sharp}}\ \underline{\text{C}\ \text{F}\sharp}\ \overline{\text{E}\ \text{B}\flat}\ \text{A}\ \overline{\text{F}\ \text{A}\flat\ \text{D}}$$

Salient harmonic details of the series are bracketed in the example: the augmented triad formed by the first three elements, the diminished triad formed by the last three, and the four tritone adjacencies.

In the penultimate variation, a special subsidiary motive and a segment of the series are employed in *stretto* at various pitch levels. Each of the other variations presents only one statement of the theme, at T(o). Segments, in particular the diminished triad, are, however, independently reiterated. Two segmented versions of the theme are of exceptional interest in that they anticipate a basic procedure of the twelve-tone system, the verticalization of linearly defined relationships (Ex. 156).

Example 156

Each of the five scenes of Act III is based on a different type of *ostinato*. In Scene 1, it is an aggregate of melodic details (the Theme); in Scene 2, a single pitch class; in Scene 3, a rhythmic figure; in Scene 4, a chord; in Scene 5, a single durational value. The initial segment of the Theme of III/1 is illustrated, together with two of its variants, in Examples 146 and 147. The remainder of the Theme is in sharp contrast with the G-minor tonality of the opening, in that a twelve-tone series is unfolded in the bass line (Ex. 157).

This series, unlike that of the Passacaglia, retains the contour of its original version (except for an occasional octave-displacement of the first and/or last note). Each statement of the series is shown in Example 158. In Variation 3 the series is transposed down a semitone, except for the third and fourth notes, which are transposed down a whole tone, and the tenth note, which remains

Example 157

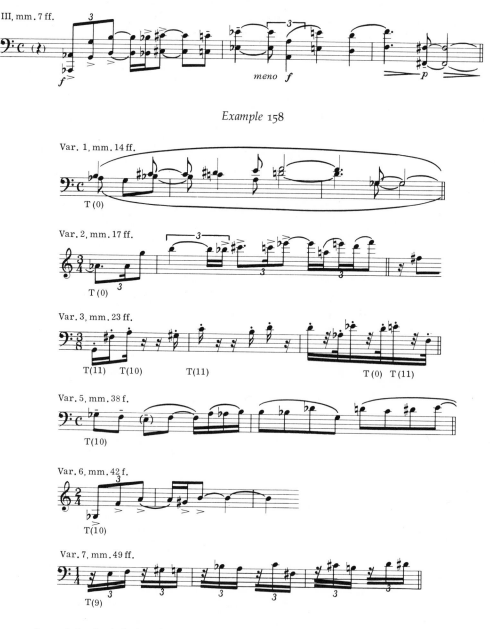

Example 158

at the original pitch-level. In Variation 6 the series is not completed. In Variation 7 the order of the first two notes is reversed.

Another component of the Theme consists of two simultaneous linear details, marked W and X in Example 159. At each restatement of W and X they
are juxtaposed in a new manner. The contour of W is repeatedly revised
through octave displacements, but is finally fixed as one of the two subjects of
the fugue with which the scene concludes. (The other subject is quoted in

Example 159, continued

Example 147b.) At several points the original intervals are modified by a semi-tonal inflection, and at one point by a whole-tone inflection. (These points are marked by an asterisk in the example.) A final component of the Theme comprises two segments which are normally stated in succession and differentiated in timbre (Ex. 160).

Example 160

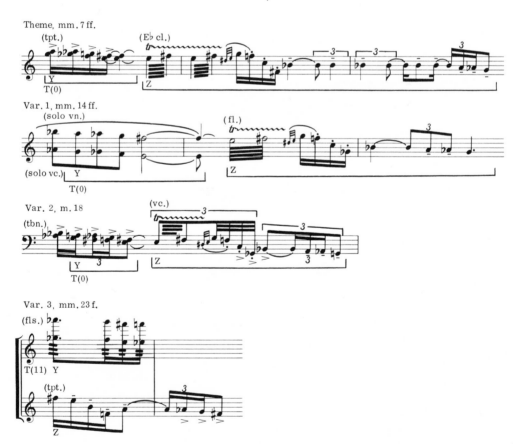

Example 160, continued

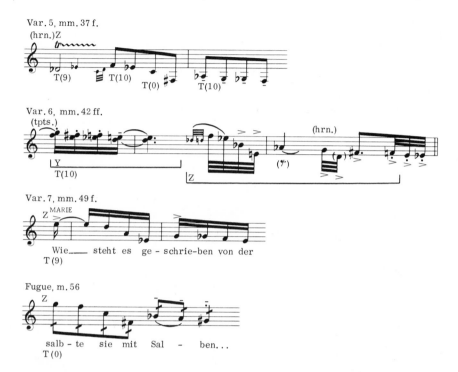

The *ostinato* as conventionally understood plays a negligible role in *Wozzeck* as compared with other music of the period. It is most significantly employed in II/4, the Scherzo movement of the Symphony in Five Movements which constitutes the formal framework of the act as a whole. In the recapitulation section of this movement, the *Ländler* which opens the scene is given to the stage band and played against a *basso ostinato* derived from the initial melodic motive of the *Ländler* in the celli of the pit orchestra (Ex. 161). Simultaneously (mm. 591ff.), in the upper strings of the pit orchestra, a chordal pattern commencing with and returning to an Eb-minor triad is progressively expanded in range and content, as illustrated in Example 162.

The focal elements of this first section of the recapitulation are the four-note *ostinato* motive of Example 161 and the Eb-minor triad. The incessant repetition of the latter against the first two statements of the *basso ostinato* (Ex. 161, mm. 589–591) establishes the keynote of this section. There is a return to both elements in the tavern scene of Act III, at Wozzeck's words, "No! No shoes! One can go to hell barefooted!" (Ex. 163). Dramatically this music refers to Wozzeck's reply, in the earlier scene, to Andres's question, "Why do you sit by the door?": "I'm sitting all right here. There are people who sit by the door and don't know it until they're carried out of the door, feet first." The incorporation of the *ostinato* motive in the vocal setting of these words is shown in Example 164.

Example 161

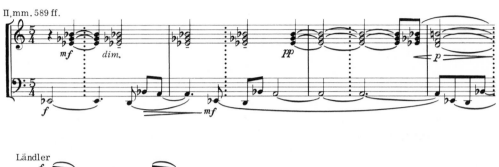

Example 162

The recapitulation of the Waltz begins with an *ostinato* figure in duple time in the pit orchestra, accompanying the stage band (Ex. 165). The reiterated minor triad plus a major seventh on Eb associates this section with the earlier recapitulation of the *Ländler*. A single augmented statement of this figure, transposed two octaves down, is a background to the music that accompanies the Drum Major's taunting of the fallen Wozzeck in the following scene (mm. 798–804).

Example 163

Example 164

Example 165

Rhythm and Tempo

The superimposition of a duple-time pattern (Ex. 165) upon the regular triple meter of the Waltz corresponds to a familiar convention, but it takes on a grotesque and obsessive quality in the closing bars of II/4. The quick closing-curtain obliterates the "real" dance-music of the stage band, and the pit or-

The Musical Language

172 chestra takes over the reprise of the Waltz in a nightmarish distortion. Through
the interposition of rests, a typical *ostinato* pattern that would characteristically
accommodate a regular four-bar phrase (Ex. 166) is extended to cover five bars
(Ex. 167).

Example 166

Example 167

II, mm. 692–696

The four remaining sections of the change-of-scene music are similarly
accompanied by progressively longer shifting *ostinato* patterns. In the first instance (Ex. 167), six groups of four eighth-notes plus one eighth-rest unfold an
ostinato melodic figure of three pitches: 6 (4 + 1) = 30 eighth-note values.
Since there are six eighth-note values per bar, five bars are required to complete the section. In each of the three following sections the *ostinato* is extended
by the addition of two more notes, and in each case there is always one
eighth-note more in the rhythmic pattern than there is in the melodic pattern,
so that there is a circular progression, the initial notes of the successive
rhythmic groupings unfolding the melodic figure in the large. Assuming that
the other numerical components remain unchanged, the following design is
implied in the overall series of *ostinato* patterns:

I. A 3-pitch melodic figure, in 6 times (4 ♪ + 1♪) = 30♪, or 5 bars.
II. A 5-pitch melodic figure, in 6 times (6 ♪ + 1♪) = 42♪, or 7 bars.
III. A 7-pitch melodic figure, in 6 times (8 ♪ + 1♪) = 54♪, or 9 bars.
IV. A 9-pitch melodic figure, in 6 times (10 ♪ + 1♪) = 66♪, or 11 bars.
V. An 11-pitch melodic figure, in 6 times (12 ♪ + 1♪) = 78♪, or 13 bars.

The composer departs from this implied series of ordered transformations only
in the third section (mm. 704–712), where instead of six groups of 8 + 1 we
have two groups of 8 + 1, followed by a group of 10 + 1, then 11 + 1, and
finally 12 + 1, and in the final section (mm. 724–736), where the melodic figure
comprises 12, rather than 11, eighth-note values and where the last of the 6
times (13 + 1) transformation patterns is cut short by the chorus of sleeping
soldiers in the following scene.

Within each section the series of ordered transformations is closed, or
circular, i.e., the progression of changes, were it to continue long enough
(which, in fact, occurs only in the first two sections), would eventually return

to the initial statement of the *ostinato* pattern. The implied design of the whole, however, is open: each section unfolds a longer *ostinato* pattern than the section that precedes it, and this progression could, in principle, continue *ad infinitum*. The *ostinato* rhythm from the Chorale of the same movement (Ex. 111) also participates in a circular series of transformations. The 9/8 of the *ostinato* pattern is notated in 4/4 (= 8/8) time, so that the barline shifts to the left by one eighth-note value relative to each statement of the *ostinato*. The section comprises nine bars (mm. 456–464), thus unfolding one complete cycle of ordered transformations. The internal rhythmic articulation of the 9/8 units is ambiguous, since the notation conforms to the 4/4 meter. Each 9/8 unit as a whole, however, is shaped by recurrent tempo and dynamic markings. Example 168 shows these markings and suggests metric subdivisions that are "natural" in terms of the distribution of long and short values, and characteristically Bergian in the successive diminution of each subdivision by subtraction of a constant value.

The 9/8 rhythmic pattern is a thematic entity in itself, independently of the pitch elements associated with it. In mm. 456ff. the rhythmic *ostinato* carries a series of chords (Ex. 110) which has already been introduced independently of this *ostinato* (mm. 447ff.), and the same rhythmic pattern returns in the retrograde (mm. ⌐474–480⌐) as the vehicle of an entirely different harmonic progression. Wozzeck's "Jawohl, Herr Hauptmann!" in I/1 is an example of a rhythmic figure whose independent thematic character is implied at once in its restriction to a single pitch. The basic motive is shown in Example 169a; this is modified by halving, relative to the motive as a whole, the rest that separates the two

Example 168

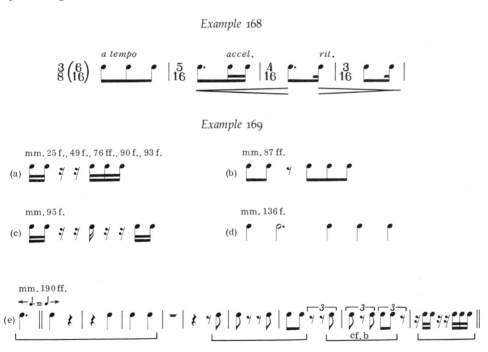

Example 169

174 figures of the motive (Ex. 169b), by breaking the second of the two figures (Ex. 169c), by augmentation (Ex. 169d), and by successive diminution (Ex. 169e).

Stroh[19] calls attention to the conversion of the motive (Ex. 170) "when Wozzeck gets furthest away from his 'Jawohl'-position with the words 'wenn wir in den Himmel kämen, so müssten wir donnern helfen' " ("If we get to heaven we'll have to help make the thunder"). (I have added the parentheses to Stroh's example in order to show how this conversion is accomplished, characteristically for Berg, by subtracting one unit at a time from the durational units that separate the two figures of the motive and from the durational units that make up the second figure.)

The thematic rhythm which is the basis of the third movement of Act III combines the character of the "Jawohl, Herr Hauptmann!" motive with that of the 9/8 *ostinato* rhythm of the Chorale: that is, it occurs both as a purely rhythmic entity (represented by a single reiterated pitch or in non-pitched instruments) and as a vehicle for various pitch-structures. The priority of the rhythmic component in determining the formal design of the movement probably has no parallel in the history of Western music apart from the pan-isorhythmic motet of the late fourteenth and early fifteenth centuries.

In the first five bars of the Interlude between the "Invention on a Note" and the "Invention on a Rhythm," the "Note" of the preceding scene and a presumably subliminal presentation[20] of the "Rhythm" of the following scene are joined. Example 171 shows the succession of *pppp* attacks in the winds and strings as the different instruments join one another in sustaining the crescendo on a unison *b* at mm. 109–113. This two-part canonic statement of the

19 Stroh 68, *PNM*.
20 See Berg's own description of this passage in his lecture on *Wozzeck*, Redlich 57b, p. 281. (The reference is to mm. 109–113, not, as indicated in Redlich, 117–121.)

Example 170

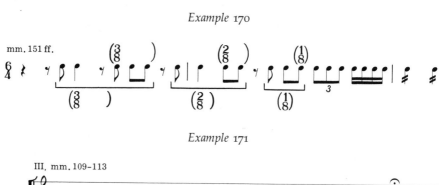

Example 171

thematic rhythm returns in the same note-values and tempo at the beginning of the concluding *stretto,* mm. 186–193. The aggregate rhythm produced by the canon is again characteristically Bergian in its progressive reduction in the number of units in each of the first three groups of attack points.

The thematic rhythm is immediately repeated in halved note-values, *fff,* in the bass drum (Ex. 172). If, as Berg suggests in his lecture on *Wozzeck,* the initial statement of the thematic rhythm hardly "reaches the level of consciousness in the listener," this second statement is directed to the opposite extreme of his "level of consciousness." In *itself* the theme is ambiguous as to pulse, internal rhythmic groupings, and meter. As a purely rhythmic entity the bass-drum figure in Example 172 is more properly notated in Example 173. Each note represents a point of attack, the durational values showing the time intervals between attacks. The tie appended to the final note indicates that its durational value is indeterminate apart from a given context.

A rhythmic pattern of this length is normally divisible into internal sub-patterns based on the relation between accented and unaccented elements. Accentuation may be dynamic, melodic, or durational. The only type of accent that is inherent in the theme is durational, but an explicit non-equivocal articulation of the theme into component patterns cannot be inferred from the distribution of these durational accents. If "meter is the measurement of the number of pulses between more or less regularly recurring accents,"[21] then the meter must be ambiguous on two counts: the ambiguity as to pulse and the absence of regularly recurring accents. The questions at issue are:

1. The assumption of a basic durational unit. In representing the Rhythm in notation we are usually concerned only with points of attack, regardless of *actual* duration of notes even where the theme is given to pitched instruments. The restatements of the bass-drum figure by the stage piano at the rise of the curtain establish the quarter-note as the "normal" durational value (Ex. 174).

21 Cooper and Meyer 60, p. 4.

Example 172

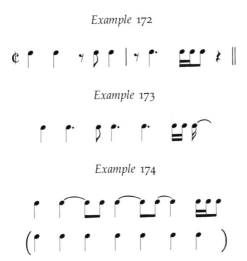

Example 173

Example 174

176   The same proportional relations are maintained in various degrees of diminution and augmentation (Ex. 175) in the remainder of the movement. These will be denoted below by the basic durational unit of a given statement. Thus, for example, the theme in double augmentation will be referred to as Rhythm ♩, in 1:2 diminution as Rhythm ♪, in 2:3 diminution as Rhythm ♪³, etc. In each case the initial element of the theme as illustrated in Example 175 is assumed as the basic durational unit.

       2. The inherent ambiguity of the final element. In the Polka, Rhythm ♩, in 2/4 time, is disposed over four-bar phrases, and Rhythm ♩ over an eight-bar period (Ex. 176). These dispositions determine the same relative metric meaning for the final element of each statement of the theme.

       In the next section (mm. 145ff.), Rhythm ♩ is disposed over a four-bar phrase in 2/2 time and repeated to form an eight-bar period, as in mm. 122–129 of Example 176 but with both theme and bar-length in double augmentation. At the same time, in the first three bars of the section, a threefold statement of Rhythm ♪ generates implied meters of 7/8 (Ex. 177).

       The distinction between the two types of metric pattern (4 × 2 units in Example 176 and 7 units in Example 177) depends on the time interval between the final attack-point of one statement and the initial attack-point of the next.

Example 175

Example 176

Example 177

In other instances the durational value to be assigned to the final element is not defined by the context, or irrelevant in that the final attack is heard as the conclusive downbeat of the given thematic statement. In Example 175 the assumption of a basic durational unit for each proportionally related version of the theme is supported by the final anapest figure, which is notated as the equivalent of that unit. This interpretation of the last three attack-points is usually, but not invariably, confirmed by the context. It is not confirmed by the representation of Rhythm Υ, for example, at mm. Υ 193–196 (Ex. 178).

Example 178

3. The relation to the barline. We have seen that the normal attributes of a rhythmic pattern of this length—pulse, internal rhythmic figures, and meter—are not definable for the theme in itself. A given statement of the theme may be inherently ambiguous as to any of these attributes, or it may express them more or less concretely in a variety of ways. The theme in itself remains a coherent unitary structure which is felt as an objective referential norm behind its explicit representations. The implications of barline and time signature as to pulse, accent, meter, and phrase will affect the character of these representations, as a comparison of Examples 172 and 173 will show. At the rise of the curtain, the rhythm of the Polka retrospectively establishes Example 172 as the correct reading of the bass-drum figure. Through the imposition of a regular phrase structure, the theme is made to conform to a popular dance in mm. 122–145 and to a folk song in mm. 145–152. There is a sudden departure from periodicity in the three overlapping statements of the theme in the orchestra at mm. $\Upsilon\Upsilon$152–159 Υ: each of these statements is in a different proportion; the proportional relations are distorted by the tempo changes in mm. 154–159; and each statement commences at a different point within the bar. Time signatures in III/3 are exclusively duple (2/4 and 2/2), but through triplets the theme is represented in what is equivalent to a triple meter in mm. 158–169 Υ. The relative time-values of the concluding anapest are doubled in this version of the theme (Ex. 179).

In mm. 180–184 there is a three-part round canon on a variant of Rhythm Υ (cf. Ex. 180 and Rhythm Υ in Ex. 175). The actual representation of the theme is given in Example 181. Each bar-length, in this instance, is metrically significant not because of its effect on the sense of accent and pulse in the theme but because it marks the time interval between the canonic parts.

Example 179

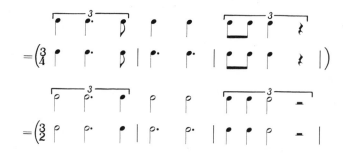

Example 180

Example 181

mm. 180–184

In the concluding section of III/3 (mm. ⌈186–211⌉) an *ostinato* 7/2 version of Rhythm ⌐ in the orchestra forms a ground above which a *stretto* on the theme unfolds in the vocal parts. The irregularity of the vocal entries and the gradual accumulation of canonic voices in different basic durational values give maximum emphasis to the inherent ambiguity of the theme as to pulse, meter, and internal rhythms, and are in maximum contrast to the regular structure of the accompanying ground in the orchestra.

4. The relation to the tempo. The versions of the theme listed in Example 175 are proportionately related in terms of corresponding note-values. Whether or not they are *actually* proportionately related depends on another dimension that is missing from the table, their respective tempi. Rhythm ⌐ at ♩ =40 and Rhythm ⌐ at ♩ = 60, for example, are identical. The two tempi overlap when Margret, accompanied by the stage piano, begins her song on the upbeat to m. 169 (Ex. 182). We have pointed out above (Ex. 179) that Rhythm ⌐ in the preceding bars is a variant of the theme,[22] in that time values of the final

[22] Our notation of Rhythm ⌐ is analogous to that which Berg employs for Rhythm ⌐ in mm. 158f. (cf. Ex. 183).

anapest are doubled. In Margret's equivalent version of the "Rhythm" the original relative values are restored.

Rhythm ⌐3⌐♪, like Rhythm ⌐3⌐♪, occurs only in the illustrated variant form, but a written-out *accelerando* gradually restores the "normal" time-values (Ex. 183). At the same time a *ritardando* from ♩ = 60 to ♩ = 40 seems to work at cross-purposes to this restoration. And what of the second statement, in the trombone, of Rhythm ⌐3⌐♪, which coincides with this *ritardando*? Since the *actual* proportions of durational values are changed, ought this to be regarded as another variant version of the theme?

Rhythm ♪ occurs in its normal notated time-values at mm. ♪ 154–159 ♪, but the tempo changes from ♩ = 60 to ♩ = 80 and back to ♩ = 60. In terms of real proportional relations, this is equivalent to a single thematic statement that vacillates between Rhythm ♪ and Rhythm ♪· , if we assume a constant tempo of ♩ = 60 (Ex. 184).

The only other statement that is concurrent with a tempo change occurs in Margret's Song (Ex. 185a). Here a diminution in the value of the fifth note of Rhythm ♪ (mm. 172f.) shifts the position of the cadential anapest relative to the barline. The return to Rhythm ♪ after the *rallentando* coincides with the return

Example 182

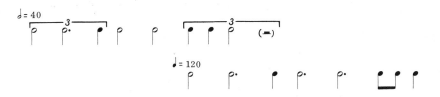

Example 183

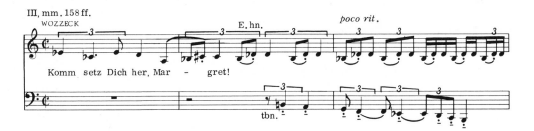

Example 184

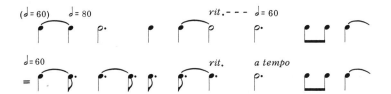

Example 185

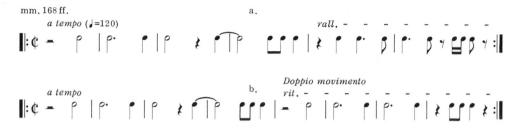

to the tempo, ♩ = 60. The real meaning of the changes in tempo emerges when the passage is rewritten in terms of a single durational unit (Ex. 185b).

The formal components of the movement, with reference only to the thematic rhythm, may be defined as follows:

Variation 1, Polka, mm. 122–145 ♪:

>   A. Rhythm ♪ (Ex. 176).
>   A. Rhythm ♪ (Ex. 176).
>   B. Rhythm ♪ (Ex. 176).
>   A. Rhythm ♪ (Ex. 176).
>   Codetta. Rhythm ♪.

Variation 2, Song, mm. 145–152 ♪:

>   A₁. Rhythm ♪, accompanied by Rhythm ♪ (Ex. 177) in side drum.
>   A₂. Rhythm ♪, in canon with stage piano.

Bridge, mm. ♪♪ 152–159 ♪:

>   (a) Overlapping statements of Rhythms ♪, ♪, ♪, in orchestra.
>   (b) Return of Polka, Rhythm ♪, in stage piano (mm. ♪ 154–157).

Variation 3, mm. 158–169 ♪ (Rhythms ♪ and ♪, in variant form, Ex. 179):

>   A. Two statements of Rhythm ♪ (Ex. 183).
>   B. a. Rhythm ♪.
>   b. Four-part canon on Rhythm ♪.
>   a. Rhythm ♪.

Variation 4, Song, mm. ♪168–179 (Ex. 185):

>   A₁. Rhythms ♪ and ♪.
>   A₂. Rhythms ♪ and ♪.

Variation 5, mm. 180–186 ♪:

>   Rhythm °; concurrently with this a three-part canon on Rhythm ♪ (Ex. 181), Rhythm ♪ (mm. ♪ 183–184), Rhythm ♪ (mm. 185–186 ♪).

Stretto, mm. ♩186–218:

A. *Ostinato* on Rhythm ♩ in orchestra (mm. 187–211♩); *stretto* on Rhythms ♩, ♩, °, and ♩, in vocal parts (mm. ♩186–212♩), taken up by the orchestra at curtain (m. ♩211) and completed in orchestra alone (m. 213).

B₁. Six-part canon on Rhythm ♩, with successive entries separated by the following durational values: ♩ ♩ ♩ ♩ ♩ ♩ (mm. 213–215).

B₂. Six-part canon on Rhythm ♩ repeated (mm. 216–218).

In Example 170 we showed how ordered-transformation procedures were applied to convert the "Jawohl, Herr Hauptmann!" rhythm into a series of equal durational values. In Change of Scene III/3–4, mm. 213–215 and 216–218, the closing anapests of the six overlapping statements of Rhythm ♩ produce a pattern which similarly generates a series of equal durational values, and this pattern is repeated independently of the thematic rhythm of III/3 as the curtain rises on the following scene (Ex. 186).

Example 186

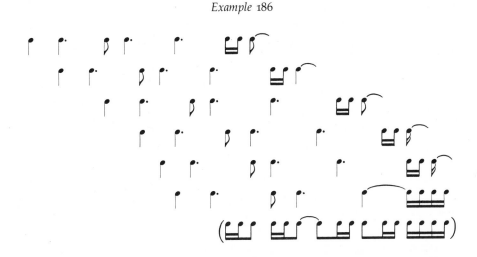

Historians of contemporary music stress a revolution in rhythmic expression in the early years of the present century. Of the classic masters of the period, Berg is entirely overlooked in this connection. If Berg's rhythmic structures do not often have the immediate impact of Stravinsky's or Bartók's or Varèse's, this is because his rhythmic language is more, rather than less, various, complex, and profound. Most obviously in the music of Stravinsky, but with other composers as well, an absolutely fixed tempo within a given time-frame is a precondition for the vitality and independence of the rhythmic dimension. It seems to have occurred to no one except Berg that the integral units of a thematic or *ostinato* rhythmic figure may be paced at different rates of speed even within a single statement of that figure (as in Examples 183–185), so that in an absolute sense the given pattern is annihilated, while in a relative sense (i.e., relative to the concurrent changes in tempo) it remains inviolate. What other composer has ever given us a *perpetuum mobile* in *tempo rubato*, like the final movement of Act III in *Wozzeck*? Yet that movement, in spite of seventeen changes of tempo within twenty-one bars, is what Berg said it was, an "Invention on a Continuous Eighth-Note Motion." There is no precedent for the scope, awareness, and invention of Berg's control of the reciprocal relation between rhythm and tempo in *Wozzeck*.

Curt Sachs has pointed out that the range between the "fastest" tempo and the "slowest" is actually much narrower than the profusion of names for the different tempi suggests. "The conductor would in a medium tempo beat quarters, in a slower tempo eighths. Therewith he would reduce an alleged difference in tempo to an actual difference in symbols."[23] As the pace of the slow eighths is increased, there comes a point where we group them in pairs and begin again in a slow tempo, imposing our beat on quarters rather than eighths. The same process is repeated in the progression from quarters to halves. Is $\quarternote$ = 60 the same tempo as $\halfnote$ = 30, where both metronome markings refer to the same music? In the first movement of Act I, the former marking is assigned to the Prelude, the latter to the Reprise. The indication "Tempo I" for the Reprise is an affirmative reply to our question. Berg's purpose in substituting the half-note for the quarter as the representative metronomic unit becomes clear only in relation to the tempi of the intervening numbers of the Suite. The successive numbers may be interpreted as projecting successively longer absolute durational values, a progression that results in a doubling of absolute values between the Prelude (MM = 60) and the Reprise (MM = 30). To say that the successive tempi are slower has no meaning unless we define the durational units that are being compared. For example, the composer calls for "very moderate quarters" in the Prelude and for "quick eighths" in the Gigue; these latter, at $\eighthnote$ = 162, move at a considerably quicker pace than the same notated values in the Prelude ($\eighthnote$ = 120). Thus, the Gigue is in a faster tempo than the Prelude. The representative durational unit in the Gigue, however, is the dotted quarter, and the metronomic indication for that value is 54, as opposed to the 60 assigned to the quarter in the Prelude. Thus, the Gigue is in a slower tempo than the Prelude. The composer's deliberate exploitation of such ambiguities explains the movement's progression from MM = 60 to MM = 30, a progression which takes us full circle to an eventual Reprise of the tempo, as well as the music, of the Prelude:

Prelude	$\quarternote$ = 60
Pavane	$\quarternote$ = 56–60
Cadenza	$\quarternote$ = 48–54
Gigue	$\dottedquarternote$ = 54
Cadenza	$\quarternote$ = 48–54

23 Sachs 53, p. 33.

Gavotte   𝅗𝅥 = 42
Double I   𝅗𝅥 = 42
Double II   ♪ = 120–138   [𝅗𝅥 = 30–34 1/2]
Air   𝅗𝅥 = 26–30
Reprise   𝅗𝅥 = 30 [♩ = 60]

In the "Invention on a Rhythm" there is a similar progression from ♩ = 160 to ♩ = 80, and a final substitution of half-note for quarter to close the circle:

Variation 1   ♩ = 160 [𝅗𝅥 = 80]
Variation 2
    A_1
    A_2 𝅗𝅥 = 70
Bridge
    (a)   𝅗𝅥 = 60
    (b)   (♩ = 160)
Variation 3
    A   𝅗𝅥 = 60
    B   𝅗𝅥 = 40
(Variation 4) (♩ = 120)
Variation 5   ♩ = 80   [𝅗𝅥 = 40]
Stretto   [𝅗𝅥 = 80]
    A
    B_1
    (B_2) (𝅗𝅥 = 50–60: transition to tempo of III/4)

The thematic rhythm generates tempo relations at another level, simultaneously with the above progession of metronomic changes. Variation 5, for example, is assigned a single metronome marking, ♩ = 80; but at the same time successive statements of the Rhythm unfold three different absolute tempi, each of which is faster than the preceding by a ratio of 2 to 3: Rhythm ♩· (= 53 1/3), Rhythm ♩ (= 80), Rhythm ♪³ (= 120). The converse obtains in Variation 3: Rhythm ♪³ is followed by Rhythm ♩³ ; the concurrent change from 𝅗𝅥 = 60 to 𝅗𝅥 = 40 means that the second tempo of the Rhythm is slower than the first by a ratio of 3 to 1 rather than 2 to 1 (the ratio of their corresponding note-values) or 3 to 2 (the ratio of the respective metronomic values); but according to the principle of substitution there is no change of tempo at all, 𝅗𝅥 = 60 being replaced by ♩³ = 60.

There are two brief interruptions of the progression from MM = 160 to MM = 80 in the "Invention on a Rhythm": the return of a fragment of the stage piano's Polka against a *quasi-rubato* statement of Rhythm ♩ (Ex. 184) in the orchestra; and Margret's Song, accompanied only by the stage piano (Ex. 185a). Both of these are musical parentheses, in which the "real" music on the stage, representing that outer world in which the murderer Wozzeck seeks refuge from his own irrevocable identity, momentarily takes precedence over the orchestra in the pit. The parenthetical character of Margret's Song is reflected at its conclusion not only in the resumption of the earlier tempo (♩ = 40 of mm. 161ff. returns as ♩ = 80 for mm. 180ff.), but also in Wozzeck's immediate repetition of the *Ländler* motive (*Leitmotiv* No. 19) in which he had previously uttered his request for Margret's Song.[24]

In both of the above scenes, changes of tempo as metronomically indicated share a common factor. In I/1 that factor is 6:

Prelude, Pavane	= 10 × 6
Cadenza, Gigue, Cadenza	= 9 × 6
Gavotte, Double I	= 7 × 6
Double II, Air, Reprise	= 5 × 6

In III/3 the common factor of the metronome markings is 10. In III/1 the metronome markings share a factor of 7. The presence of such a common factor facilitates the compositional exploitation of proportional relations between different tempi, as in the curtain music of Change of Scene III/1–2. By the simple device of allowing seven quarters for the falling and six quarters for the rising curtain, both curtains are given the same duration, though the tempo has changed from ♩ = 49 to ♩ = 42.

The composer's motivation in assigning ♩ = 62 1/2 to a phrase merely six quarters in duration, of which only three quarters are in tempo, is rather more difficult to discover. The phrase occurs in the *Melodram* of II/4, the tempi of which are metronomically represented as follows:

m. 605	♩ = 75	(6 × 12 1/2)
m. ⌐ 610	♩ = 100	(8 × 12 1/2)
m. 618	♩ = 75	(6 × 12 1/2)
m. ⌐ 622	♩ = 112 1/2	(9 × 12 1/2)
m. ⌐ 625	♩ = 62 1/2	(5 × 12 1/2)
m. 627	♩ = 75	(6 × 12 1/2)
m. 633	♩ = 100	(8 × 12 1/2)

These proportional relations allow for an overlapping of the tempi of different sections in terms of equivalent durational elements:

$$♩ = 75 \quad ♩ = 100 \quad ♩ = 75 \quad ♩ = 112\ 1/2$$

The durational value of the dotted half-note is projected within the 4/4 meter at mm. 605–608, where the 3/4 *Ländler* tune, returning in the stage band at the close of the preceding dialogue between Wozzeck and Andres, continues in spite of

24 The "real" character of the stage music is also shown in the stage accompanist's "grace notes" as he catches up with the singer in m. 169, and in Margret's disorientation as to pitch, in her repetition of the tune a semitone lower in mm. 174–179.

the entrance of the ♩ Chorale melody. In mm. 606–608 and again in m. 618 there are quarter-note triplets which anticipate the "Marschtempo," ♩ = 112 1/2. The following *subito largo*, ♩ = 62 1/2, is heard, rather, as a *poco più mosso*, if the "counted" durational value is halved: 𝅗𝅥 = 56 1/4 is replaced by ♩ = 62 1/2. The *ritardando* in m. 626 will lead into the return of the faster original tempo, 𝅗𝅥 = 75, at mm. 627ff., if we assume that the slackening quarter-note is replaced by the half-note (= 37 1/2) at the *a tempo*. The *subito largo* is exceptional in that there is no equivalence of durational units between this tempo and the other tempi of the *Melodram*. (The composer has here preferred to imply this non-equivalence by multiplying the common factor, 12 1/2, by a number, 5, that occurs nowhere else as a multiple of the common factor and that is prime to the other multiples of 12 1/2 in the metronome markings of the *Melodram*, rather than by discarding the common factor of the whole section.)[25]

Conclusion

If I have not attempted to establish the coherence and unity of the work as a whole in terms of the interdependence and interaction of all the structural elements discussed in the foregoing survey, it is not because I am unaware of the importance and desirability of doing so. But the criteria upon which overall continuity depends cannot be determined apart from a fuller and more systematic presentation of such elements than can be offered here and now. Premature generalizations will not only fail to elucidate the larger relationships: they must also ignore or distort the very details whose integration into the total work it is their chief business to explain.

Perhaps it is in any case tendentious to assume that the many different compositional procedures and techniques in *Wozzeck* must be integrated as components of a single comprehensive system. We see the analyst's responsibility as the explication of such a system because of our training and experience with a vast musical literature in which every simultaneity and every progression are referable to a single type of chord structure and a few fundamental principles of voice leading.[26] But is such an approach productive when we are confronted with such an amalgam of styles and methods as we find, for example, in III/1: triadic tonality, non-serial "atonal" elements, an ordered twelve-tone set, and a variety of chordal patterns moving in strictly parallel motion?

In our first chapter we described the Three Pieces for Orchestra as an essential preparation for the composition of *Wozzeck* and cited a number of strikingly similar passages in the two works. There is nevertheless an all-important distinction in basic technical procedures. In *Wozzeck* the composer

25 Given Berg's proclivity for seeing omens in numbers, he might have been influenced in his decision to maintain 12 1/2 as a factor even here, where it has no practical meaning, and to ask for 62 1/2 rather than a more conventional metronome mark—that in performance would have been indistinguishable from 62 1/2—by the number of the bar (625) in which the tempo change occurs.

26 Cf. Perle 77b, p. 162.

faced "the necessity of giving each scene and each accompanying interlude an unmistakable aspect, a rounded-off and finished character."[27] In fulfilling this "necessity" he evolved a harmonic language that was far more differentiated, a language that provided articulative means which were not yet available to him at the time of the Three Pieces. In *Wozzeck* unity and contrast are no longer dependent on large-scale thematic connections, thematic transformations, and contrapuntal thematic operations. Indeed, the autonomy of each scene depends not only on characteristic and differentiated formal and structural procedures, but also on certain "rounded-off and finished" themes and motives that remain self-contained and independent of one another in a way that the themes and motives of the Three Pieces do not.

A development in the same direction—toward greater clarity and differentiation—is found in the respective scoring of the two works. In his lecture Berg himself speaks of his endeavor

> to satisfy my desire for unity and integration, as well as for variety and multiplicity of form, by utilizing possibilities of orchestration and of instrumental combination. You will find not infrequently in this opera sections or even whole scenes (like this one [II/3]) to which a specific sonorous body remains attached. In this way a small instrumental group—in the manner of an "obbligato"—is attached to the little Suite-movement of scene 1, Act I, for instance: five woodwinds and three kettledrums and a harp, or three flutes, or four brass instruments only, or the quartet of strings. One self-contained section of scene 2, Act I, is entirely concerned with the sonority of muted brass and strings playing col legno; a fugal episode of scene 1, Act III is limited to the sound of five solo strings only. Finally the orchestration of the very last scene of the opera might be mentioned, the scene of the playing children, from which oboes, bassoons, trombones and doublebasses are totally excluded.[28]

A similar diversity of timbre is called for in the vocal parts as well. Aside from the general distinction between *Sprechstimme* (according to the principles first formulated by Schoenberg for *Pierrot lunaire*) and the singing voice, there are the distinctions in tonal quality implied in the terms "spoken," "half-sung," "*parlando,*" and "*cantabile,*" and still more subtle timbral contrasts that cannot be explicitly indicated but which the composer suggests by the liberal use of such emotive terms as "anxiously," "coyly," "ironically," "admiringly," "urgently," "mysteriously," "passionately," etc.[29]

Here the principles that govern the musical language of the opera and those that govern the very utterance of the text itself converge. And indeed, in his essay, "The Preparation and Staging of Wozzeck," Berg insists that for the production and staging of the opera "not only is a precise knowledge of the Büchner drama assumed, but also of the music, at least so far as its character

27 Berg 27, MM.　　28 Redlich 57b, pp. 276f.
29 Cf. Berg's criticism of a famous Wagnerian soprano in a letter to his wife: "A very good voice . . . but completely soulless . . . completely colorless, without any modulation or adaptability to such simple musical qualities as you can find in the music: e.g., tragic, heroic, frightening, grand, lyrical, etc." (Berg 71, p. 336).

and its language, its dramatic style, is concerned. . . . Knowledge of the music and of the diversity that has been sought in every respect, and which is also found in the musical language of the individual scenes, will lead in itself to a similar diversity (in every respect) in the stage design."[30]

30 Appendix I.

"EINS NACH DEM ANDERN"

"It has been months now since I've done any more work on *Wozzeck.* Everything suffocated, buried!" These despairing words to his wife in a letter dated August 22, 1916, suggest that at least at times during the earlier months of his first year of military service Berg had found it possible to put in some work on the opera. Because of his preoccupation with the Three Pieces for Orchestra, which was only completed about the time of his induction in August of 1915, he had not been able before that date to continue beyond the first sketches that he had attempted fifteen months earlier, immediately after viewing the Viennese première of the drama. The composer's own chronology dismisses whatever work he did on the composition before 1917: in his 1927 article on *Wozzeck*[1] he wrote, "It has been ten years since I started to compose it," and two years later in another version of the same article this is changed to "twelve years."[2] The inception of the composition is thus placed in the period of the first letter to Schoenberg, written during a leave of absence from military service in August, 1917, in which he referred to this project "planned more than three years ago." His expectation that his return to "slavery" would preclude "the coherent writing down of any considerable section" was confirmed, according to a letter dated July 23, 1918, in which he informed Schoenberg that he was once more at work on *Wozzeck* after a "year-long interruption" and "several unsuccessful attempts to write some piano pieces, or chamber music." This resumption of work on the opera was again made possible by a leave of absence, spent, like the preceding, at the home of his wife's parents at Trahütten in southwest Styria. Here he remained until the end of August, and managed, as he was

1 Berg 27, MM.   2 Berg 30, *Anbruch.*

already able to write to Webern on August 19, to "get something finished."[3] According to Reich,[4] he had commenced his work on the opera in the previous summer with the second scene of Act II, and it is perhaps to that scene that this statement refers. This supposition is supported by a letter to his wife in which he described his return alone to the family home after seeing her off on a brief journey: "I myself walked uphill very slowly, frequently resting, 'according to regulations,' and finally, as I proceeded with heavy steps, there actually occurred to me—though I wasn't planning to work—a long-sought idea for an entrance of Wozzeck's." In all probability the reference is to Wozzeck's theme in the triple fugue of II/2, the character of which conforms to this description of its inception and to which he assigns the tempo-marking *schwer* (Ex. 21). It was in this same letter to Helene that the composer spoke of his identification, "during these years of war," with the protagonist of his opera.[5]

With the end of the war in November, 1918, and his release from military service, Berg continued to be beset by obligations that left him little time to devote to composition. Some months earlier he had written to his wife of Schoenberg's "magnificent idea of founding, in the coming season, a society which would offer its members weekly performances of compositions dating from 'Mahler to the present,' and possibly more than one performance of the same work, if it is a difficult one."[6] As soon as the war was over, this "Society for Private Musical Performances" was formed in Vienna, under the permanent presidency of Schoenberg. The management of the Society, including organizational work, supervision of rehearsals, etc., was largely Berg's responsibility. The small monthly stipend for this time-consuming work was supplemented by the income that Berg received from a few private students of composition and from money contributed by his family, on whose behalf he undertook the management of several houses that they owned in Vienna.[7] Writing from the Berghof, the family estate in Carinthia, in the summer of 1919 he was able to report to Schoenberg that he was slowly making progress on the composition of *Wozzeck*, having completed the first act and a large scene (presumably Scene 2) of the second act.

A few months later he found himself " 'commanded,' by a power just as questionable as that of the military in its time,"[8] to return to the Berghof in order to assume, at the urgent insistence of his mother, the management of the estate—a responsibility which not only left him no time whatsoever for composition but which also forced him to give up, for the time being, the other musical activities that he had pursued in Vienna. His letters to Helene, who remained in Vienna, reflected his anxiety for her safety and welfare in view of the appalling difficulties and uncertainties of living conditions in the capital of post-war Austria, "where everything is shut down and life becomes more impossible every day."[9] On April 19, 1920, he wrote to Schulhoff:

3 Reich 53, *SM*, p. 50.   4 Reich 65, p. 45.   5 Berg 65, p. 376.
6 Ibid., p. 364.   7 Reich 65, p. 50, and Berg 65, p. 414.   8 Reich 63, p. 48.
9 Berg 65, p. 424.

My stay here, which is devoted to the settlement of family affairs, is coming to an end, thank God. Now I'll be able to attend once more to *myself* and *my own* affairs. After four months! *Surely* my physical ailments could all be lanced like a cyst once I were permitted to compose. But the world around me (whether it be the military, family, earning a living, etc.) has robbed and continues to rob me of more than half my life, and it is *this* which makes me sick. Nothing else! Now I have hope that I will get better.[10]

The sale of the Berghof brought Berg's exile to an end. During July and August he was again at Trahütten, at work on *Wozzeck* and uneasily anticipating a career as a musical journalist upon his return to Vienna at the end of the summer, having accepted the editorship of the semi-monthly *Musikblättern des Anbruch*, published by Universal Edition. On August 14 he wrote to Webern:

If I didn't *have* to do it, if I didn't stand before the necessity of scraping some means of existence, I would write to Hertzka today and throw the whole thing over, come what might, and spend the winter here and compose my opera and finish the instrumentation. But as it is, I have to stake my immediate future (or my whole future?) on a "career" (horrible word) that means nothing to me but the bare possibility of existence.[11]

Berg's plan to assume the editorship of *Anbruch* did not materialize. Writing to Schulhoff on December 16, he explained his lapses as a correspondent:

During the autumn, except for a few interruptions, I was very sick for three months. Twice in the sanitorium. A sort of nervous breakdown connected with my constant affliction of asthma. Afterward my ability to work (something that was more than ever necessary for my livelihood) was so diminished that in general I could attend to correspondence only when the water was up to my mouth—no, over my head. Now, when things are going better with me again, I'm working as usual: giving lessons, doing musical literary work,[12] directing Schoenberg's Society during his absence (he is in Amsterdam for six months). Besides, I have just had two things of mine published (at my own expense! A pair of antique objects from the house had to pay for it): one quartet (score and parts) and four short clarinet pieces. So in addition there was the killing task of proof-reading![13]

Thanks to his wife's stay at the Alpine health resort, Bad Hofgastein, we have between June 9 and July 4, 1921, a series of letters from Berg that are in effect a detailed personal diary. There are numerous references to his work on the scene that he found "most difficult of all," the tavern scene of Act II. "What I have in mind to write is slowly, quite slowly, taking shape. (Don't mention anything about this to Mathilde. Her husband [Schoenberg] thinks I'm working on the book!)"[14] The "book" in question was to be a study of the life and work of Schoenberg, a project to which Berg had apparently more or

10 Vojtěch 65, p. 58.   11 Reich 65, pp. 52f.
   12 Though Berg did not assume the position of editor, he "was still working for 'Anbruch' in 1921" according to Reich 65, p. 53, who, however, does not specify the nature of this work. The "musical literary work" that Berg mentions may be in connection with his projected book on Schoenberg, mentioned below.
   13 Vojtěch op. cit., pp. 59f.   14 Berg 65, pp. 456 and 457.

less committed himself, but which he found it impossible to realize. On June 11 he was able to report more progress on the opera: "When my thoughts are not quite completely with you, as they are now after your two mournful letters, I am continually preoccupied with *Wozzeck*. This tavern scene is going slowly, but it's going. If it succeeds as I now dimly imagine it, the biggest hurdle is overcome and the rest a game in comparison."[15] (The same scene was to prove the "biggest hurdle" again four-and-a-half years later, when the work was in rehearsal for its first performance.)[16]

"I spent the afternoon after 4 o'clock at home and wrote something for the Society again," he wrote on June 23. "Unfortunately, this interferes with my work, so that I get fearfully depressed." A further cause of depression was the news that Helene had to remain at Hofgastein longer than they had anticipated. But—significantly, for Berg, on the 23rd of the month[17]—he had "reason to be in a better mood," for he had joyful news for Helene:

> The American Relief Administration, which recently sent me a form to fill out, has sent me a kind invitation . . . to fetch two packages of provisions: altogether, 22 kg flour, 9 kg rice, 10 kg bacon, 2 dozen corned beef (that's 6 1/2 kg), 2 1/4 kg lard, 12 dozen milk, 6 kg sugar, 1 kg cocoa, 3 3/4 kg oil, and 10 dozen salmon. What do you say to that?!!! That comes to about 80 kg of provisions! I can't even calculate the value. Perhaps 10,000 to 20,000 crowns (or more?).[18]

As late as June of 1921 Berg was still preoccupied with the "disposition of the scenes in *Wozzeck*," according to his letter of the 17th. So far as Act I was concerned, this problem had already been solved. The completion of this act had been reported to Schoenberg in Berg's letter of July 29, 1919.[19] His hope, expressed in that letter, that he would complete Act II during the same summer was still unrealized almost two years later, as we know from his letters of June, 1921, to Helene, in which he referred to his work on the *Wirtshausszene*. From Berg's letter to Schoenberg of July 27, 1920, in which he illustrated a musical conceit that he used in *Wozzeck*—although he made no reference to the opera[20]—we can perhaps surmise that he was at work on the third scene of Act II during his summer months at Trahütten that year. In August of 1921 he was again at Trahütten, nearing, at last, the completion of the short score, and asking Schoenberg to grant him an extension of his leave of absence from the Society since he would not be able to achieve this, as he had hoped, by September 1. According to Reich, the short score was completed in October.[21]

Even before completing the instrumentation and preparing a proper vocal score of the opera, Berg made some attempt to interest opera directors in the work. In December Eduard Steuermann performed the Piano Sonata in Darmstadt and Frankfurt, and Berg travelled with him, having taken advantage

15 Ibid., p. 458.   16 Ibid., pp. 545–552 *passim*.   17 See pp. 127ff., above.
18 Berg 65, p. 470. The continuing hardship of life in Vienna almost two years later is indicated in Schoenberg's letter of April 24, 1923, in which he recommended Berg, Webern, and Hauer as "cases of extreme need" to the American Relief Fund for German and Austrian Musicians (Schoenberg 65, pp. 87f.).   19 See p. 28, above.
20 See pp. 124f., above.   21 Reich 65, p. 55, but see Chapter Two, fn. 19.

of the occasion to arrange for Steuermann to play the work from the short score for directors of the opera houses in both cities. The full score was completed in the following spring.[22] Berg's letters to Helene during May, 1922, refer to revisions in the libretto, the preparation (under the composer's direction) of the vocal score by his pupil, Fritz Heinrich Klein, the binding of the full score, and the Frankfurt Stadttheater's refusal to accept the work for performance. To Helene he wrote:

> To whom, other than yourself, am I indebted for *Wozzeck!* To you, because you gave me the *inner* and *outer* peace, through five years, without which I couldn't have written a single bar! And which no one in the world, except *you*, could have given to or taken from me. I will write this to Jeannette [Berg's mother, who had written to congratulate him on the completion of the opera], and tell her at the same time that, apart from the dear Lord, I am grateful to three persons for *Wozzeck:* to Schoenberg (as my teacher, even though he tried to discourage me from doing it);[23] to Jeannette, because she made it possible for me to work on it during the past year-and-a-half without any pecuniary concerns; and to my darling, for the reasons I mentioned earlier! As to the interlude at the end, that I owe *only to you, you composed it* and I only wrote it down. *That's the way it is.* [24]

By the time Berg completed the opera, interest in *Woyzeck* and its author was no longer limited to a small circle of avant-garde enthusiasts. The increasing influence of social-democratic cultural and political attitudes in the postwar period and the rise of the expressionist theater had converged to make Büchner a subject of topical concern both for scholars and for the general public.[25] New editions of the collected works appeared in 1916 (Hausenstein), 1922 (Bergemann), and 1923 (A. Zweig). There were numerous separate reprints of *Woyzeck* in both practical and scholarly editions, as well as dissertations, monographs, and articles. The foremost director of the time, Max Reinhardt, staged his much discussed version of the drama for the first time on April 5, 1921. A growing public shared the excitement of discovering a still controversial work of the most striking contemporary relevance by a genius who had only

---

22 Berg's letters of May, 1922, refer to the "completed" full score. He continued to retouch the work—making numerous small changes in metronome and dynamic markings, for example—after the publication of the vocal score.

23 Karl Rankl, a pupil of Schoenberg's when Berg was working on the opera, recalls that "Schoenberg disapproved of Berg's choice [of a subject], and argued that music should deal 'rather with angels than with batmen'" (Rankl 52, *Score*, p. 43). Another reason for Schoenberg's disapproval of the subject is reported by Berg's pupil, Gottfried Kassowitz (68, *ÖM*): "Berg was once quite upset, after he had already been working on *Wozzeck* for a while. In answer to my question he told me that he had just spoken of *Wozzeck* to Schoenberg for the first time and that Schoenberg had expressed the opinion that it was impossible to make something good of it. Why? Because 'Wozzeck' was an antimusical, unsingable name! Berg was so much under Schoenberg's influence that at first he was actually hesitant." Even after the opera was finished Schoenberg persisted in his negative attitude for a time. In a letter to his wife on April 8, 1923, Berg described a visit with Schoenberg: "[He] was impossible again, and criticized everything about me: that I am still always working on *Wozzeck* ('This is Karl Krausish, this continual revising!'); that I smoke; that I *should not imagine that I will have a success with Wozzeck,* because it's too difficult."

24 Berg 65, p. 487. The source of the D minor theme of the final interlude is discussed above, p. 12, fn. 28.

25 See Strudthoff 57.

just emerged from obscurity eighty years after his death at the age of 23 and was already assured of a place in the pantheon of German literature.

Given the importance of the operatic theater in the cultural and social life of Germany and Austria, the news that Büchner's drama had been made into an opera could not fail to arouse interest, in spite of the obscurity of the composer. Berg, upon completing the work, reported this fact to a number of musical journals and came to the daring decision to publish the vocal score himself, as he had each of his earlier works that had so far appeared in print. The money for this could not be raised by selling "a pair of antique objects from the house," as it had been for the publication of the quartet and the clarinet pieces. Berg borrowed the necessary funds from his sister's close friend, May Keller, and by the end of the year the engraved vocal score was ready. Alma Mahler, the composer's widow and a close friend of the Bergs, repaid the debt, as she reports in her memoirs:

> Now the opera was finished. Alban and Helene Berg came to me, showed me the score, and asked me to accept the dedication of the work. They were in trouble: a friend who had lent them money to have the score printed was pressing for repayment. The matter weighed heavily on the Bergs, and having taken up collections in the past for Schoenberg and others, I went on another begging tour and raised the missing sum in short order.[26]

In January, 1923, Berg sent out printed cards announcing the publication of the vocal score: "Permit me to inform you that the vocal score of my opera *Wozzeck* (after the drama by Georg Büchner) has just appeared. The edition consists of 230 large quarto pages, costs 150,000 Austrian crowns, and may be obtained directly from me. Respectfully yours, Alban Berg, Vienna XIII, Trauttmansdorffgasse 27." In the same month Erwin Stein's three-page introduction to the music of Berg and Webern was published in *Anbruch*.[27] *Wozzeck* is described as an innovative work in that it returns to the concept of closed forms in dramatic music. The design of each act and each scene is named and the dramatic and musical purpose of the formal plan is summarized: "By reason of the fact that they contain something organically necessary and are thus drama in themselves, [the forms] create a sense of outward concentration of

26 Werfel 58, p. 181. These memoirs are also published in a German version (Mahler 60) which differs in numerous particulars from the English. In respect to the publication of the vocal score of *Wozzeck* we read in the German (p. 77): "Since Universal Edition didn't want to print *Wozzeck* at its own expense, the money for the publication was advanced by a friend of Berg's sister—to be sure, only for a limited time, and then she asked for repayment ahead of time. Now I went on a begging tour again and raised the money in short order, so that it was possible finally to get on with the printing." However, it does not appear that Berg had any serious discussion with Emil Hertzka, director of Universal Edition, prior to the appearance of the privately printed score. He signed an agreement with Hertzka on April 13, 1923, after having approached the American firm, G. Schirmer, at Alma Mahler's suggestion. (In both the English and the German version of her memoirs, a faulty recollection respecting Berg is reported on the same page from which each of the above quotations is taken. It was not Berg but Webern who had presumably "wavered between Schoenberg and Hans Pfitzner" in seeking a teacher, and it was not Webern but Berg who had composed "Altenbergs Ansichtskarten.")

27 Stein 23, *Anbruch*.

the dramatic moments."[28] In thus stressing the formal aspects of the work, Stein struck the keynote for all subsequent critical discussion. Clearly, Berg himself must have regarded this emphasis as appropriate and useful: Stein was a friend and had been a fellow-student under Schoenberg, and we can assume that the line he followed in introducing the opera must have had Berg's approval and may even have been prompted by the composer, a probability suggested by the fact that Berg saw fit to include a facsimile of the formal outline prepared by his pupil, Fritz Mahler, in each distributed copy of the published vocal score. This assumption finds further support in an article published in October of the same year by another of Berg's pupils, Fritz Heinrich Klein, the arranger of the piano reduction.[29] Four years later, in "A Word About *Wozzeck*,"[30] Berg denied that the individuation of formal units in the opera was motivated by any purpose that transcended the specific problems created by his text, but his implied disclaimer of any responsibility for the emphasis placed by the critics on this aspect of the work seems a bit disingenuous. In any event, the thesis that the employment of forms traditionally associated with "absolute" music represented a post-Wagnerian operatic "reform" provided a useful handle for the journalists in a domain—the musical theater —where publicity is the life-blood of a new work.

In April of 1923 the earliest article exclusively devoted to *Wozzeck* was published, an enthusiastic appraisal of the vocal score that was all the more appreciated by Berg because the author was personally unknown to him. Viebig's remarkably perceptive and comprehensive essay[31] and Universal Edition's acceptance at this time of both *Wozzeck* and the Three Pieces for Orchestra led Berg, as he wrote to his wife on April 11, to anticipate

> a worthy première in the coming season. . . . The article in *Die Musik* is fabulous. Three pages of the most devoted praise, then, in conclusion, the usual grumbling about performance problems, to be sure, so that the striking effect of the article is somewhat weakened, but hopefully made up again by the musical supplement, a photographically reduced reproduction of the Cradle Song, of which the author says: "It is one of the greatest lyrical inspirations to be found in recent operatic literature." . . . If only [Schoenberg] knew about the article in *Die Musik*, which speaks continuously of the *novelty* in everything that belongs to this style, and which discloses all of its *formal secrets* (the Suite, etc.)! I'm so glad that *Klein* comes out so fabulously in the article (and with him the arrangement)! The content is also very well reported, that is to say, what is purely human (the common folk) is stressed, rather than the fate of an individual. He especially praises my stage adaptation into three acts (15 scenes out of Büchner's 25 scenes). And *everything so right*, as though I had told him. I hadn't thought it possible that anyone could come upon it by *himself, everything* that I had intended in *Wozzeck*: morally, theatrically, musically, etc., etc.[32]

28 Stein 22, *Chesterian*, p. 35 (an English translation of the article subsequently printed in *Anbruch*).

29 Klein 23, *Anbruch*. For a reprint of the outline see Mahler 57.

30 Berg 27, *MM*.   31 Viebig 23, *M*.   32 Berg 65, pp. 507f.

Though Berg was disappointed in his hope that Viebig's article would help to bring the opera to the stage in the coming season, it did lead to further publicity for the work, in the form of a polemical attack against Viebig's position in the February, 1924, issue of *Die Musik*[33] and a rejoinder by Berg in the same magazine three months later.[34]

Meanwhile, "after standing still for fifteen years," Berg's career was about to "move forward with giant strides," as he wrote to Helene upon concluding his agreement with Universal Edition.[35] In June, 1923, eight years after their completion, the orchestra pieces were performed for the first time when Webern conducted the first and second movements in Berlin. Two months later the Quartet was performed with great success in Salzburg at the first annual festival of the International Society for Contemporary Music. Among the auditors was Hermann Scherchen, already well known for his sponsorship of new music, who expressed an interest in conducting excerpts from *Wozzeck* in a concert version during the following season. The "Three Excerpts for Voice and Orchestra from *Wozzeck*" owes its origin to Scherchen's request. Comprising the music of Change of Scene I/2–3 through the conclusion of the Cradle Song, the opening scene and following interlude of Act III, and Change of Scene III/4–5 through the final scene (with the soprano soloist taking the vocal part assigned to the children), it was premièred in Frankfurt in June, 1924, and was an immediate and extraordinary success with critics and public alike.

Some months before this, Erich Kleiber had given Berg assurances of his intention to produce the opera. Considering the controversy that had surrounded his appointment as musical director of the Berlin State Opera in the previous season, at the age of only thirty-three, Kleiber's decision was a bold and courageous one. In welcoming him to his post, the Intendant, Max von Schillings, had written: "We must realise that a part of the press will be very much in arms against you. Already they are creating a most horrible atmosphere in readiness for your arrival. . . . But once you are really installed we will make it clear that you can revise the whole repertory as you like."[36] The difficulties culminated in Schillings's sudden resignation less than three weeks before the première of *Wozzeck*, presumably because of a dispute with the agency responsible for the state subsidy. John Russell, in his biography of Kleiber, suggests that the widely accepted fiction that "137 full rehearsals" preceded the first performance was invented by those who

> would have liked to see Kleiber follow Schillings into retirement. . . . For months beforehand it had been put about that *Wozzeck* was occupying a disproportionate amount of the Staatsoper's time. Rehearsals beyond number were said to be throwing the rest of the repertory into disorder: and even today, in serious histories of the period, there is talk of "137 full rehearsals." Those who were in the original production remember that there were, on the contrary, no more than

33 Petschnig 24, *M.*   34 Berg 24, *M.*
35 Berg 65, p. 510.   36 Russell 57, p. 65.

thirty-four orchestra rehearsals for what is still a prodigiously difficult piece: and Kleiber himself once pointed out that when *Wozzeck* was revived in 1926 only one full rehearsal had to be called.[37]

Kleiber's opponents went so far, according to Russell, as to circulate false rumors to the effect that he secretly wished to be rid of Schillings and had intrigued behind the scenes toward this end. It seems altogether improbable that Kleiber could have been thus preoccupied while preparing the première performance of Berg's "unperformable" opera, or that he could have wished to add to the controversy that already surrounded the work by secretly provoking a serious crisis at this very moment.

In the event, the forthcoming production became a central issue in the campaign against Kleiber. Berg arrived in Berlin to attend rehearsals only three days after Schillings's dismissal. He wrote to Helene on December 2, just thirteen days before the scheduled première:

> The press puts out nothing that is favorable to Kleiber. Pieces cut out of the latest local rags! There's still time to call it off. Until the 14th Kleiber conducts three more times at the Opera. *There* we'll find out whether or not the public is *against* him. There's *no sign* of opposition on the part of the personnel and orchestra. *On the contrary!* Their awareness of the kind of individual this is is far too powerful. And to give up, because of anxiety, a performance like what we'll have with Kleiber —Schützendorf[38]—*this* orchestra—*this* direction, would be insanity. To do that, as I've said, there's still time. Even if it were 6 o'clock on the evening of December 14th! Besides, at the same time there will be a big *orchestral concert* with *Siegfried Wagner* and Kemp![39] That's where all our adversaries will be!!![40]

Ten years later, after Kleiber had resigned his post in protest against the *Kulturpolitik* of the Nazi dictatorship and *Wozzeck* had been banned from every German stage, the following authorized account of the circumstances that surrounded the Intendant's dismissal was published in *Max von Schillings: der Kampf eines deutschen Künstlers*:

> The degeneration of German cultural life now stretched without hindrance over ever widening circles. The hegemony of atonality in music was now assured. In the State Opera every available means to do honor to the Schoenbergian, Alban Berg, is set up. Kleiber and Hörth, both appointed by Schillings, to his own misfortune, compete in their ardent efforts on behalf of the most consummate presentation of a stage work that drives the German spirit out of the temple of the State Opera with an unequivocal gesture. Kleiber triumphs once again over the dismissed Intendant, who had opposed the acceptance of *Wozzeck* and is blameless for the unique scandal evoked by the première of an opera that had until then been characterized as "unplayable."[41]

In fairness to the man who had appointed Kleiber as musical director of the State Opera and who had promised him a free hand to "revise the whole rep-

---

37 Ibid., p. 94.

38 Leo Schützendorf and Sigrid Johanson played the leading roles at the première.

39 Barbara Kemp, the wife of Schillings and a celebrated dramatic soprano, was originally supposed to create the part of Marie (Adorno 68, p. 37).

40 Berg 65, p. 549.   41 Raupp 35, p. 274.

ertory," it should be pointed out that he had died two years before the publication of his official "biography."

The reviews of the open dress-rehearsal that preceded the première show to what an extent *Wozzeck* had become a touchstone of attitudes on various intersecting ideological, aesthetic, social, political, professional, and personal issues.[42] The critics who wished to use Berg as a club with which to beat Schoenberg described him as "the most intransigent of all the Schoenbergians." (Later, after the indisputable and continuing success of the opera, they were to describe him, for the same reason, as "the *least* intransigent.") Parallels were drawn between the political and the musical situation: "Where anarchism in political life will take the nations may be a question of the future for politicians. Where it has taken us in art is already manifest. The young talents have had their fling and left us a rubbish dump, on which for years henceforth nothing will grow or prosper."

Berg had written to his wife on December 6: "Whether Kleiber stands or falls depends on the success of this première." Those who looked forward to Kleiber's fall were already committed in their judgment of the opera. Ultimately, neither the propaganda of its opponents nor the counter-propaganda of those who had reason to hope that the work would be well received could influence its fate. But there were newspapers that went so far as to publish false news-reports in what can only have been a deliberate attempt to provoke a scandal that would force the work and its conductor from the stage. The *Berliner Lokalanzeiger* covered the dress rehearsal under the headings, "Scandal in the State Opera House—Riot at the Dress Rehearsal—The *Wozzeck* Performance Leads to Heated Altercations." The trouble was supposed to have been initiated by Schoenberg's followers, whose applause provoked a "passionate counter-demonstration." In another paper the distinguished critic, art historian, and musicologist, Oskar Bie, urged the public not to be disturbed by "exaggerated reports that may have their origin in circumstances that have to do with certain personal motivations. I can already say that in producing this work our opera house is offering one of its most creditable and successful achievements. Therefore, remain calm and objective!"

Even after the première and three subsequent performances had been received with enormous acclaim by the public, a section of the press continued to publish fabricated accounts of disturbances at the opera house. The *Lokalanzeiger* falsely reported that the fourth performance on January 7 was terminated before the completion of the third act because of demonstrations in which even some members of the orchestra were supposed to have taken part. The *Deutsche Zeitung* warned of the imminent economic collapse of the state theaters, but drew some hopeful conclusions from the alleged disruptions of the performance:

42 The reviews of the Berlin production from which the following quotations are taken were collected and republished in the pamphlet, *Alban Bergs "Wozzeck" und die Musikkritik*, by *Musikblätter des Anbruch* [1926].

After the first performance of *Wozzeck* our music critic, in connection with his complete rejection of the work, wrote as follows:

"The only hope that remains is that the public in its overwhelming majority will not be prepared to take a seat in the Augean stable of Berg's art, that it will not quietly submit to the vulgarity that goes hand-in-hand with tediousness in the scenes of *Wozzeck*, and that an indefinable but sure instinct will prevent it from following the road down which Mr. Kleiber is descending. The forthcoming performances must show whether this instinct still endures, or whether the pestilence continues to devour everything around it."

We have, in fact, nothing more to add to this today. The hope expressed in these statements has not been vain. The public is prepared to defend itself. The opera *Wozzeck* has been dispatched and Mr. Erich Kleiber has been given a lesson which will surely wipe the smile from his face. If the work is scheduled again, further disturbances should not be ruled out.

In spite of this campaign to incite disruptions that would prevent a repetition, *Wozzeck* received six more performances in Berlin during its first season. By and large, both the public and the critics sensed with Dr. Adolf Aber, chief critic of a Leipzig paper, that the work before them was one "whose great intrinsic qualities will still be valid when there will be no one left who remembers the current crisis of the Berlin Opera." There were even those who knew at once that *Wozzeck* was an event in the general cultural history of the period, not merely another successful opera. Max Lesser, cultural critic of the *Neue Wiener Tagblatt*, described the impact of the first performance only at second hand, as one who judged the significance of the work by its effect upon those who had seen it—as he had not—and who were more gifted with musical insight than himself:

What has happened? A composer whose name has not yet penetrated beyond a circle of professional musicians goes from Vienna to Berlin and has a work performed. The event occurs on December 14, 1925, and the next day the cultural world knows the name of Alban Berg. . . . Once again we witness the rare and thus all the more gladdening spectacle of a great spirit coming into view. We live to see that an artistic achievement of the highest order needs only to be presented in order to win the hearts of all that are susceptible to it. . . . One feels that the expressive possibilities of art have been enlarged, and one is grateful and delighted, not less as an observer standing outside than as a connoisseur who possesses the means of understanding.

Even before *Wozzeck* had been put to the test in Berlin, Otakar Ostrčil, principal conductor of the Czech National Opera, had expressed his intention to produce the opera, as we learn from the letter that Berg, in Prague to attend the third ISCM Festival and to hear Zemlinsky conduct the excerpts from *Wozzeck*, wrote to Helene on May 16, 1925. The Prague production, the first outside of Berlin, opened on November 11, 1926. Here, as in Berlin, there was a politically motivated campaign against the opera—a campaign organized, ironically enough, by Czech nationalists who chose to demonstrate their *anti*-Germanic sentiment by an attack on the same work (in spite of its translation into Czech) that the German nationalists had attacked as being non-representative of German art. Describing the situation in Prague in a letter to Kleiber, Berg wrote: "Most of the Czech nationalists' agitation was and is directed against [Ostrčil], because he doesn't put on the *Bartered Bride* seven evenings a week."[43] An unfortunate coincidence, the fatal apoplectic stroke suffered by the deputy mayor while attending the opera, played into the hands of the nationalists. Disorders during the third performance, which took place on the day of the funeral, caused the police to clear the theater after the second act and to place a ban on further performances.

A third production opened in Leningrad on June 13, 1927. The performance, according to Berg's wire to his wife, was "a huge, tumultuous success." The few days that the composer spent in Leningrad were a memorable and gratifying experience, as he recalled in a subsequent interview:

> On the way from the station to my lodging house I was truly dismayed: my name and the name of my work stared down at me in giant letters from every street corner, every hoarding and every advertising pillar. That taught me straight away that in Leningrad a première is not a matter that concerns only a couple of experts whose reports then decree whether or not a larger public will interest itself in the following performances.[44]

The work had been in preparation for six months and Berg was pleased with every aspect of the production, including, though he knew no Russian, "the poet Kusmin's translation of the text [which] was proclaimed masterly. I can report with satisfaction that the thing was a success and that the reviews were good without exception. A toast proposed by a young Russian composer at the banquet given in my honor is enough to show how they appreciate modern music in Russia: the toast ended 'Bottoms up to Arnold Schoenberg, the teacher of all living composers!' " Other observers gave a rather different picture of the reception accorded the opera. A report from Leningrad in the September, 1927, issue of *Die Musik* summed up the impression made by the work as follows:

> At the close of this year's season Alban Berg's *Wozzeck* was given as the final novelty, with the composer present. The impression is a very diversified one: enthusiastic acceptance and decisive rejection. The presence of the composer was not least in contributing to its success. In spite of every objection to the generally disagreeable music—to which our ears, accustomed as they are to tonal devices of another sort, have still to be recruited—one cannot deny that this music arouses interest.

In the January, 1928, issue of the same journal a tentative prospectus for the forthcoming (1927–28) Leningrad season concludes: "Among last year's productions *Wozzeck* had poor success and will probably have to give way to another work." A projected production at the Bolshoi Theater in Moscow did not materialize.

43 Russell 57, p. 121.
44 Reich 65, p. 69. Reich does not give the source of his quotation.

The contrast between Berg's view of the success of the Russian première of his opera and the view expressed by the Leningrad correspondent of *Die Musik* six months later may be a reflection of changing forces in Russian musical life rather than of different interpretations of the same objective event. Russian musical culture during the mid-twenties was marked by intense partisan activity in support of *various* tendencies in contemporary music and *different* evaluations of the relevance and significance of these tendencies for "proletarian culture." Even in the more susceptible field of literature, it was not yet assumed that styles and techniques could be defined and controlled by bureaucratic injunctions. "Art must make its own way and by its own means," wrote Trotsky in 1924. ". . . The domain of art is not one in which the Party is called upon to command."[45] In the same year the monthly journal *Musical Culture*, edited by the modernist composer Nicolai Roslavetz, published its first issue, bearing the slogan "Music is music, not ideology." In an earlier essay on *Pierrot lunaire* Roslavetz had predicted that "Schoenberg's principles and methods will gradually conquer the thoughts of contemporary artistic youth; already now we can speak of a 'Schoenbergian School' as of a fact, which is of decisive importance for the immediate future of music."[46] Roslavetz opposed the view of the Russian Association of Proletarian Musicians that advanced musical idioms must be rejected because of their inaccessibility to the masses:

> Naturally, I am not a "proletarian composer" in the sense that I compose familiar music in the style of Bortniansky or Galuppi. On the contrary, to such an extent have I become a "bourgeois" that I regard the Russian proletariat as the rightful heir of all of past culture, and it is precisely because of this that I compose my symphonies, quartets, trios, songs, and similar "problems," as [my] critics, in their blessed ignorance, call them. And I am convinced that I will live to see the day when the proletariat will find my music as accessible and comprehensible as it now is to the best representatives of progressive Russian musical society.[47]

Wozzeck was only one among many operas by contemporary composers of Western Europe to be produced in the Soviet Union between 1925 and 1929, with the support of the Association for Contemporary Music. The promotional activities of the ACM on behalf of new music by both native and foreign composers played a leading role in Russian musical life during these years, but then it had to give way to the increasing authority of the Russian Association of Proletarian Musicians as current Soviet culture became increasingly regimented in the name of what the RAPM, in its "Ideological Platform" of 1929, called the "enforcement of hegemony of the proletariat."[48] *Wozzeck*—though neither it nor any other specific work, nor, for that matter, any specific composer, was explicitly cited in this manifesto—would obviously have been condemned by implication as a supposed product of "modern decadent bourgeois art." To this day it has not been revived in the Soviet Union.[49]

45 Trotsky 57, p. 218.   46 Schwarz 65, *PNM*, p. 88.   47 Prieberg [65], p. 57.
48 The complete document is given in Slonimsky 49, pp. 655ff.
49 The dominance of RAPM was short-lived. In 1932 a decree of the Central Committee of the Communist Party established a single Union of Soviet Composers and liquidated RAPM, which was found to be guilty of "all kinds of 'leftist' distortions of Marxism-Leninism, vulgarization, and

Just as the German nationalists' denunciation of *Wozzeck* as a work that was not representative of authentic German culture did not prevent the Czech nationalists from denouncing it for the opposite reason, its exclusion from the Soviet Union because of its "bourgeois decadence" did not inhibit the Nazis, when they came to power in 1933, from banning it in Germany as an example of *Kulturbolschewismus*. Meanwhile, *Wozzeck* had a few more years to make its triumphant way and to earn for Berg an income that at last permitted him, for a time, to concentrate on his work without the distractions and interruptions of pressing material concerns. These few years, "the short decade between 1924 and 1933, from the end of the German inflation to Hitler's seizure of power," were a time—so Berg's friend and compatriot, Stefan Zweig, recalled shortly before his suicide in 1942—that "represents—in spite of all—an intermission in the catastrophic sequence of events whose witnesses and victims our generation has been since 1914."[50] The successful production of *Wozzeck* that opened in Oldenburg on March 5, 1929, proved that this once "unplayable" work was not necessarily beyond the means of a provincial theater. (It was in connection with this production that Berg first presented his musically illustrated public lecture on the opera.)[51] In the following season alone, there were forty performances in eight German opera houses, and by the end of 1932 *Wozzeck* had been staged in seventeen cities in Germany. Characteristically, the composer's home town, Vienna, did not produce the work until March 20, 1930, only one year before the American première in Philadelphia under Leopold Stokowski. Of a performance that he attended in Berlin in the autumn of 1928, Berg remarked that it "was put on without any humbug, just like every other opera in the repertory." Listening to it from the gallery, he found the music "often really *lovely*, even to my present tastes, which have otherwise taken me rather far from this way of composing."[52]

---

pseudo-simplification" (Slonimsky 49, p. 358). But at the same time there was to be no relaxation in the "relentless battle" against "rightist musicians," who, "under the pretense of study of Western-European technique . . . are smuggling in the ideological baggage of the rotting bourgeois world, all these 'atonalities,' jazz harmonies, etc." The decree of 1932, which liquidated not only RAPM but also its "proletarian" counterparts in literature and art, coincided with a political turn away from ultra-leftism and toward the stabilization of relations with other European countries, just as the 1929 manifesto of RAPM had coincided with a political move in the opposite direction: the end of the New Economic Policy and the inauguration of the first Five-Year Plan.

50 Zweig 43, pp. 315f., 326. 51 Redlich 57b, pp. 261ff. 52 Berg 65, pp. 568f.

Appendix I / "THE PREPARATION AND STAGING OF *WOZZECK*"

BY ALBAN BERG

Alban Berg's "Praktische Anweisungen zur Einstudierung des *Wozzeck*," written in 1930 and intended for distribution with the performance materials of *Wozzeck*, was published shortly after the composer's death in Reich 37. In June of 1968 (in *The Musical Times*), the International Alban Berg Society was privileged to offer this important essay, the German edition of which had long been out of print, in an English translation for the first time, with the kind permission of the composer's widow, Frau Helene Berg.

THE MUSIC

The following are essential for the study and performance of the music: (a) the full score incorporating the important corrections given in the list of errata published late in December 1929; (b) the new edition of the vocal score, the title page of which contains the following note: 'This edition revised and provided with additional markings for the vocal parts by the composer'.*

*This sentence was deleted from subsequent printings of the revised edition. (G. P.)

These corrections, or retouchings, concern on the one hand the voice parts, which have been supplied with dynamic indications and the terms 'Recitative', 'Parlando', and 'Cantabile'[1]; and on the other hand revisions of tempo and corrections of metronome marks. The latter are to be taken in a relative rather than in an absolute sense. From performances of recent years I have come to feel that the work as a whole should unfold in a more leisurely manner. I mention this goal of a generally more relaxed presentation because the text and content tend to suggest the opposite conception. Consider for example the last scene of the first act, where the tempo, Andante, is not to be forsaken in spite of the indication 'affettuoso'. Or the last scene of the second act, which one is likely to take too fast, instead of permitting the 'Rondo martiale' to maintain a more bombastic, coarser, almost more portly character. Not to speak of the 'In-

[1] It is important to differentiate between these directions, which indicate where a *cantabile*, that is, a *bel canto* treatment of the voice, is clearly required and feasible, and where it is not.

203

troduction' (Act II, bars 737/744 to 760), the performance of which cannot be too calm and controlled.

The same, it seems to me, applies to the murder scene (III/2), which—in keeping with the very slow tempo of the organ point of 40 bars—suggests a certain solemnity that ought probably not to be interrupted until the moment of the murder!

This new requirement of a generally more leisurely presentation has to do not only with the tempo, but also with the dynamics of the work, which, with the exception, naturally, of the explosions that eventually occur in each scene, is to be thought of as a *'piano* opera'. The achievement of this *piano* requires special attention. The many 'espressivos' of the individual voices (as well as those of the solo strings!) can easily lead one to exaggerate the dynamic indications. In the case of the winds (especially with orchestras that have small string sections) one may easily be misled by the many small crescendo signs. These must be understood within the context of the indicated *pp*, *p*, or *mp*. Special attention is to be paid to *fp*. This dynamic mark actually signifies—when it is found within a soft phrase—not *forte*, but at most a small *sforzando*, whose subsequent *piano* is of the essence. On the other hand, the dynamic indications in my score have given rise to quite a different sort of misunderstanding. For example, where the muted horns are marked *pp* they are often completely inaudible. It will always be clear (as, for example, through the marking of parts as principal or subordinate, or with the sign, ⌐)[2] where the composer's intention is rather to be realized through a stronger or only half-muted tone.

The same often applies to the *col legno* (bowed or struck) strings, where more tone may be achieved through a partial use of the hair of the bow.

In large opera houses, if possible, a

2 In the score and performance material, ⌐ means that the part so designated proceeds in the same rhythm as and constitutes chord-factors with a principal part (**H**) or a subordinate part (**N**). Principal and subordinate parts must be allowed to come through, however.

third pair of horns! They are in any case available in the stage music (Military March in I/3). This will usually be required for the sake of clarity in *tutti* passages, as for example in the change-of-scene music of Act II, bars 713–723, *etc.*

Likewise, wherever possible, two harps! The two parts must naturally be prepared in advance, on the basis of the *one* part now provided in the performance material. It is obvious that the second part should not be a merely mechanical doubling of the first, but that the present part should be distributed between two instruments. Such an arrangement for two harps is planned for the projected performance of *Wozzeck* in Vienna under Professor Franz Jellinek. This arrangement will thereafter be generally applicable.

It is very important that study of the *Wirtshausmusik* (II/4) be begun in good time, and not only in the rehearsal room but also on the stage. The reason for this precaution is that one must make a decision about the size of the instrumental group while there is still time, and this decision depends on the placing of the small ensemble on the stage and on the acoustics of the house. It will then become clear, above all, how many violins (fiddles) and how many guitars may be needed, for these instruments can be doubled as required. A special role in the *Wirtshausmusik* is played by the accordion. Here one must also know in good time what degree of accomplishment may be counted on from the available instrument and performer(!). In case no adequate players are available for this instrument and for the guitars, some temporary rearrangement of their parts will have to be made. From the score of this *Wirtshausmusik* one can infer the composer's intentions. In any event, the above remarks regarding the small ensemble show why one must begin early in preparing it. This applies also to the so-called 'sermon' (Act II, bar 605) which, in particular, must be rehearsed as chamber music and then synchronized with the speaker's part (again, not only in the rehearsal room, but also on the stage).

The following remarks amplify the instructions for the execution of the

Sprechstimme as given in both the full score and the vocal score. No singing, under any circumstances! Still, the pitches are to be stated and held exactly as indicated by the notes, but held with the tone quality of the speaking voice. To be sure, such a speaking voice need not be restricted to chest tone throughout. Head tones are also possible, even necessary, since the normal speaking voice is often too low and of too limited a compass. For this reason these spoken pitches are placed where they will cause the singer no more difficulty or harm than the sung tones suitable to the different registers and to various changes in expression.

Only in those cases where, in spite of these directions, an unnatural and mannered timbre (either in the high or low register) is unavoidable, is it permitted to execute the spoken melody in a narrower compass, within which, however, 'the relationship of the individual pitches to one another' must be absolutely maintained.

PRODUCTION AND STAGING

Not only is a precise knowledge of the Büchner drama assumed, but also of the music, at least so far as its character and its language, its dramatic style, is concerned. In spite of this unconditional requirement, the designer will be left sufficient scope for applying his own manner and style to his task. And this is so even if a realistic representation prevails throughout, as I think necessary, so that an immediate and unambiguous recognition and overall view of the place in which each scene is set is assured.

Knowledge of the music and of the diversity that has been sought in every respect, and which is also found in the musical language of the individual scenes, will lead in itself to a similar diversity (in every respect) in the stage design. This diversity will manifest itself as much in the distinctions between the three rooms (Marie's, the Captain's, the Doctor's), as in those between the street scenes (in the town and before the door of Marie's house), or between the large open space in which the tavern garden scene of Act II

is placed and the narrow corner of the low dive of III/3. What possibilities for contrast, for example, between the latter scene and the landscapes in Acts I and III, especially that of the 'open field', in which the sky, with its phenomena, spans the whole stage!

The scenic representation of these natural phenomena (the sunset that, to Wozzeck, is so uncanny) must likewise unfold with the utmost clarity imaginable (for the spectator as well), as, for instance, in the scenes at the pond, where the moon that is first seen near the horizon (III/2) again breaks through the clouds, but now higher in the sky (III/4). The water in the pond should also be recognizable as such. At one of the performances it was found to be very effective—and in complete correspondence with the music—to have the water in the pond begin to move gently at bar 275, to have this movement of the waves reach a climax at bars 285/286, and then to let it slowly subside, all movement ceasing completely at bar 302.

An exception to the demand for the greatest possible realism may perhaps be made in the low tavern scene (III/3). This scene, placed between the two scenes at the pond, may be given an immaterial, ghostly effect, for which it would suffice to have a mere suggestion of the place. This would permit the change of scene preceding and following to be managed within the unusually short period of time indicated. It should not be necessary to say so, but changes of scene here, as everywhere in the work, must be managed strictly within the time allowed by the continuous and uninterrupted music between the scenes. Now as ever, I must stress the importance of a precise observance of the stage directions regarding the curtain and changes of scene. And to this I must add that by 'curtain' I literally mean only the principal curtain at the close of each act, whereas I have thought of the conclusions of the scenes within the acts in a less restrictive sense, as marked by drop-curtains, gauze screens, blackouts (?), *etc.* In any case, at the exact place where the direction 'Change of Scene' appears the stage must become invisible

206

(also inaudible!), and only where the direction 'Curtain rises' is given is it to be visible again. (It has been proved to be practical to direct the manipulation of the curtain from the orchestra rather than from the stage, where because of the physical activity in scene-shifting the orchestra is often not heard and the required connection between the curtain and the music therefore almost impossible to realize.)

It is also important to observe the hour represented in the individual scenes. These changing times of the day and night must be clearly recognizable. For example, the twilight in the 5th scene of Act I must be substantially differentiated in its lighting from the other scenes that are played in the same setting, II/3 and III/5. It is likewise well to differentiate between the gradually fading evening light of I/3 and the morning sunlight in the same setting of II/1, as well as the night-time candle light of III/1.

NB: The night scene (II/5) in the barracks becomes brighter at bar 761, since the returning Drum Major enters with a light and puts it down somewhere. When he disappears with it at bar 808 the gloom of the beginning of the scene is restored.

The work of the stage-manager also demands an intimate knowledge of the music. The general meaning of a stage direction in Büchner* is often only made explicit through the music. Marie's murder, for example, occurs at the moment that Wozzeck—once only—'plunges the knife into her throat' (bar 103). Everything that follows (bars 104–106) refers musically only to Marie and to her death. Any further carnage must therefore be avoided!

Likewise, in the next to last scene (III/4) Marie's corpse should dominate the scene only in bars 239–249, in correspondence with the course of the music, which is devoted entirely to Wozzeck except for these bars. The corpse must therefore remain almost invisible (perhaps in the shadow of the willows) the whole time.

On the other hand there are other scenes in which the fantasy of the producer is given much greater leeway. For example, in the scene in the Doctor's study it would not be unsuitable to have the action made more lively by a medical examination, temperature-taking, etc, in keeping with and parallel to the dialogue. Similar liberties may be taken in the two tavern scenes, in which, however, the seemingly harmless fun of the first (II/4) and the uncanny, almost daemonic exuberance of the second (III/3) should be well differentiated.

But even in such scenes, which from the point of view of stage-direction are more freely composed, the demands made by the musical characterization of certain roles must be taken into consideration. For example, with the appearance of the Idiot (Act II, bar 643) it gradually becomes quiet and at bar 651 every distraction through noisy and otherwise importunate activity on the part of the other guests at the inn should be avoided. A similar instance is found in the dialogue between the Captain and the Doctor at the forest path near the pond (III/4). Both of them, standing the whole while more or less aside, should perform this dialogue in a quasi-muted manner, for the main thing here is the music and the visual aspect of the scene.

Finally, and most important of all: the preparation of the scenes in which Marie's child appears (preferably played by a little girl, since girls are much more gifted than boys of that age), and above all the preparation of the final scene (with the important ensemble of the other children) cannot begin too early! These scenes must be absolutely secure by the time the general rehearsals on stage begin, and by that time they should also have been completely rehearsed on stage and with the orchestra. Otherwise the scenes with the children will not only slow up rehearsals in the final period before the opening night, but it will no longer be possible to get these scenes ready through extra rehearsals. Such extra rehearsals, which usually can only be given with coach and piano, are no substitute for the contact between the orchestra and the children.

*Cf. pp. 40f., above. (G. P.)

Zimmer

DER HAUPTMANN. WOZZECK

HAUPTMANN *(auf einem Stuhl)*. WOZZECK *(rasirt ihn)*.

HAUPTMANN. Langsam, Wozzeck, langsam; eins nach dem andern. Er macht mir ganz schwindlig. Was soll ich denn mit den zehn Minuten anfangen, die Er heut zu früh fertig wird? Wozzeck! bedenk' Er, Er hat noch seine schönen dreißig Jahre zu leben! Dreißig Jahr! macht dreihundert und sechzig Monate und erst wie viel Tage, Stunden, Minuten! Was will Er denn mit der ungeheuren Zeit all anfangen! Theil Er sich ein, Wozzeck!

WOZZECK. Ja wohl, Herr Hauptmann!

HAUPTMANN. Es wird mir ganz angst um die Welt, wenn ich an die Ewigkeit denke. Beschäftigung, Wozzeck, Beschäftigung! Ewig, daß ist ewig!—

Das sieht Er ein. Nun ist es aber wieder nicht ewig, und das ist ein Augenblick, ja, ein Augenblick!—Wozzeck, es schaudert mich, wenn ich denke, daß sich die Welt in einem Tage herumdreht. Was für eine Zeitverschwendung!— Wo soll das hinaus? So geschwind geht alles!—Wozzeck, ich kann kein Mühlrad mehr sehen, oder ich werd' melancholisch!

WOZZECK. Ja wohl, Herr Hauptmann!

HAUPTMANN. Wozzeck, Er sieht immer so verhetzt aus! Ein guter Mensch thut das nicht, ein guter Mensch, der sein gutes Gewissen hat, thut alles langsam . . . . Red' Er doch was, Wozzeck. Was ist heut für Wetter?

WOZZECK. Schlimm, Herr Hauptmann, schlimm. Wind!

HAUPTMANN. Ich spür's schon, 's ist so was Geschwindes draußen; so ein Wind macht mir den Effect, wie eine Maus. *(Pfiffig.)* Ich glaub', wir haben so was aus Süd-Nord?

WOZZECK. Ja wohl, Herr Hauptmann.

HAUPTMANN. Ha! ha! ha! Süd-Nord! Ha! ha! ha! O, Er ist dumm, ganz abscheulich dumm! *(Gerührt.)* Wozzeck,

*Except for the substitution of roman for the obsolete gothic type, the text is given as it appears in the Landau edition of 1909, which reproduces Franzo's original text literally except for the ordering of the scenes.

207

208

Er ist ein guter Mensch, aber *(mit Würde)*, Wozzeck, Er hat keine Moral! Moral, das ist, wenn man moralisch ist, versteht Er? Es ist ein gutes Wort. Er hat ein Kind ohne den Segen der Kirche, wie unser hochwürdiger Herr Garnisonsprediger sagt, "ohne den Segen der Kirche"—das Wort ist nicht von mir.

WOZZECK. Herr Hauptmann! Der liebe Gott wird den armen Wurm nicht drum ansehen, ob das Amen darüber gesagt ist, eh' er gemacht wurde. Der Herr sprach: Lasset die Kleinen zu mir kommen!

HAUPTMANN. Was sagt Er da? Was ist das für eine kuriose Antwort? Er macht mich ganz confus mit seiner Antwort. Wenn ich sage: Er, so meine ich Ihn, Ihn . . .

WOZZECK. Wir arme Leut! Sehen Sie, Herr Hauptmann, Geld, Geld! Wer kein Geld hat!—Da setz' einmal einer Seinesgleichen auf die moralische Art in die Welt! Man hat auch sein Fleisch und Blut! Unsereins ist doch einmal unselig in dieser und der anderen Welt! Ich glaub', wenn wir in den Himmel kämen, so müßten wir donnern helfen.

HAUPTMANN. Wozzeck! Er hat keine Tugend, Er ist kein tugenhafter Mensch! Fleisch und Blut? Wenn ich am Fenster lieg', wenn's geregnet hat, und den weißen Strümpfen so nachseh', wie sie über die Gasse springen—verdammt! Wozzeck, da kommt mir die Liebe! Ich hab' auch Fleisch und Blut! Aber Wozzeck, die Tugend! die Tugend! Wie sollte ich dann die Zeit herumbringen? —ich sag' mir immer: du bist ein tugendhafter Mensch, *(gerührt)* ein guter Mensch, ein guter Mensch!

WOZZECK. Ja, Herr Hauptmann, die Tugend—ich hab's noch nicht so aus. Sehn Sie, wir gemeine Leut'—das hat keine Tugend; es kommt einem nur so die Natur. Aber wenn ich ein Herr wär und hätt' einen Hut und eine Uhr und ein Augenglas und könnt' vornehm reden, ich wollt' schon tugendhaft sein. Es muß was Schönes sein um die Tu-

gend, Herr Hauptmann, aber ich bin ein armer Kerl.

HAUPTMANN. Gut, Wozzeck, Er ist ein guter Mensch, ein guter Mensch. Aber Er denkt zu viel, das zehrt; Er sieht immer so verhetzt aus. Der Diskurs hat mich angegriffen. Geh' Er jetzt, und renn' Er nicht so, geh' Er langsam, hübsch langsam die Straße hinunter, genau in der Mitte!

Freies Feld.
Die Stadt in der Ferne.

WOZZECK *(und)* ANDRES *(schneiden Stöcke im Gebüsch).*

WOZZECK. Du, der Platz ist verflucht!

ANDRES. Ach was! *(Singt:)*

Das ist die schöne Jägerei,
Schießen steht jedem frei!
Da möcht ich Jäger sein,
Da möcht ich hin!

WOZZECK. Der Platz ist verflucht. Siehst du den lichten Streif da über das Gras hin, wo die Schwämme so nachwachsen? Da rollt abends ein Kopf. Hob ihn einmal einer auf, meint', es wär' ein Igel. Drei Tage und drei Nächte drauf, und er lag auf den Hobelspänen.

ANDRES. Es wird finster, das macht dir angst. Ei was! *(Singt:)*

Läuft dort ein Has' vorbei,
Fragt mich, ob ich Jäger sei?
Jäger bin ich auch schon
    gewesen,
Schießen kann ich aber nit!

WOZZECK. Still Andres! Das waren die Freimaurer, ich hab's, die Freimaurer! Still!

ANDRES. Sing' lieber mit. *(Singt:)*

Saßen dort zwei Hasen,
Fraßen ab das grüne, grüne Gras.

WOZZECK. Hörst du, Andres, es geht was?! *(Stampft auf dem Boden.)* Hohl! Alles hohl! ein Schlund, es schwankt . . . Hörst du, es wandert was mit uns, da unten wandert was mit uns!

ANDRES *(Singt:)*

Fraßen ab das grüne Gras
Bis auf den Rasen!

WOZZECK. Fort, fort! *(Reißt ihn mit sich.)*
ANDRES. He! bist du toll?
WOZZECK *(bleibt stehen)*. 's ist kurios still.
Und schwül. Man möcht den Athem
halten! Andres!
ANDRES. Was?
WOZZECK. Red' was! *(Starrt in die Gegend.)*
Andres! wie hell! Ein Feuer fährt von
der Erde in den Himmel und ein Getös
herunter, wie Posaunen. Wie's
heranklirrt!
ANDRES. Die Sonn' ist unter. Drinnen
trommeln sie.
WOZZECK. Still, wieder alles still, als wär'
die Welt tot!
ANDRES. Nacht! Wir müssen heim!

Die Stadt

MARIE *(mit ihrem Kinde am Fenster).*
MARGARETH.——*(Der Zapfenstreich geht
vorbei)*, (der) Tambourmajor (voran).

MARIE *(das Kind auf dem Arm wiegend)*. He,
Bub! Sa sa! Ra ra ra! Hörst! Da kommen
sie!
MARGARETH. Was ein Mann! wie ein
Baum!
MARIE. Er steht auf seinen Füßen, wie
ein Löw—*(Tambourmajor grüßt.)*
MARGARETH. Ei, was freundliche Augen,
Frau Nachbarin! So was is man an ihr
nit gewohnt.
MARIE *(Singt)*:

Soldaten, das sind schöne
Bursch—
Soldaten, Soldaten!——

MARGARETH. Ihre Augen glänzen ja
noch—
MARIE. Und wenn! Was geht Sie's an?
Trag' Sie Ihre Augen zum Juden und laß
Sie sie putzen, vielleicht glänzen sie
auch noch, daß man sie für zwei Knöpf'
verkaufen könnt.
MARGARETH. Was Sie, Sie Frau Jungfer!
Ich bin eine honette Person, aber Sie,
das weiß jeder, Sie guckt sieben Paar
lederne Hosen durch.

MARIE. Luder! *(Schlägt das Fenster zu.)*
Komm, mein Bub! Was die Leut' wollen!
Bist nur ein arm Hurenkind und machst
deiner Mutter doch so viel Freud' mit
deinem unehrlichen Gesicht! Sa! sa!
(Singt:)

Mädel, was fangst du jetzt an?
Hast ein klein Kind und kein
Mann!
Ei, was frag' ich darnach,
Sing' ich die ganze Nacht:
Eia, popeia, mein Bub, juchhu!
Gibt mir kein Mensch nix dazu!

Hansel! spann deine sechs
Schimmel an,
Gib sie zu fressen auf's neu—
Kein Haber fresse sie,
Kein Wasser saufe sie,
Lauter kühle Wein muß es sein,
Juchhe!
Lauter kühle Wein muß es sein!
(Es klopft am Fenster.)

MARIE. Wer da? Bist du's, Franz? Komm
herein!
WOZZECK. Kann nit. Muß zum Verles!
MARIE. Hast Stecken geschnitten für den
Major?
WOZZECK. Ja, Marie. Ach . . .
MARIE. Was hast du, Franz, du siehst so
verstört?
WOZZECK. Pst, still! Ich hab's aus! Es war
ein Gebild am Himmel, und alles in
Gluth. Ich bin vielem auf der Spur!
MARIE. Mann!
WOZZECK. Und jetzt alles finster, finster
. . . Marie, es war wieder was, viel . . .
(Geheimnisvoll.) Steht nicht geschrieben:
"Und sieh, es ging der Rauch auf vom
Land, wie ein Rauch vom Ofen."
MARIE. Franz!
WOZZECK. Es ist hinter mir hergegangen
bis vor die Stadt. Was soll das werden?
MARIE. Dein Bub—
WOZZECK. Hei, Jung! Heut abend wieder
auf die Meß! Ich hab' noch was gespart!
Jetzt muß ich fort. *(ab.)*
MARIE *(allein)*. Der Mann! So vergeistert!
Er hat sein Kind nicht angesehen! Er
schnappt noch über mit den Gedanken!

Was bist so still, Bub. Fürcht'st dich? Es wird so dunkel, man meint, man wird blind. Sonst scheint doch die Laterne herein! Ach! wir armen Leut. Ich halt's nit aus, es schauert mich . . .

Studierstube des Doctors.

WOZZECK. DER DOCTOR.

DOCTOR. Was erleb' ich, Wozzeck? Ein Mann von Wort? Ei! ei! ei!

WOZZECK. Was denn, Herr Doctor?

DOCTOR. Ich habs gesehen, Wozzeck! Er hat auf die Strasse gep—t, an die Wand gep—t, wie ein Hund! Geb' ich Ihm dafür alle Tage drei Groschen? Wozzeck! Das ist schlecht, die Welt wird schlecht, sehr schlecht. O!

WOZZECK. Aber, Herr Doctor, wenn einem die Natur kommt!

DOCTOR. Die Natur kommt! die Natur kommt! Aberglaube! abscheulicher Aberglaube! Die Natur! Hab' ich nicht nachgewiesen, daß der *musculus sphincter vesicae* dem Willen unterworfen ist? Die Natur! Wozzeck! Der Mensch ist frei! In dem Menschen verklärt sich die Individualität zur Freiheit! Den Harn nicht halten können! (*Schüttelt den Kopf, legt die Hände auf den Rücken und geht auf und ab.*) Hat er schon seine Erbsen gegessen, Wozzeck? Nichts als Erbsen, nichts als Hülsenfrüchte, merk' Er sich's! Die nächste Woche fangen wir dann mit Hammelfleisch an. Es gibt eine Revolution in der Wissenschaft, ich sprenge sie in die Luft. Harnstoff, salzsaures Ammonium, Hyperorydul! —Wozzeck, kann Er nicht wieder p—n? Geh' Er einmal da hinein und probir Er's.

WOZZECK. Ich kann nit, Herr Doctor!

DOCTOR (*mit Affekt*). Aber an die Wand p—n! Ich hab's schriftlich, den Accord in der Hand! Ich hab's geseh'n, mit diesen Augen gesehen, ich steckte gerade die Nase zum Fenster hinaus und ließ die Sonnenstrahlen hineinfallen, um das Niesen zu beobachten, die Entstehung des Niesens. Man muss alles beobachten. Hat er mir Frösche gefangen? Laich? Süsswasser-Polypen? *Cristatellum?* Hat Er? Stoß' Er mir nicht ans Mikroskop, ich habe den linken Backenzahn eines Infusoriums darunter. Aber (*tritt auf ihn los*). Er hat an die Wand gep—t!—Nein!—ich ärgere mich nicht, ärgern ist ungesund, ist unwissenschaftlich! Ich bin ruhig, ganz ruhig, mein Puls hat seine gewöhnlichen 60, und ich sag's Ihm mit der größten Kaltblütigkeit. Behüte, wer wird sich über einen Menschen ärgern, einen Menschen! Wenn es noch ein Proteus wäre, der einem unpäßlich wird! Aber, Wozzeck, Er hätte doch nicht an die Wand p—n sollen!

WOZZECK. Seh'n Sie, Herr Doctor, manchmal hat man so 'nen Charakter, so 'ne Struktur.—Aber mit der Natur ist's was anders, sehen Sie, mit der Natur (*er kracht mit den Fingern*), das ist so was, wie soll ich doch sagen—zum Beispiel—

DOCTOR. Wozzeck, Er philosophirt wieder!

WOZZECK. Ja, Herr Doctor, wenn die Natur aus ist—

DOCTOR. Was, wenn die Natur—

WOZZECK. —die Natur aus ist, wenn die Welt so finster wird, daß man mit den Händen an ihr herumtappen muß, daß man meint, sie verrint wie ein Spinnengewebe. Ach, wenn was is und doch nicht is! Ach, Marie! Wenn alles dunkel is, und nur noch ein rother Schein im Westen, wie von einer Esse, an was soll man sich da halten? (*Schreitet im Zimmer auf un ab.*)

DOCTOR. Kerl! Er tastet mit seinen Füßen herum, wie mit Spinnfüßen.

WOZZECK (*vertraulich*). Herr Doctor, haben Sie schon was von der doppelten Natur gesehen? Wenn die Sonne im Mittag steht, und es ist, als gieng' die Welt im Feuer auf, hat schon eine fürchterliche Stimme zu mir geredet.

DOCTOR. Wozzeck, Er hat eine *aberratio.*

WOZZECK (*legt den Finger an die Nase*). Die Schwämme! Haben Sie schon die Ringe von den Schwämmen am Boden gesehen? Linienkreise—Figuren—da steckts, da—wer das lesen könnte!

DOCTOR. Wozzeck, Er kommt ins Narrenhaus. Er hat eine schöne fixe Idee, eine köstliche *aberratio mentalis partialis*, zweite Spezies! Sehr schön ausgebildet! Wozzeck, Er kriegt noch mehr Zulage! Zweite Spezies: Fixe Idee bei allgemein vernünftigem Zustand! Er thut noch alles, wie sonst? rasirt seinen Hauptmann?

WOZZECK. Ja wohl!

DOCTOR. Ißt seine Erbsen?

WOZZECK. Immer ordentlich, Herr Doctor! Das Geld für die Menage kriegt das Weib——Darum thu' ich's ja!

DOCTOR. Thut seinen Dienst?

WOZZECK. Ja wohl!

DOCTOR. Er ist ein interessanter Casus! Er kriegt noch einen Groschen Zulage die Woche. Wozzeck, halt' Er sich nur brav! Seh' Er mich an: was muß Er thun?

WOZZECK *(stöhnend)*. Die Marie . . .

DOCTOR. Erbsen essen, dann Hammelfleisch essen, sein Gewehr putzen, dazwischen die fixe Idee pflegen. O, meine Theorie! O, mein Ruhm! Ich werde unsterblich! Unsterblich!

WOZZECK. Ja! die Marie . . und der arme Wurm.

DOCTOR. Unsterblich, Wozzeck! Zeig' er die Zunge!

Oeffentlicher Platz. Buden.

VOLK. WOZZECK. MARIE.

ALTER MANN *(und)* KIND *(tanzen und singen):*

Auf der Welt ist kein Bestand,
Wir müssen alle sterben, das
ist uns wohlbekannt.
Heißaßa! Hopßaßa!

WOZZECK. He! Marie, lustig! Schöne Welt! Gelt?

AUSRUFER *(vor einer Bude)*. Meine Herren und Damen! Hier sind zu sehen das astronomische Pferd und der geographische Esel! Die Kreatur, wie sie Gott gemacht hat, ist nix, gar nix! Sehen Sie die Kunst! Schon der Affe hier! Geht aufrecht, hat Rock und Hosen, hat einen Säbel! He, Michel! mach Kompliment! So ist's brav! Gib' Kuß. Da! *(Der Affe trompetet.)* Meine Herren und Damen!

Hier sind zu sehen das historische Pferd und der philosophische Esel. Sind Favorits von allen Potentaten Europas, Afrikas, Australiens. Mitglieder von allen gelehrten Gesellschaften, waren früher Professoren an einer Universität. Der Esel sagt den Leuten alles, wie alt, wie viel Kinder, was für Krankheiten! Kein Schwindel, alles Erziehung! Der Esel hat eine viehische Vernunft, auch vernünftige Viehigkeit, ist nicht viehdumm, wie die Menschen, das geehrte Publikum abgerechnet. Der Aff' geht aufrecht, schiesst eine Pistole los, ist musikalisch. *(Der Affe trompetet wieder.)* Meine Herren und Damen! Hier sind zu sehen der astrologische Esel, das romantische Pferd, der militärische Affe! Hereinspaziert, meine Herrschaften, gleich ist der Anfang vom Anfang. Hereinspaziert, kost einen Groschen!

ERSTER ZUSCHAUER. Ich bin ein Freund vom Grotesken. Ich bin ein Atheist.

ZWEITER ZUSCHAUER. Ich bin ein christlich-dogmatischer Atheist. Ich muß den Esel sehen. *(Gehen in die Bude.)*

WOZZECK. Willst auch hinein?

MARIE. Mein'twegen. Was der Mensch Quasten hat, und die Frau hat Hosen. Das muß ein schön Ding sein. *(Gehen hinein.)*

Das Innere der Bude.

AUSRUFER *(den Esel produzierend)*. Zeig dein Talent! zeig deine viehische Vernünftigkeit. Beschäme die menschliche *Société.* Meine Herrschaften, das ist ein Esel, hat vier Hufe und einen Schweif und das sonstige Zubehör! War Professor an einer Universität, die Studenten haben bei ihm Reiten und Schlagen gelernt! Er hat einen einfachen Verstand und eine doppelte Raison. Was machst du, wenn du mit der doppelten Raison denkst? *(Der Esel p—t.)* Wenn du mit der doppelten Raison denkst?! Sage, ist unter der geehrten *Société* da ein Esel? *(Der Esel schüttelt den Kopf.)* Sehen Sie, das ist Vernunft. Was ist der Unterschied zwischen einem Menschen und einem Esel? Staub, Sand, Dreck sind beide. Nur das Ausdrücken ist verschieden.

Der Esel spricht mit dem Huf. Sag' den Herrschaften, wie viel Uhr es ist! Wer von den Herrschaften hat eine Uhr?

EIN ZUSCHAUER *(reicht die seine)*. Hier!

MARIE. Das muß ich sehen! *(Klettert auf eine Bank.)*

WOZZECK. ——————

Straße.

MARIE. TAMBOURMAJOR.

TAMBOURMAJOR. Marie.

MARIE *(ihn anschauend, mit Ausdruck)*. Geh' einmal vor dich hin!—Ueber die Brust wie ein Rind und ein Bart wie ein Löwe. So ist Keiner!—Ich bin stolz vor allen Weibern!

TAMBOURMAJOR. Wenn ich erst am Sonntag den großen Federbusch hab' und die weißen Handschuh! Donnerwetter! Der Prinz sagt immer: Mensch! Er ist ein Kerl!

MARIE *(spöttisch)*. Ach was! *(Tritt vor ihn hin.)* Mann!

TAMBOURMAJOR. Und du bist auch ein Weibsbild! Sapperment! Wir wollen eine Zucht von Tambourmajors anlegen. He! *(Er umfaßt sie.)*

MARIE. Laß mich!

TAMBOURMAJOR. Wildes Thier!

MARIE *(heftig)*. Rühr' mich nicht an!

TAMBOURMAJOR. Sieht dir der Teufel aus den Augen?

MARIE. Meinetwegen. Es ist alles eins!——

Der Hof des Doctors.

STUDENTEN *(und)* WOZZECK *(unten)*. DER DOCTOR *(am Dachfenster)*.

DOCTOR. Meine Herren! Ich bin auf dem Dache wie David, als er die Bathseba sah; aber ich sehe nichts, als die *culs de Paris* der Mädchenpension im Garten trocknen. Meine Herren! Wir sind an der wichtigen Frage über das Verhältniß des Subjekts zum Objekt. Wenn wir eins von den Dingen nehmen, worin sich die organische Selbst-Affirmation des Göttlichen auf einem so hohen Standpunkte manifestirt, und ihr Verhältniß zum Raum, zur Erde, zur Zeit untersuchen, meine Herren, wenn ich also diese Katze zum Fenster hinauswerfe, wie wird diese Wesenheit sich zum Gesetz der Gravitation und zum eigenen Instinkt verhalten? He, Wozzeck! *(brüllt)* Wozzeck!

WOZZECK *(hat die Katze aufgefangen)*. Herr Doctor, sie beißt!

DOCTOR. Kerl! Er greift die Bestie so zärtlich an, als wär's seine Großmutter.

WOZZECK. Herr Doctor, ich hab' Zittern.

DOCTOR *(ganz erfreut)*. Haha! schön, Wozzeck. *(Reibt sich die Hände.)*

WOZZECK. Mir wird dunkel!

DOCTOR *(erscheint im Hofe, nimmt die Katze)*. Was seh' ich, meine Herren? Eine neue Species Hasenlaus. Eine schönere Species als die bekannte. *(Zieht eine Lupe heraus.)* Hasenlaus, meine Herren! *(Die Katze läuft fort.)* Meine Herren! Das Thier hat keinen wissenschaftlichen Instinkt. Hasenlaus, die schönsten Exemplare trägt es im Pelzwerk.—Meine Herren! Sie können dafür was anderes sehen. Sehen Sie diesen Menschen! Seit einem Vierteljahr ißt er nichts als Erbsen! Bemerken Sie die Wirkung—fühlen einmal den ungleichen Puls, und dann die Augen—

WOZZECK. Herr Doctor, mir wird ganz dunkel! *(Setzt sich.)*

DOCTOR. Courage, Wozzeck, noch ein paar Tage, und dann ist's fertig. Fühlen Sie, meine Herren, fühlen Sie! *(Die Studenten betasten dem Wozzeck Schläfen, Puls, und Brust.)* A propos, Wozzeck, beweg' er vor den Herren doch einmal die Ohren. Ich hab's Ihnen schon zeigen wollen—zwei Muskeln sind dabei tätig. Allons! frisch!

WOZZECK. Ach, Herr Doctor!

DOCTOR. Bestie! Soll ich dir die Ohren bewegen! Willst du's machen, wie die Katze? So, meine Herren, das sind so Uebergänge zum Esel, häufig auch infolge weiblicher Erziehung und der Muttersprache. Wozzeck! Deine Haare hat die Mutter zum Abschied schön ausgerissen aus Zärtlichkeit. Sie sind ja ganz dünn geworden. Oder ist's erst seit ein paar Tagen, machen's die Erbsen? Ja, meine Herren, die Erbsen, die Erbsen! Die Wissenschaft!

Stube.
MARIE *(sitzt, ihre Kind auf dem Schooß, ein Stückchen Spiegel in der Hand. Bespiegelt sich.)* Was die Steine glänzen? Was sind's für welche? Was hat er gesagt?— Schlaf, Bub! Drück die Augen zu, fest. *(Das Kind versteckt die Augen hinter den Händen.)* Noch fester! Bleib so—still! oder er holt Dich! *(Singt):*

> Mädel, mach's Lädel zu!
> 's kommt ein Zigeunerbu,
> Führt dich an seiner Hand
> Fort ins Zigeunerland.

(Spiegelt sich wieder.) 's ist gewiß Gold! Unsereins hat nur ein Eckchen in der Welt und ein Stückchen Spiegel, und doch hab' ich einen so rothen Mund, als die großen Madamen mit ihren Spiegeln von oben bis unten und ihren schönen Herren, die ihnen die Händ' küssen, und ich bin nur ein arm Weibsbild! . . . *(Das Kind richtet sich auf.)* Still, Bub, die Augen zu! Das Schlafengelchen! . . . *(Sie blinkt mit dem Glas)* . . . wie's an der Wand läuft!—Die Augen zu, oder es sieht dir hinein, daß du blind wirst. *(Wozzeck tritt herein, hinter sie. Sie fährt auf, mit den Händen nach den Ohren.)*
WOZZECK. Was hast da?
MARIE. Nix!
WOZZECK. Unter deinen Fingern glänzt's ja.
MARIE. Ein Ohr-Ringlein—hab's gefunden—
WOZZECK. Ich hab so noch nix gefunden!—Zwei auf einmal!
MARIE. Bin ich ein schlecht Mensch?
WOZZECK. 's ist gut, Marie.—Was der Bub schläft! Greif ihm unters Aermchen, der Stuhl drückt ihn. Die hellen Tropfen stehen ihm auf der Stirn . . . Alles Arbeit unter der Sonne, sogar Schweiß im Schlaf. Wir arme Leut! . . . Da ist wieder Geld, Marie, die Löhnung und was von meinem Hauptmann und vom Doctor.

MARIE. Gott vergelt's, Franz.
WOZZECK. Ich muß fort. Heut Abend, Marie, Adies!
MARIE *(allein, nach einer Pause).* Ich bin doch ein schlecht Mensch. Ich könnt mich erstechen.—Ach! Was Welt! Geht doch alles zum Teufel, Mann und Weib!

Straße.

HAUPTMANN. DOCTOR.

HAUPTMANN. Wohin so eilig, geehrtester Herr Sargnagel?
DOCTOR. Wohin so langsam, geehrtester Herr Exercizengel?
HAUPTMANN. Nehmen Sie sich Zeit! Laufen Sie nicht so! Uff!
DOCTOR. Pressirt! pressirt!
HAUPTMANN. Laufen Sie nicht! Ein guter Mensch geht nicht so schnell. *(Heftig schnaufend.)* Ein guter Mensch—ein guter—Sie hetzen sich ja hinter dem Tod d'rein—Sie machen mir Angst!
DOCTOR. Ich stehle meine Zeit nicht.
HAUPTMANN. Ein guter Mensch—*(Erwischt den Doctor beim Rock.)* Herr Doctor, die Pferde machen mir ganz Angst, wenn ich denke, daß die armen Bestien zu Fuß gehen müssen. Rennen Sie nicht so, Herr Sargnagel! Rudern Sie mit dem Stock nicht so in der Luft! Sie schleifen sich ja Ihre Beine auf dem Pflaster ab. *(Hält ihn fest.)* Erlauben Sie, daß ich ein Menschenleben rette—
DOCTOR. Frau in vier Wochen todt, *cancer uteri*. Habe schon zwanzig solche Patienten gehabt—in vier Wochen—
HAUPTMANN. Doctor! erschrecken Sie mich nicht, es sind schon Leute am Schreck gestorben, am puren hellen Schreck!
DOCTOR. In vier Wochen!—Giebt ein interessantes Präparat.
HAUPTMANN. Oh! Oh!
DOCTOR. Und Sie selbst! Hm! aufgedunsen, fett, dicker Hals, apoplektische Konstitution! Ja, Herr Hauptmann, Sie können eine *apoplexia cerebri* kriegen, Sie können sie aber vielleicht nur auf der einen Seite bekommen. Ja, Sie können

nur auf der einen Seite gelähmt werden
oder im besten Falle nur unten!

HAUPTMANN. Um Gottes—

DOCTOR. Ja! das sind so ungefähr Ihre
Aussichten auf die nächsten vier
Wochen! Uebrigens kann ich Sie ver-
sichern, daß Sie einen von den interes-
santen Fällen abgeben werden, und
wenn Gott will, daß Ihre Zunge zum
Theile gelähmt wird, so machen wir die
unsterblichsten Experimente. *(Will gehen.)*

HAUPTMANN. Halt, Doctor! Ich lasse Sie
nicht! Sargnagel! Todtenfreund! in vier
Wochen?—Es sind schon Leute am
puren Schreck—Doctor! Ich sehe schon
die Leute mit den Citronen in den
Händen, aber sie werden sagen: er war
ein guter Mensch *(gerührt)*, ein guter
Mensch—

DOCTOR *(thut, als hätte er ihn just bemerkt,
schwenkt den Hut)*. Ei! guten Morgen,
Herr Hauptmann! *(Hält ihm den Hut
hin.)* Was ist das? Herr Hauptmann,
das ist—Hohlkopf!

HAUPTMANN *(macht am Rock eine Falte)*.
Und was ist das, Herr Doctor? Das
ist Einfalt! Hahaha! Aber nichts für
ungut! Ich bin ein guter Mensch, aber
ich kann auch, wenn ich will! Herr Doctor, ich sag' Ihnen, wenn ich will—
(Wozzeck geht rasch vorbei, salutiert.)

HAUPTMANN. He! Wozzeck! Was hetzt Er
sich so an uns vorbei? Bleib Er doch,
Wozzeck! Er läuft ja wie ein offenes
Rasirmesser durch die Welt, man
schneidet sich an Ihm! Er läuft, als hätte
er ein Regiment Katzenschweife zu
rasiren, und würde gehenkt, so lange
noch ein letztes Haar—aber über die
langen Bärte—was wollte ich doch
sagen—die langen Bärte—

DOCTOR. Ein langer Bart unter dem
Kinn—schon Plinius spricht davon—
man muß es den Soldaten abge-
wöhnen—

HAUPTMANN. Ha, die langen Bärte! Was
ist's, Wozzeck? Hat Er nicht ein Haar
aus einem Bart in seiner Schüssel
gefunden? Haha!—Er versteht mich
doch? Ein Haar von einem Menschen!

Vom Bart eines Sapeurs—oder eines
Unteroffiziers—oder eines Tambourmajors. He, Wozzeck? Aber Er hat ein
braves Weib, he?

WOZZECK. Ja wohl! Was wollen Sie damit
sagen, Herr Hauptmann?!

HAUPTMANN. Was der Kerl ein Gesicht
macht! Nun haha! wenn auch nicht
gerade in der Suppe, aber wenn Er sich
eilt und um die Ecke geht, so kann Er
vielleicht noch auf einem paar Lippen
eins finden! Ein Haar nämlich! Uebrigens ein paar Lippen, Wozzeck, ein
paar Lippen!—o! ich habe auch einmal
die Liebe gefühlt!—Aber, Kerl, Er ist ja
kreideweiß!

WOZZECK. Herr Hauptmann, ich bin ein
armer Teufel! Hab' sonst nichts auf der
Welt! Herr Hauptmann, wenn Sie Spaß
machen—

HAUPTMANN. Spaß' ich? Daß dich! Spaß!
Kerl—

DOCTOR. Den Puls, Wozzeck! Klein, hart,
hüpfend—

WOZZECK. Herr Hauptmann! Die Erd' ist
Manchem höllenheiß—die Hölle ist kalt
dagegen—

HAUPTMANN. Kerl, will Er sich erschie-
ßen? Er sticht mich mit seinen Augen!
Ich mein's gut mit ihm, weil er ein
guter Mensch ist, Wozzeck, ein guter
Mensch!

DOCTOR. Gesichtsmuskeln starr, ges-
pannt, Auge stier. Hm!

WOZZECK. Ich geh'—es ist viel möglich!
Der Mensch—es ist viel möglich! Ja oder
nein? Gott im Himmel! Man könnt' Lust
bekommen, einen Kloben hineinzu-
schlagen und sich dran aufzuhängen.
Dann wüßt' man, woran man ist! Ja
oder nein? *(Geht rasch ab.)*

DOCTOR. Er ist ein Phänomen, dieser
Wozzeck!

HAUPTMANN. Mir wird ganz schwindlig
von dem Menschen! Wie der lange
Schlingel läuft und sein Schatten hin-
terdrein! Und so verzweifelt! Das hab
ich nicht gerne! Ein guter Mensch ist
dankbar gegen Gott. Ein guter Mensch
hat auch keine Courage! Nur ein
Hundsfott hat Courage! Ich bin auch

manchmal schwermütig; ich hab' in meiner Natur so was Schwärmerisches, ich muß immer weinen, wenn ich meinen Rock an der Wand hängen sehe! Aber der Mensch ist dazu da, um seinen Schöpfer zu preisen und sich in der Liebe zum Leben zu befestigen. Nur ein Hundsfott hat Courage! Nur ein Hundsfott!

Mariens Stube.

MARIE. WOZZECK.

MARIE. Guten Tag, Franz.

WOZZECK (*sieht sie starr an und schüttelt den Kopf*). Hm! ich seh' nichts, ich seh' nichts. O, man müßt's seh'n, man müßt's greifen können mit Fäusten!

MARIE. Was hast, Franz?

WOZZECK (*wie früher*). Bist du's noch, Marie?!—Eine Sünde, so dick und breit—das müßt stinken, daß man die Engelchen zum Himmel hinausräuchern könnt'. Aber du hast einen rothen Mund, Marie! Einen rothen Mund— keine Blase drauf?

MARIE. Du bist hirnwüthig, Franz, ich fürcht' mich . . .

WOZZECK. Du bist schön—"wie die Sünde." Aber kann die Todsünde so schön sein, Marie? (*Auffahrend.*) Da!— Hat er da gestanden, so, so?

MARIE. Ich kann den Leuten die Gasse nicht verbieten . . .

WOZZECK. Teufel! Hat er da gestanden?

MARIE. Dieweil der Tag lang und die Welt alt ist, können viel Menschen an einem Platze stehen, einer nach dem andern.

WOZZECK. Ich hab ihn gesehen!

MARIE. Man kann viel sehen, wenn man zwei Augen hat, und wenn man nicht blind ist, und wenn die Sonn' scheint.

WOZZECK. Du bei ihm!

MARIE (*keck*). Und wenn auch!

WOZZECK (*geht auf sie los*). Mensch!

MARIE. Rühr' mich nicht an. Lieber ein Messer in den Leib, als eine Hand auf mich. Mein Vater hat's nicht gewagt, wie ich zehn Jahr alt war . . .

WOZZECK (*sieht sie starr an, läßt langsam die Hand sinken*). Lieber ein Messer! (*Nach*

einer Pause, scheu flüsternd:) Der Mensch ist ein Abgrund, es schwindelt einem, wenn man hinunterschaut . . . Mich schwindelt . . .

Die Wachtstube.

WOZZECK. ANDRES.

ANDRES (*singt:*)

> Frau Wirthin hat eine brave Magd,
> Sie sitzt im Garten Tag und Nacht,
> Sie sitzt in ihrem Garten—

WOZZECK. Andres!

ANDRES. Nu!

WOZZECK. Was meinst, wo sie . . . Schön Wetter!

ANDRES. Sonntagswetter! Musik vor der Stadt. Vorhin sind die Weibsbilder hin . . . Tanz . . . die Bursche dampfen, das geht!

WOZZECK (*unruhig*). Tanz, Andres, sie tanzen!

ANDRES. Im Rößl und im Stern.

WOZZECK. Was glaubst, wo sie—ich muß sehen, wo sie tanzen!

ANDRES. Meinetwegen. (*Singt.*)

> Sie sitzt in ihrem Garten,
> Bis daß das Glöcklein zwölfe schlägt,
> Und paßt auf die Soldaten.

WOZZECK. Andres, ich hab keine Ruh.

ANDRES. Narr!

WOZZECK. Ich muß hinaus. Es dreht sich mir vor den Augen. Tanz! Wird sie heiß haben! Verdammt!—Adies!

ANDRES. Was willst du?

WOZZECK. Ich muß fort, muß sehen.

ANDRES. Wegen dem Mensch!

WOZZECK. Hinaus, hinaus!

Wirthshaus.
Abend. Fenster offen. Tanz. Bursche.
Soldaten. Mägde.

Bänke vor dem Haus.

ERSTER HANDWERKSBURSCHE (*singt*):

216

Ich hab ein Hemdlein an, das ist
nicht mein,
Meine Seele stinket nach
Branntewein!

ZWEITER HANDWERKSBURSCHE. Vergiß-
meinnicht! Freundschaft! Bruder, soll
ich dir aus Freundschaft ein Loch in die
Natur machen? Bruder! ich will ein Loch
in deine Natur machen, ich will dir alle
Flöh' am Leib totschlagen. Bruder, ich
bin auch ein Kerl, du weißt—

ERSTER HANDWERKSBURSCHE. Meine Seele,
meine unsterbliche Seele stinket nach
Branntwein! Sie stinket, und ich weiß
nicht warum. Warum ist die Welt!
Selbst das Geld geht in Verwesung
über! Der Teufel soll den lieben Herrgott
holen! Bruder, ich muß ein Regenfaß
voll greinen.

ZWEITER HANDWERKSBURSCHE. Vergiß-
meinnicht! Warum ist die Welt so
schön!—Ich wollt', unsere Nasen wären
zwei Bouteillen, und wir könnten sie
uns einander in den Hals gießen. Die
ganze Welt ist rosenroth! Branntwein,
das ist ein Leben.

ERSTER HANDWERKSBURSCHE. Meine Seele
stinket, oh! ich lieg mir selbst im Weg
und muß über mich springen! Das ist
traurig!

*(Wozzeck stellt sich an's Fenster, blickt hinein.
Marie und der Tambourmajor tanzen vorbei,
ohne ihn zu bemerken.)*

WOZZECK. Er! Sie! Teufel!

MARIE *(im Vorbeitanzen).* Immer zu! Immer
zu!

WOZZECK. Immer zu—immer zu! *(Sinkt auf
die Bank vor dem Hause.)* Immer zu!
(Schlägt die Hände ineinander.) Dreht
euch, wälzt euch! Warum löscht Gott
nicht die Sonne aus! Alles wälzt sich in
Unzucht über einander! Mann und
Weib und Mensch und Vieh! Sie thun's
am hellen Tag, sie thun's schier einem
auf den Händen, wie die Mücken.
Weib! Weib! Immer zu. *(Fährt heftig auf.)*
Wie er an ihr herumgreift! An ihrem
Leib! Und sie lacht dazu! Verdammt!
Ich—

BURSCHE *(drinnen, singen im Chor):*

Ein Jäger aus der Pfalz
Ritt einst durch den grünen
Wald!
Halli, halloh! Halli, halloh!
Ja lustig ist die Jägerei
Allhie auf grüner Haid'.
Das Jagen ist mein Freud'.

ANDERE BURSCHE *(singen):*

O Tochter, meine Tochter—
Was hat sie gedenkt,
Daß sie sich an die Kutscher
Und die Schiffsleut' hat gehängt?!

(Soldaten gehen hinaus, an Wozzeck vorbei.)

EIN SOLDAT *(zu Wozzeck).* Was machst du?

WOZZECK. Wie viel Uhr?

SOLDAT. Elf Uhr!

WOZZECK. So? Ich meint', es müßt später
sein! Die Zeit wird einem lang bei der
Kurzweil—

SOLDAT. Was sitzest du da vor der Thür?

WOZZECK. Ich sitz' gut da. Es sind manche
Leut' nah an der Thür und wissen's
nicht, bis man sie zur Thür hinausträgt,
die Füß' voran!

SOLDAT. Du sitzest hart.

WOZZECK. Gut sitz ich, und im kühlen
Grab da lieg' ich dann noch besser—

SOLDAT. Bist besoffen?

WOZZECK. Nein! Leider! Brings nit
zusamm!

ERSTER HANDWERKSBURSCHE *(drinnen, hat
sich auf den Tisch gestellt und predigt).*
Jedoch, wenn ein Wanderer, der
gelehnt steht an dem Strom der Zeit
oder aber sich die göttliche Weisheit
beantwortet und fraget: Warum ist der
Mensch? Aber wahrlich, geliebte Zuhörer, ich sage Euch, es ist gut so, denn
von was hätten der Landmann, der
Faßbinder, der Schneider, der Arzt
leben sollen, wenn Gott den Menschen
nicht geschaffen hätte? Von was hätte
der Schneider leben sollen, wenn er
nicht dem Menschen die Empfindung
der Schamhaftigkeit eingepflanzt hätte?
von was der Soldat und der Wirth,
wenn er ihn nicht mit dem Bedürfniß
des Todtschlagens und der Feuchtigkeit
ausgerüstet hätte? Darum zweifelt nicht,

Geliebteste, ja! ja! es ist alles lieblich und fein, aber alles Irdische ist eitel, selbst das Geld geht in Verwesung über, und meine unsterbliche Seele stinket sehr nach Branntewein. Zum Schluß, meine geliebten Zuhörer, lasset uns noch über's Kreuz p—n, damit ein Jud' stirbt!

WOSSECK. Sie hat rothe Backen, und er einen schönen Bart! Warum nicht? Warum also nicht?

EIN IRRSINNIGER (*drängt sich neben Wozzeck ans Fenster*). Lustig, lustig, aber es riecht—

WOZZECK. Narr, was willst du?

IRRSINNIGER. Ich riech, ich riech Blut!

WOZZECK. Blut! Ha, Blut! Mir wird roth vor den Augen. Mir ist, als wälzten sie sich alle in einem Meer von Blut übereinander.

Freies Feld.
Nacht.

WOZZECK.

WOZZECK. Immer zu! Immer zu! Still Musik! Ha! was sagt Ihr? So—lauter! lauter! Jetzt hör' ich's. Stich—stich die Zickwölfin todt—Stich—stich—die—Zickwölfin todt—soll ich?—muß ich? Ich hör's immer, immer zu—stich todt —todt—Da unten aus dem Boden heraus spricht's, und die Pappeln sprechen's—stich todt—stich—

Kaserne.
Nacht.

ANDRES (*und*) WOZZECK (*schlafen in einem Bett*).

WOZZECK (*fährt auf*). Andres! Andres! ich kann nicht schlafen, wenn ich die Augen zumach', dann seh ich sie doch immer und ich hör' die Geigen immer zu, immer zu. Und dann sprichts aus der Wand heraus—hörst du nix, Andres? Und das geigt und springt!

ANDRES (*murmelt*). Ja!—laß sie tan—zen—

WOZZECK. Und dazwischen blitzt's mir immer vor den Augen, wie ein Messer! wie ein breites Messer, und bald liegt's

auf einem Tisch in einem Laden in einer dunklen Gass', und bald hab' ich's in der Hand und—oh!

ANDRES. Schlaf, Narr!

WOZZECK. "Und führe uns nicht in Versuchung!" Mein Herr und Gott, "und führe uns nicht in Versuchung, Amen!"

*Kasernenhof.**

TAMBOURMAJOR. ANDRES. WOZZECK (*abseits*).

TAMBOURMAJOR. Ich bin ein Mann! Ich hab' ein Weibsbild, ich sag' Ihm, ein Weibsbild!—Zur Zucht von Tambourmajors! Ein Busen und Schenkel! Und alles fest! Die Augen wie glühende Kohlen. Ein Weibsbild, sag' ich Ihm . . .

ANDRES. He! He! Wer is es denn?

TAMBOURMAJOR. Frag' Er den Wozzeck da! Hehe! Ich bin ein Mann, ein Mann! (*Ab.*)

WOZZECK (*zu Andres*). Er hat von mir geredt? Was hat er gesagt?

ANDRES. Ich sollt' dich fragen, wer sein

*(Scene variant included in the Landau edition of 1909.)

Wirthshaus.

TAMBOURMAJOR. WOZZECK. ANDRES. LEUTE.

TAMBOURMAJOR. Ich bin ein Mann! (*Schlägt sich auf die Brust.*) Ein Mann, sag' ich. Wer will was? Wer kein besoffener Herrgott ist, der laß sich von mir—. Ich will ihm die Nas ins A—loch prügeln. Ich will—(*Zu Wozzeck.*) Da Kerl, sauf'—ich wollt', die Welt wäre Schnaps, Schnaps, der Mann muß saufen— da Kerl, sauf'—

WOZZECK (*blickt weg, pfeift*).

TAMBOURMAJOR. Kerl, soll ich dir die Zung' aus dem Hals zieh'n und sie dir um den Leib wickeln? (*Sie ringen, Wozzeck unterliegt.*) Soll ich dir noch so viel Athem lassen, als ein Altweiberf—z? Soll ich—

WOZZECK (*sinkt erschöpft auf eine Bank*).

TAMBOURMAJOR. Jetzt soll der Kerl pfeifen, dunkelblau soll er sich pfeifen! He! Branntwein das ist mein Leben! Branntwein das giebt Courage!

EINER. Der hat sein Fett!

ANDRES. Er blut'.

WOZZECK. Einer nach dem Andern.

Mensch ist. Hätt ein prächtig Weibsbild—die hätt' Schenkel—

WOZZECK (ganz kalt). So? Hat er das
gesagt? Was hat mir heut Nacht ge-
träumt, Andres? War's nicht von einem
Messer?—Was man doch närrische
Träume hat! Oder kluge Träume? (Will
fort.)

ANDRES. Wohin, Kamerad?

WOZZECK. Meinem Hauptmann Wein holen. Ach! Andres, sie war doch ein ein-
zig Mädel!

ANDRES. Wer war? War? Ist nicht mehr?

WOZZECK. Wird bald nicht mehr sein.
Adies!

Mariens Stube.

MARIE (allein, blättert in der Bibel). "Und ist
kein Betrug in seinem Munde erfunden
worden" . . . Herrgott, Herrgott! Sieh
mich nicht an! (Blättert weiter.) "Aber die
Pharisäer brachten ein Weib zu ihm, so
im Ehebruch lebte und stelleten sie vor
ihm." (Liest murmelnd weiter, dann mit
gehobener Stimme): "Jesus aber sprach:
So verdamme ich dich auch nicht, geh'
hin und sündige hinfort nicht mehr."
(Schlägt die Hände zusammen.) Herrgott!
Herrgott!—ich kann nicht—Herrgott!
gieb mir nur so viel, daß ich beten kann.
(Das Kind drängt sich an sie.) Der Bub
giebt mir einen Stich ins Herz. Fort! Das
brüst' sich in der Sonne! Nein komm,
komm her! (Beginnt zu erzählen.) Es war
einmal ein König. Der Herr König hatt'
eine goldene Kron und eine Frau Köni-
gin und ein klein Büblein. Und was
aßen sie alle?—Sie aßen alle Leber-
würst . . . Der Franz ist nit gekommen,
gestern nit, heut nit . . . Mir wird heiß,
heiß! (Reißt das Fenster auf.) Wie steht es
geschrieben von der Magdalena—wie
steht es geschrieben? . . . Und kniete
hin zu seinen Füßen und weinte und
küßte seine Füße und netzte sie mit
Thränen und salbte sie mit Salben" . . .
(Schlägt sich auf die Brust.) Heiland! ich
möchte dir die Füße salben—Heiland,
du hast dich ihrer erbarmt, erbarme
dich auch meiner!——

Kramladen.

WOZZECK. EIN JUDE.

WOZZECK. Das Pistölchen ist zu theuer.

JUDE. Nu, kauft's nur—gaude Waar'!
Kauft's nit? Was anders?

WOZZECK. Was kost' das Messer?

JUDE. Zwei Gulden! 'Sist gaud! a gaud's
Messer. Wollt Ihr Euch den Hals mit
abschneiden? Nun, was is? Ich geb's
Euch so wohlfeil wie ein Anderer! Ihr
sollt Euren Tod wohlfeil haben, aber
doch nicht umsonst. Ihr kauft's? Nu?

WOZZECK. Das kann mehr als Brod
schneiden—

JUDE. Ja, Herrche!

WOZZECK. Da! (wirft das Geld hin, nimmt
das Messer, ab.)

JUDE. Da! Hihi! Als ob's nix wär! Und s'is
doch Geld. Hihi.

Straße.
Sonntag nachmittags.

MARIE (vor der Hausthür, ihr Kind auf dem
Arm. Neben ihr eine alte Frau. Kinder
spielen auf der Straße).

KLEINE MÄDCHEN (gehen paarweise und
singen):

> Wie heute schön die Sonne
> scheint,
> Wie steht das Korn im Blüh'n!
> Sie gingen über die Wiese hin,
> Sie gingen zwei und zwei.
> Die Pfeifer gingen vorne,
> Die Geiger hinterdrein,
> Sie hatten alle rothe Schuh
> Und gingen immer zu.

ERSTES MÄDCHEN. (tritt aus der Reihe).
Was Anderes!

ALLE. Was Anderes! Was?

ERSTES MÄDCHEN. Ich weiß nit. Was
Anderes!

MARIE. Kommt—alle im Kreis (singt, die
Kinder singen nach und drehen sich).

> "Ringel, Ringel, Rosenkranz,
> Ringel, Ringel!"

ERSTES MÄDCHEN (zur alten Frau). Großmutter, warum scheint heute die Sonn'?

ALTE FRAU. Darum!

ERSTES MÄDCHEN. Aber warum—darum?

ZWEITES MÄDCHEN. Großmutter, erzählt was!

MARIE. Ja, erzählt was, Base.

ALTE FRAU (erzählt). Es war einmal ein arm Kind und hatt' keinen Vater und keine Mutter—war alles todt und war niemand auf der Welt, und es hat gehungert und geweint Tag und Nacht. Und weil es niemand mehr hatt' auf der Welt, wollt's in den Himmel geh'n. Und der Mond guckt' es so freundlich an, und wie's endlich zum Mond kommt, ist's ein Stück faul Holz. Da wollt's zur Sonne geh'n, und die Sonn' guckt' es so freundlich an, und wie's endlich zur Sonne kommt, ist's ein verwelkt Sonnblümlein. Da wollt's zu den Sternen geh'n, und die Sterne gucken es so freundlich an, und wie's endlich zu den Sternen kommt, da sind's goldene Mücklein, die sind aufgespießt auf Schlehendörner und sterben. Da wollt' das Kind wieder zur Erde, aber wie's zur Erde kam, da war die Erde ein umgestürzt Häfchen. Und so war das Kind ganz allein und hat sich hingesetzt und hat geweint: Hab' nicht Vater noch Mutter, hab' nicht Sonne, Mond und Sterne und nicht die Erde. Und da sitzt es noch und ist ganz allein.

MARIE (drückt angstvoll ihr Kind an die Brust). Ach! wenn ich todt bin! Bas', sie hat mir das Herz schwer gemacht. Mein armer Wurm! Wenn ich todt bin!

Kaserne.

ANDRES. WOZZECK (kramt in seinen Sachen).

WOZZECK. Das Kamisölchen, Andres, gehört nit zur Montur. Du kannst's brauchen, Andres! Das Kreuz ist meiner Schwester und das Ringlein, ich hab' auch noch zwei Herzen, schön Gold. Das da lag in meiner Mutter Bibel, und da steht:

> Leiden sei all men Gewinnst,
> Leiden sei mein Gottesdienst,

> Herr! wie Dein Leib war roth und wund,
> So laß mein Herz sein alle Stund.

ANDRES (ganz starr, sieht ihn verwundert an, schüttelt den Kopf, sagt zu allem). Jawohl!

WOZZECK (zieht ein Stück Papier hervor). Johann Franz Wozzeck, Wehrmann und Füselier im 2. Regiment, 2. Bataillon, 4. Compagnie, geboren Maria Verkündigung 20. Juli (murmelt die Jahreszahl). Ich bin heut alt 30 Jahr, 7 Monat und 12 Tag.

ANDRES. Franz, du kommst ins Lazareth. Du mußt Schnaps trinken und Pulver drin, das tödt' das Fieber.

WOZZECK. Ja, Andres, wenn der Schreiner die Hobelspäne sammelt, da weiß niemand, wer seinen Kopf darauf legen wird.

Waldweg am Teich.
(Es dunkelt.)

WOZZECK. MARIE.

MARIE. Dort links geht's in die Stadt. S'ist noch weit. Komm schneller.

WOZZECK. Du sollst da bleiben, Marie. Komm, setz' dich.

MARIE. Aber ich muß fort.

WOZZECK. Komm. (Sie setzten sich.) Bist weit gegangen, Marie. Sollst dir die Füße nicht mehr wund laufen. S'ist still hier! Und so dunkel.—Weißt noch, Marie, wie lang es jetzt ist, daß wir uns kennen?

MARIE. Zu Pfingsten drei Jahr.

WOZZECK. Und was meinst, wie lang es noch dauern wird?

MARIE (springt auf). Ich muß fort.

WOZZECK. Fürchst dich, Marie? Und bist doch fromm? (lacht) Und gut! Und treu! (Zieht sie wieder auf den Sitz.) Fürchst dich?—Was du für süße Lippen hast, Marie! (küßt sie). Den Himmel gäb' ich drum und die Seligkeit! wenn ich dich noch oft so küssen dürft. Aber ich darf nicht!—Was zitterst?

MARIE. Der Nachtthau fällt.

WOZZECK (flüstert vor sich hin). Wer kalt ist, den friert nicht mehr! Dich wird beim

220 Morgenthau nicht frieren.—Aber mich!
Ach! es muß sein!

MARIE. Was sagst du da?

WOZZECK. Nix. *(Langes Schweigen.)*

MARIE. Wie der Mond roth aufgeht!

WOZZECK. Wie ein blutig Eisen! *(zieht ein Messer.)*

MARIE. Was zitterst so? *(springt auf.)* Was willst?

WOZZECK. Ich nicht, Marie! und kein anderer auch nicht! *(stößt ihr das Messer in den Hals.)*

MARIE. Hilfe! Hilfe! *(Sie sinkt nieder.)*

WOZZECK. Todt! *(beugt sich über sie.)* Todt! Mörder! Mörder! *(stürzt davon.)*

Wirthshaus.

(Bursche, Dirnen, Tanz.) WOZZECK *(abseits an einem Tische).*

WOZZECK. Tanzt alle; tanzt nur zu, springt, schwitzt und stinkt, es holt Euch doch noch einmal alle der Teufel! *(leert sein Glass, singt:)*

> Es ritten drei Reiter wohl an den Rhein,
> Bei einer Frau Wirthin da kehrten sie ein.
> Mein Wein ist gut, mein Bier ist klar,
> Mein Töchterlein liegt auf der—

Verdammt! *(springt auf.)* He, Käthe! *(tanzt mit ihr.)* Komm, setz dich! *(führt sie an seinen Tisch.)* Ich hab heiß, heiß! *(zieht den Rock aus.)* S'ist einmal so! Der Teufel holt die Einen und läßt die Andern laufen. Käthe, du bist heiß! Wart nur, wirst auch noch kalt werden! Kannst nicht singen?

KÄTHE *(singt:)*

> In's Schwabenland, da mag ich nit,
> Und lange Kleider trag ich nit,
> Denn lange Kleider, spitze Schuh
> Die kommen keiner Dienstmagd zu.

WOZZECK. Nein! keine Schuh, man kann auch bloßfüßig in die Höll' geh'n! *(singt:)*

> O pfui mein Schatz, das war nicht fein!
> Behalt den Thaler und schlaf allein!

Ich möcht heut raufen,—raufen—

KÄTHE. Aber was hast du da an der Hand?

WOZZECK. Ich? ich?

KÄTHE. Roth! Blut!

(Es stellen sich Leute um sie.)

WOZZECK. Blut? Blut?

WIRTHIN. Freilich—Blut.

WOZZECK. Ich glaub', ich hab' mich— geschnitten, da an der—rechten— Hand—

WIRTHIN. Wie kommts aber an den Ellenbogen?

WOZZECK. Ich habs abgewischt.

WIRTHIN. Mit der rechten Hand am rechten Arm?

BAUER. Puh! was stinkt da Menschenblut!

WOZZECK *(springt auf).* Was wollt Ihr? Was geht's Euch an? Bin ich ein Mörder? Was gafft Ihr? Platz—oder es geht jemand zum Teufel! *(stürzt hinaus.)*

Waldweg am Teich.
Nacht.

WOZZECK *(kommt herangewankt.)*

Das Messer?—Wo ist das Messer?—Ich hab's da gelassen.—Näher, noch näher. —Mir graut's—Da regt sich was. Still!— Alles still und todt.—Mörder! Mörder! Ha! da ruft's. Nein—ich selbst. *(stößt auf die Leiche)*—Marie! Marie! Was hast du für eine rothe Schnur um den Hals? Hast dir das rothe Halsband verdient, wie die Ohr-Ringlein, mit deiner Sünde! Was hängen dir die schwarzen Haare so wild—?!—Mörder!— Mörder—Sie werden nach mir suchen. Das Messer verräth mich! Da, da ist's —Leute!—fort!

(Am Teich.)

So! da hinunter! *(wirft das Messer hinein.)* Es taucht ins dunkle Wasser wie ein Stein. Aber der Mond verräth mich—der Mond ist blutig. Will denn die ganze Welt es ausplaudern?!—Das Messer, es liegt zu weit vorn, sie findens beim Baden oder wenn sie nach Muscheln tauchen. *(geht in den Teich hinein.)* Ich find's nicht. Aber ich muß mich waschen. Ich bin blutig. Da ein Fleck—und noch einer. Weh! weh! ich wasche mich mit Blut—das Wasser ist Blut . . . Blut . . . *(ertrinkt.)*

(Es kommen Leute.)

ERSTER BÜRGER. Halt!

ZWEITER BÜRGER. Hörst du? Dort!

ERSTER BÜRGER. Jesus! das war ein Ton.

ZWEITER BÜRGER. Es ist das Wasser im Teich. Das Wasser ruft. Es ist schon lange niemand ertrunken. Komm—es ist nicht gut zu hören.

ERSTER BÜRGER. Das stöhnt—als stürbe ein Mensch. Hans! da ertrinkt jemand.

ZWEITER BÜRGER. Unheimlich! Der Mond roth und die Nebel grau. Hörst?—jetzt wieder das Aechzen.

ERSTER BÜRGER. Stiller,—jetzt ganz still. Komm! komm schnell. *(Eilen der Stadt zu.)*

Früher Morgen. Vor Mariens Hausthür.

KINDER *(spielen und lärmen.)*

ERSTES KIND. Du Margreth!—die Marie

ZWEITES KIND. Was is?

ERSTES KIND. Weißt es nit? Sie sind schon alle 'naus.

DRITTES KIND *(zu Mariens Knaben.)* Du! Dein Mutter is todt!

DER KNABE *(auf der Schwelle reitend.)* Hei! Hei! Hopp! Hopp!

ERSTES KIND. Wo is sie denn?

ZWEITES KIND. Draus liegt sie, am Weg, neben dem Teich.

ERSTES KIND. Kommt—anschaun! *(laufen davon.)*

DER KNABE. Hei! Hei! Hopp! Hopp!

Secirsaal.

CHIRURG. ARZT. RICHTER.

RICHTER. Ein guter Mord, ein ächter Mord, ein schöner Mord, so schön, als man ihn nur verlangen kann. Wir haben schon lange keinen so schönen gehabt.

ARZT. ————————

The list that follows is almost entirely restricted to writings to which reference is made in the present volume. In the footnote references magazine articles are indicated by author, the year of issue, and an abbreviated title of the journal; books are indicated by author and the year of publication.

Adorno, Theodor W. 1968. *Alban Berg.* Vienna: Elisabeth Lafite.

Albrecht, Otto E. 1953. *A Census of Autograph Music Manuscripts of European Composers in American Libraries.* Philadelphia: University of Pennsylvania Press.

Anbruch, Musikblätter des. [1926]. *Alban Bergs "Wozzeck" und die Musikkritik.* Vienna: Universal Edition.

Archibald, Bruce. 1968. "The Harmony of Berg's 'Reigen,' " *Perspectives of New Music,* VI/2 (Spring/Summer): 73ff.

Berg, Alban. 1924. "Die Musikalischen Formen in meiner Oper 'Wozzeck,' " *Die Musik,* XVI/8 (May): 587ff.

——. 1927. "A Word about 'Wozzeck,' " *Modern Music,* V/1 (November/December): 22ff.

——. 1930. "*Wozzeck:* Bemerkungen von Alban Berg," *Musikblätter des Anbruch,* XII (February): 52f. (German version of the preceding. Another English translation can be found in Reich 65, pp. 64–66.)

——. 1965. *Briefe an seine Frau.* Munich: Langen-Müller Verlag.

——. 1971. *Letters to His Wife.* Trans. Bernard Grun. New York: St. Martin's Press.

——. 1978. A letter to Hanna Fuchs-Robettin. *International Alban Berg Society Newsletter,* 6 (June): 2f.

Berger, Arthur. 1963. "Problems of Pitch Organization in Stravinsky," *Perspectives of New Music,* II/1 (Fall/Winter): 11ff.

Bieber, Hugo. 1914. "Wozzeck und Woyzeck," *Literarisches Echo,* XVI: 1188ff.

Blaukopf, Kurt. 1953. "New Light on 'Wozzeck,' " *Saturday Review,* Sept. 26, pp. 62f.

——. 1954. "Autobiographische Elemente in Alban Berg's 'Wozzeck,' " *Österreichische Musikzeitschrift,* IX/5 (May): 155ff.

Büchner, Georg. 1850. *Nachgelassene Schriften,* ed. Ludwig Büchner. Frankfort: Sauerländer.

——. 1879. *Sämtliche Werke und handschriftlicher Nachlass,* ed. Karl Emil Franzos. Frankfort: Sauerländer.

224

1909. *Gesammelte Schriften*, ed. Paul Landau. Berlin: P. Cassirer.

1913. *Wozzeck-Lenz: Zwei Fragmente*, ed. Wilhelm Hausenstein. Leipzig: Insel-Verlag.

[1916]. *Gesammelte Werke*, ed. Wilhelm Hausenstein. Leipzig: Insel-Verlag.

[1919]. *Wozzeck: Ein Fragment*. Berlin: A. Juncker Verlag.

1920. *Woyzeck*, ed. Georg Witkowski. Leipzig: Insel-Verlag.

1923. *Sämtliche poetische Werke nebst einer Auswahl seiner Briefe*, ed. Arnold Zweig. Munich and Leipzig: Rösl.

1928. *The Plays of Georg Büchner*, trans. and ed. Geoffrey Dunlop. New York: Viking.

[1936]. *Woyzeck*, ed. Ernst Hardt. Leipzig: Insel-Verlag.

1954. *Danton's Tod and Woyzeck*, ed. Margaret Jacobs. Manchester: The University Press.

1955. *Woyzeck*, trans. Theodore Hoffman. In Volume 1 of *The Modern Theatre*, ed. Eric Bentley. Garden City, N.Y.: Doubleday and Anchor.

1958 [1st ed. 1922]. *Werke und Briefe*, ed. Fritz Bergemann. Wiesbaden: Insel-Verlag.

1963. *Woyzeck*, trans. John Holmstrom. In *Three German Plays*. London: Penguin Books.

1965. *Complete Plays and Prose*, trans. and ed. Carl Richard Mueller. New York: Hill and Wang.

1967. *Sämtliche Werke und Briefe*, ed. Werner R. Lehmann. Volume 1. Hamburg: Christian Wegner Verlag.

1969. *Woyzeck*, trans. Henry J. Schmidt. New York: Avon Books.

Carner, Mosco. 1975. *Alban Berg*. London: Duckworth.

Chadwick, Nicholas. 1971. "Berg's Unpublished Songs in the Österreichische Nationalbibliothek," *Music and Letters*, LII/2 (April): 123ff.

Colacicchi, Luigi. 1943. "La Stagione di opere contemporanee all Teatro Reale dell' Opera," *Musica* (Florence: Sansoni), II: 214ff.

Cooper, Grosvenor, and Leonard B. Meyer. 1960. *The Rhythmic Structure of Music*. University of Chicago Press.

Dam, Hermann van. 1954. "Zu Georg Büchners 'Woyzeck,' " *Akzente*, I: 82ff.

DeVoto, Mark. 1966a. "Alban Berg's Picture Postcard Songs." Dissertation, Princeton University.

———. 1966b. "Some Notes on the Unknown *Altenberg Lieder*," *Perspectives of New Music*, V/1 (Fall/Winter): 37ff.

Eliot, T. S. 1958. " 'Ulysses,' Order, and Myth." Reprinted in *Criticism: The Foundations of Literary Judgment*, ed. Mark Schorer et al. New York, Chicago, and Burlingame: Harcourt, Brace and World.

Fink, G.-L. 1961. "Volkslied und Verseinlage in den Dramen Büchners," *Deutsche Vierteljahrschrift*, XXXV: 558ff.

Fox, Charles Warren. 1948. "Modern Counterpoint: A Phenomenological Approach," *Notes*, VI/1 (December): 46ff.

Franzos, Karl Emil. 1901. "Über Georg Büchner," *Deutsche Dichtung*, XXIX: 195ff., 289ff.

Hauch, Edward Franklin. 1929. "The Reviviscence of Georg Büchner," *Publications of the Modern Language Association of America*, XLIV: 892ff.

Hilmar, Ernst. 1975. *Wozzeck von Alban Berg*. Vienna: Universal Edition.

Jarman, Douglas. 1979. *The Music of Alban Berg*. Berkeley: University of California Press.

Kassowitz, Gottfried. 1968. "Lehrzeit bei Alban Berg," *Österreichische Musikzeitschrift*, XXIII/6–7 (June/July): 323ff.

Keller, Hans. 1952. "Alban Berg and the C Major Triad," *Music Review*, XIII/4 (November): correspondence.

Klein, Fritz Heinrich. 1923. "Alban Bergs 'Wozzeck,' " *Musikblätter des Anbruch*, V (October): 216ff.

Knight, A. H. J. 1951. *Georg Büchner*. Oxford: Basil Blackwell.

Lindenberger, Herbert. 1964. *Georg Büchner*. Carbondale: Southern Illinois University Press.

Mahler, Alma (see also Werfel). 1960. *Mein Leben*. Berlin: S. Fischer Verlag.

Mahler, Fritz. 1957. *Zu Alban Bergs Oper "Wozzeck". Szenische und musikalische Übersicht*. Vienna: Universal Edition.

Martens, Wolfgang. 1960. "Der Barbier in Büchners 'Woyzeck,' " *Zeitschrift für deutsche Philologie*, LXXIX: 361ff.

Mautner, Franz H. 1961. "Wortgewebe, Sinngefüge und 'Idee' in Büchners 'Woyzeck,' " *Deutsche Vierteljahrschrift*, XXXV: 521ff.

Mayer, Hans. 1960. *Georg Büchner und seine Zeit*. Wiesbaden: Limes Verlag.

Perle, George. 1965. "Pierrot lunaire." In *The Commonwealth of Music*, ed. Gustave Reese and Rose Brandel. New York: Free Press.

1967a [1977]. *The String Quartets of Béla Bartók*. New York: Dover. (A pamphlet accompanying a recording of the six quartets.) Reprinted in *A Musical Offering: Essays in Honor of Martin Bernstein*, ed. Edward H. Clinkscale and Claire Brook. New York: Pendragon.

1967b. "The Musical Language of Wozzeck," *Music Forum* (New York: Columbia University Press), I: 204ff.

1967c. "Woyzeck and Wozzeck," *Musical Quarterly*, LIII/2 (April): 206ff.

1967d. "Three Views of Wozzeck," *Saturday Review*, Dec. 2, pp. 54f.

1968. "Wozzeck. Ein Zweiter Blick auf das Libretto," *Neue Zeitschrift für Musik*, CXXIX/5 (May): 218ff.

1971. "Representation and Symbol in the Music of Wozzeck," *Music Review*, XXXIII/4 (November): 281ff.

1977a. *Serial Composition and Atonality*. 4th ed., revised. Berkeley: University of California Press.

1977b. *Twelve-Tone Tonality*. Berkeley: University of California Press.

1977c. "Berg's Master Array of the Interval Cycles," *Musical Quarterly*, LXIII/1 (January): 1ff.

1977d. "The Secret Program of the *Lyric Suite*," *International Alban Berg Society Newsletter*, 5 (June): 4ff.

1978. "Mein geliebtes Almschi . . .," *International Alban Berg Society Newsletter*, 7 (Fall): 5ff.

Petschnig, Emil. 1924. "Atonales Opernschaffen," *Die Musik*, XVI/5 (February): 342ff.

Ploebsch, Gerd. 1968. *Alban Bergs "Wozzeck."* Strasbourg and Baden-Baden: Heitz.

Prieberg, Fred K. [1965]. *Musik in der Sowjetunion*. Cologne: Verlag Wissenschaft und Politik.

Rankl, Karl. 1952. "Arnold Schoenberg," *Score*, 6 (May): 40ff.

Raupp, Wilhelm. 1935. *Max von Schillings: der Kampf eines deutschen Künstlers*. Hamburg: Hanseatische Verlagsanstalt.

Redlich, H. F. 1952. "Alban Berg and the C Major Triad," *Music Review* XIII/3 (August): correspondence.

1955, 1960. "Appendix" to 2 *Lieder* by Alban Berg. Vienna: Universal Edition.

1957a. *Alban Berg: Versuch einer Würdigung*. Vienna: Universal Edition.

1957b. *Alban Berg: The Man and His Music*. London: John Calder.

Reich, Willi. 1930. "Alban Berg," *Die Musik*, XXII/5 (February): 347ff.

1937. *Alban Berg. Mit Bergs eigenen Schriften und Beiträgen von Theodor Wiesengrund-Adorno und Ernst Křenek*. Vienna, Leipzig, and Zurich: Herbert Reichner Verlag.

1953. "Aus unbekannten Briefen von Alban Berg an Anton Webern," *Schweizerische Musikzeitung*, XCIII/2 (February): 49ff.

1963. *Alban Berg*. Zurich: Atlantis Verlag.

1965. *Alban Berg*, trans. Cornelius Cardew. London: Thames and Hudson.

1968. *Arnold Schönberg oder der konservative Revolutionär*. Vienna, Frankfort, and Zurich: Verlag Fritz Molden.

1971. *Schoenberg: A Critical Biography*, trans. Leo Black. New York: Praeger.

Rilke, Rainer Maria. 1948. *Letters of Rainer Maria Rilke*. Volume II. New York: W. W. Norton.

Russell, John. 1957. *Erich Kleiber*. London: Andre Deutsch.

Sachs, Curt. 1953. *Rhythm and Tempo*. New York: W. W. Norton.

Schäfke, Rudolf. 1926. "Alban Bergs Oper 'Wozzeck,' " *Melos*, V/5 (May): 267ff.

Scherliess, Volker. 1975. *Alban Berg*. Reinbek bei Hamburg: Rowohlt Taschenbuch Verlag.

Schoenberg, Arnold. 1965. *Letters*, selected and ed. Erwin Stein. New York: St. Martin's Press.

Schwarz, Boris. 1965 [1972]. "Arnold Schoenberg in Soviet Russia," *Perspectives of New Music*, IV/1 (Fall/Winter): 86ff. Reprinted in

226

Perspectives on Schoenberg and Stravinsky, ed. Benjamin Boretz and Edward T. Cone. New York: W. W. Norton.

Schweizer, Klaus. 1970. *Die Sonatensatzform im Schaffen Alban Bergs.* Stuttgart: Musikwissenschaftliche Verlags-Gesellschaft.

Sessions, Roger. 1951. *Harmonic Practice.* New York: Harcourt, Brace.

Slonimsky, Nicholas. 1949. *Music since 1900.* 3rd ed. New York: Coleman-Ross.

Sokel, Walter H. 1959. *The Writer in Extremis: Expressionism in Twentieth-Century German Literature.* Stanford: Stanford University Press.

Stein, Erwin. 1922. "Alban Berg and Anton von Webern," *The Chesterian* (October): 33ff.

——— 1923. "Alban Berg—Anton v. Webern," *Musikblätter des Anbruch,* V (January): 13ff.

——— 1927. "Preface" to *Lyrische Suite* by Alban Berg. Vienna: Universal Edition.

Steiner, George. 1961. *The Death of Tragedy.* New York: Alfred A. Knopf.

Stravinsky, Igor. 1947. *The Poetics of Music.* Cambridge: Harvard University Press.

Stravinsky, Igor, and Robert Craft. 1959. *Conversations with Igor Stravinsky.* Garden City, N.Y.: Doubleday.

——— 1960. *Memories and Commentaries.* Garden City, N.Y.: Doubleday.

——— 1963. *Dialogues and a Diary.* Garden City, N.Y.: Doubleday.

——— 1966. *Themes and Episodes.* New York: Alfred A. Knopf.

Stroh, Wolfgang Martin. 1968. "Alban Berg's 'Constructive Rhythm,'" *Perspectives of New Music,* VII/1 (Fall/Winter): 18ff.

Strudthoff, Ingeborg. 1957. *Die Rezeption Georg Büchners durch des deutsche Theater.* Berlin: Colloquium Verlag.

Treitler, Leo. 1976. "'Wozzeck' et l'Apocalypse," *Schweizerische Musikzeitung,* CXVI/4 (July/August): 249ff.

Trotsky, Leon. 1957 (originally published in 1925). *Literature and Revolution.* New York: Russell and Russell.

Viebig, Ernst. 1923. "Alban Bergs 'Wozzeck': ein Beitrag zum Opernproblem," *Die Musik,* XV/7 (April): 506ff.

Viëtor, Karl. 1949. *Georg Büchner: Politik, Dichtung, Wissenschaft.* Bern: A. Francke.

Vogelsang, Konrad. 1977. *Dokumentation zur Oper "Wozzeck" von Alban Berg.* Laaber-Verlag.

Vojtěch, Ivan. 1965. "Arnold Schoenberg, Anton Webern, Alban Berg. Unbekannte Briefe an Erwin Schulhoff." In Volume 18 of *Miscellenea Musicologica,* Prague: Universita Karlova.

Werfel, Alma Mahler. 1958. *And the Bridge Is Love.* New York: Harcourt Brace and Company.

Willnauer, Franz. 1966. "Alban Berg über Musik und Musiker," *Neue Zeitschrift für Musik,* 127/4 (April): 128ff.

Zweig, Stefan. 1943 [1964]. *The World of Yesterday.* New York: Viking. (Reprinted in paperback, University of Nebraska Press.)

Aber, Adolf, 198
Adler, Guido, 2
Adorno, Theodor W., 7, 11, 223
Albrecht, Otto E., 223
Altenberg, Peter, 7, 10
American Relief Fund, 191
Anbruch, 190, 193, 223
Aravantinos, Panos, illus. 17
Archibald, Bruce, 223
Association for Contemporary Music, 200
Atonality, 99, 130f., 132f., 163, 164

Bach, Johann Sebastian, 124
Bartók, Béla, 129, 164, 181
Beethoven, Ludwig van, xvi
Benn, Maurice R., 37, 223
Berg, Alban
  correspondence: to Helene Berg, 18, 20f., 28, 30, 72, 129, 186, 188, 189, 190f., 192, 194, 195, 196, 197, 199; to Hanna Fuchs-Robettin, xvi; to Kassowitz, 56; to Kleiber, 199; to Schoenberg, 7f., 12, 19f., 28, 125, 188, 191; to Schulhoff, 21, 189f.; to Webern, 19, 20, 30, 189, 190
  influenced: by Mahler, 12–14, 16, 17; by Schoenberg, 6, 15, 17f.
  life: acceptance of *Wozzeck* by Kleiber for performance, 195; completion of *Wozzeck*, 192; composition of *Wozzeck*, xvi, 19f., 30, 164, 188–192; difficulties following the war, 189–191; Director of Society for Private Musical Performances, 189, 190, 191; early support for the war, 12, 20f.; health problems, 19, 21, 190; military service,

19–21, 56, 129, 188f.; post-war politics' effect on *Wozzeck*, 192, 196–201 *passim*, illus. 19; publication of *Wozzeck*, 193, 194, illus. 1, 2, 13, 14, 20, 21; studies with Schoenberg, 1–4, 6f.; supposed suicide attempt, xvii; trip to Amsterdam, 18; views against militarism, 21
  literary works, 223; analyses of Schoenberg's music, 4; analysis of *Wozzeck*, 43, 128; *Anbruch*, 190; essay on *Wozzeck*, 89, 186f., 194, 203–206; lecture on *Wozzeck*, 43, 73, 89, 99, 174, 186; projected biography of Schoenberg, 190f.
  manuscripts, early works, 1, 3
  premières: *Altenberg Lieder*, 8; *Three Pieces for Orchestra*, 19, 195
  style: form, 3f., 7, 11, 16f., 20, 37, 46–49, 89, 93f., 120, 126, 145, 193f.; orchestration, 9, 47–49, 68, 74; twelve-tone music, xv; twelve-tone sets, xv, 10, 164
  views: about atonality, 99; about opera, xiv
  works: *Altenberg Lieder*, Op. 4, xii, 7–11, 13, 15, 17, 19, 37, 165; *An Leuken*, 1; arrangements of Schoenberg's music, 4, 11; Concerto for Violin and Orchestra, 13, 37; early songs, 1; Four Pieces for Clarinet and Piano, Op. 5, 8, 11, 13, 190, 193; Four Songs, Op. 2, 2, 4–6, 11; *Lulu*, xiiif., xv, xvii, 3f., 10, 13, 29, 89; *Lyric Suite* for String Quartet, xvi, 6, 8, 129; piano variations, 1; projected symphony, 12; *Schliesse mir die Augen beide*, 3; *Sieben frühe Lieder*, 3; Sonata for Piano, Op. 1, 2, 4, 13, 17, 191; String Quartet, Op. 3, 6f., 11, 13, 17, 190, 193, 195; Three Excerpts for

227

Index

Mahler, Fritz, 43, 48, 194, 224
Mahler, Gustav, 4, 12–14, 16, 17, 189
Martens, Wolfgang, 34, 43, 224
Marx, Karl, 23
Massey, Max, xii
Mautner, Franz H., 224
Mayer, Hans, 225
Metaphors and symbols. *See* under *Wozzeck*
Meyer, Leonard B., 224
Mitropoulos, Dimitri, xi
Mombert, Alfred, 4
Motet, panisorhythmic, 174
Motives, rhythmic. *See* tempo and rhythm
Mozart, Wolfgang Amadeus: operas, xvii, 36, 74, 123
Mueller, Carl Richard, 224
Musica reservata, 124. *See also* metaphors and symbols
Musical Culture, 200
Die Musik, 194f., 199
Mussolini, Benito, illus. 19

Nader, Michael, illus. 6
Number symbolism, 128f., 185

Octave register, 131
Opera, xiv, 36
Orchestration, 9, 47–49, 68, 74, 95, 110, 112, 120, 124, 127f., 186, 204
Ostinato, 9, 15, 81, 93, 97, 100, 106, 124, 126, 131, 135, 139, 164–171, 172–174, 178, 181
Ostrčil, Otakar, 198f.

Passacaglia, 11, 17, 94, 126
Pekary, Stefano, illus. 19
Performance problems. *See* under *Wozzeck*
Perle, George, xif., xiv-xvii, 28f., 225
Petschnig, Emil, 46, 195, 225
Pfitzner, Hans, 193
Philadelphia Grand Opera Company, illus. 18
Ploebsch, Gerd, 28f., 225
Politics: Communism, 200f.; Nazism, 196f., 201, illus. 19
Polytonality, 73, 99
Prieberg, Fred K., 225

Quotation, 74, 123

Rankl, Karl, 192, 225
Raupp, Wilhelm, 225
Ravel, Maurice, 18
Redlich, H. F., xi, 2, 3, 11, 29, 225
Reich, Willi, xivf., xvi, xvii, 2f., 8, 27, 29, 189, 191, 203, 225
Reinhardt, Max, 192
Rhythmic motives. *See* Tempo and rhythm
Rilke, Rainer Maria, 23, 79, 225
Roslavetz, Nicolai, 200
Russell, John, 195f., 225
Russian Association of Proletarian Musicians, 200f.

Sachs, Curt, 182, 225
Scales: diatonic, 155, 161f.; segments, 155–163; semitonal, 142, 155, 158–161, 164;

whole-tone, 4, 6f., 95, 99, 133, 141, 155–158, 161, 164
Schäfke, Rudolf, 27, 225
Scherchen, Hermann, 195
Scherliess, Volker, 225
Schillings, Max von, 195–197
Schindler, Anton Felix, xvi
Schirmer, G., 193
Schoenberg, Arnold: influence on Berg, 3f., 6
life: conducting of *Altenberg Lieder*, 8; founding of Society for Private Musical Performances, 189; projected biography by Berg, 190f.
style: form, 3f.; twelve-tone works, xv
views: about *Altenberg Lieder*, 8; about Berg, 1f.; about Berg's String Quartet, 7; about producers, xvii; about *Tristan und Isolde*, 122; about *Wozzeck*, 192
works: Book of the Hanging Gardens, Op. 15, 6; Chamber Symphony No. 1, Op. 9, 3f., 17, 123; *Die Glückliche Hand*, Op. 18, 13, 18; *Erwartung*, Op. 17, 6, 13, 18, 20, 37; Five Piano Pieces, Op. 23, 164; Five Pieces for Orchestra, Op. 16, 6, 11, 13, 17, 18, 123; *Gurrelieder*, 3f., 11; *Pelleas und Melisande*, Op. 5, 4, 17; Piano Suite, Op. 25, 164; *Pierrot lunaire*, Op. 21, 8, 13, 15, 91, 128, 186, 200; Serenade, Op. 24, 164; Six Little Pieces for Piano, Op. 19, 8; String Quartet No. 1, Op. 7, 3, 17; String Quartet No. 2, Op. 10, 4, 11, 17; Three Piano Pieces, Op. 11, 6
mentioned, xiv, 12, 18, 19, 125, 188, 193, 194, 197, 199, 225
Schulhoff, Erwin, 21, 189f.
Schützendorf, Leo, 196
Schwartz, Boris, 225
Schweizer, Klaus, 226
Scriabin, Alexander, 142, 164
Serafin, Tullio, illus. 19
Sessions, Roger, 132, 226
Shirley, Wayne D., 125
Slonimsky, Nicholas, 226
Society for Private Musical Performances, 189, 190, 191
Sokel, Walter H., 9, 14, 226
Spies, Claudio, xii
Sprechstimme, 186
Stage directions. *See* under *Wozzeck*
Stein, Erwin, 6, 8, 193f., 226
Steiner, George, 37, 226
Steuermann, Eduard, 191f.
Stokowski, Leopold, 201, illus. 18
Strauss, Richard, 4, 74
Stravinsky, Igor, 8, 129, 164, 181, 226; viewed by Berger, 131; views about Berg, 8, 16, 73; views about Wagner, 94
Stroh, Wolfgang Martin, 174, 226
Strudthoff, Ingeborg, 226
Symbolism. *See* Metaphors and symbols; Number symbolism
Symmetry, 11, 16, 69, 91, 124f., 127, 139, 146, 150f., 159f., 163f.

Teatro Reale dell' Opera, illus. 19
Tempo and rhythm, 6, 15f., 84, 89, 90f., 128f., 142, 171–185, 203f.

229

Designer: Al Burkhardt
Compositor: Interactive Composition Corp.
Printer: Malloy Lithographing
Binder: John H. Dekker & Sons
Text: VIP Palatino
Display: Phototypositor Palatino
Cloth: Elephant Hide Paper and
Joanna Arrestox B 19990
Paper: 55 lb. Glatfelter and
70 lb. Old Forge Enamel